Basics

by Simon Fischer

300

exercises

and practice

routines

for the violin

EDITION PETERS

LONDON FRANKFURT LEIPZIG NEW YORK

Peters Edition Limited
10–12 Baches Street
London
N1 6DN

First published 1997; reprinted 1997
© 1997 by Hinrichsen Edition, Peters Edition Limited, London

ISBN 1 901507 00 9

A catalogue record for this book is
available from the British Library

Cover: Juan Gris, *Le violon*. (1916 oil on wood panel)
© ADAGP, Paris and DACS, London 1997
Öffentliche Kunstsammlung Basel, Kunstmuseum
Gift of Dr H. C. Raoul La Roche, 1952
Photo: Öffentliche Kunstsammlung Basel, Martin Bühler

Music-setting by Maud Hodson and Tina Jones
Photographs by Derrick Witty

Designed by Riley Associates, London
Printed in Great Britain by St Edmundsbury Press,
Bury St Edmunds, Suffolk
Set in Adobe Systems Frutiger and Monotype Plantin

Contents

Introduction

Basic technical exercises can be used by players of all levels because most of the technical issues remain the same – e.g., intonation, tone production, rhythm and articulation, co-ordination, relaxation, as well as the easiest possible working of arms, hands and fingers.

Violin playing is complex because to play even a simple phrase a large number of quite different techniques must be performed one after another, often at great speed. Each note in a succession of notes may need to be produced in a fundamentally different way from the others. For example, to play the first note the bow may have to be placed on the string and then 'bite' the beginning of the note; to play the second note the bow may have to pivot smoothly across to another string; to play the third note a finger may have to be lifted, to play the fourth note the hand may have to shift up or down, and so on.

On their own, most of the separate techniques are very simple. It is only when we try to perform several of them at the same time that they can appear to become more difficult. To a certain extent, an 'easy' piece is easy because very few actions have to be performed at the same time; a 'difficult' piece is difficult because ten or twenty actions may have to be performed at the same time or in close succession. (The easiest 'piece' of all must therefore be just one open string played pizzicato, because it consists of only one action.)

Many of the individual actions that make up technique can themselves be broken down into several elements. This book deals with these elements, large or small, one at a time, which is the quickest way to build technique.

The exercises in *Basics* can be used in a number of different ways. First, they provide an easy and direct way to build, one at a time, the simple actions that together are called 'technique'. Second, many of them double as useful warm-up exercises. Third, even a player with the finest technique has to continue to practise in order not to lose it, and *Basics* exercises are an effective and time-efficient way to work on specific areas.

Well-aimed exercises develop individual parts of technique. The next step is to combine the individual techniques in countless different ways by playing scales, studies and pieces. But many of the difficulties of everyday playing simply vanish if you regularly practise key individual techniques separately.

The most important thing is to have so much technique that you don't have to think about it. If you are too conscious of the 'how', it can make playing almost impossible, just as any actions that normally happen automatically – walking, talking, eating, etc. – become stilted and awkward when we try to perform them consciously. Children learn quickly because the 'how' goes straight into the unconscious. It is through the adult knowing ever more clearly and consciously what to do, that finally technique becomes automatic and is then naturally forgotten. Then the player can really be free to make music.

Sources

Many of the exercises in this collection have been used widely for decades, and in some cases for centuries. Their exact origin is difficult to trace because they have been so widely practised. Others have been used so much by certain teachers, though not necessarily invented by them, that the exercises have become associated with them: Galamian-type tone production exercises, Flesch Urstudien-type finger tapping (repeated by Yost and Dounis), Ševcík or Schradieck-type finger patterns, Dounis-type shifting or finger action exercises, etc.

Some of the exercises are adaptations of traditional methods, while others are my own. But in a field as old and widespread as violin playing, new ideas usually turn out to have been thought of before. As a student I 'invented' the exercise in which the player runs his or her hand up and down the stationary bow (Exercise 36). I showed it to a Bulgarian violinist who said she had been taught that same exercise in Sofia fifteen years earlier. Later I came across a similar exercise in *Six Lessons with Yehudi Menuhin* (Faber, London, 1971), and again in Tortelier's *How I Play, How I Teach* (Chester Music, London, 1975).

Some of the exercises originally appeared in serialised form in *The Strad* magazine. The first of these was a tone production exercise that I learnt from Dorothy DeLay. Before sending the article to the magazine, I telephoned Miss DeLay in New York to ask her permission, explaining that I did not want to 'steal' her exercise. She laughed and said: 'Don't worry. I learnt it from Galamian, and he learnt it from Capet, so feel free – what is important is that these exercises become known!'

Acknowledgements

My thanks to Dorothy DeLay, whose basic exercises were not only the inspiration but also the starting point for this book, as well as my gratitude for her support and encouragement for the project over the years.

I am indebted to the many friends and colleagues, notably Emanuel Hurwitz, who have looked through or used early drafts of the book, and whose suggestions have always been so helpful; and in particular to Kyra Humphreys and Veronika Weise whose painstaking work in trying out exercises and checking text was invaluable.

Thanks also to all the many students over the fifteen-year period during which the book has developed, who have acted as willing and enthusiastic 'guinea pigs', making it possible to refine and redesign each exercise countless times. Without them, few of the exercises could have evolved into their final form.

Finally, I am grateful to Jennifer King who modelled so patiently for the photographs.

How to use *Basics*

Which exercise to practise?
How long to practise it for?
How often to practise it?

Everybody's needs are different, and an exercise that may be relevant for one player may be irrelevant for another. *Basics* can be used in any number of ways according to preference.

The exercises fall into several categories. Some are intended simply to illuminate a particular aspect of playing, e.g., nos. 1, 2, 6, 19, 54, 55. These can be returned to from time to time, but do not need to be practised regularly.

Some of the exercises are designed to give a different feel to the hands and arms in all the different aspects of playing, for example: the feel of each finger on the bow; of raising and dropping the fingers; of drawing a straight bow, and so on. Most of these are very short and simple, and do not require more than sixty or ninety seconds, e.g., nos. 3, 4, 5, 9, 56, 89, 98, 128. They do not need to be practised every day, although many players find that different exercises become 'favourites' to which they return again and again. They can be used daily for building technique; or, by returning to them regularly, used as a quick way to ensure that everything stays in good working order.

Other exercises are solid practice routines that constantly develop technique and, like playing scales, may become part of everyday practice. Some of the key exercises in this category are tone production, shifting, intonation and vibrato. Used again and again, these improve the player's technique on a continual basis.

Many *Basics* exercises can be used in daily practice to save time. Intonation exercises, for instance,

save time by 'tuning' the hand so that fewer intonation problems are likely to arise in subsequent practice. Fifteen minutes spent on an intonation exercise can mean that you spend one hour instead of two working on intonation in a piece. Many of the shifting exercises include all possibilities of shifting from one finger to another. Once you have practised them for an hour, or for ten minutes, the repertoire you play afterwards feels more secure because, in effect, you have already worked on all the shifts in one go.

Some players like to spend all the practice in a day just playing, for example, shifting exercises or tone production exercises. The improvement in the general level of playing that results from working like this can be felt for a long time to come.

Although *Basics* is not a book to play through from cover to cover, one approach is to practise something from each section every day. Some exercises will take thirty seconds, and some will take thirty minutes; what is practised depends entirely on the individual's needs and availability of time.

Keep a record of what you have practised. For example, in a row of alternative key signatures (such as on page 142), tick each key signature as you play it. Mark each exercise with a tick each time you do it. Practising a tone production exercise, make a note of 'A string, low position', 'D string, high position', and so on.

Right Arm and Hand

Bow hand

Thumb counter-pressure

Counter-pressure is sometimes very little, and at other times much more, depending on the amount of pressure into the string, and which part of the bow is used. At the heel the thumb's contact with the bow can be very light, even in the loudest playing. At the point, the thumb has to work hard against the downward pressure of the fingers into the bow. However much it is, counter-pressure should always be as little as possible.

Counter-pressure is automatic and unconscious, but conscious releasing can be helpful. The most common thumb tension problems do not come from counter-pressing, but from not letting the thumb release when less counter-pressure is needed.

Place the thumb at an angle of about 45° to the bow, so that the tip of the left side of the thumb (as seen from the player's viewpoint) is on the stick and the right side is against the nut. The thumb should always bend outwards.

This exercise shows how much counter-pressure the thumb has to give in every part of the bow.

Fig. 1

(a)

Light and relaxed thumb despite the pressure into the string

(b)

At the point the thumb counter-presses more

1   Place the bow on the string at the heel, just in front of the first finger, holding the bow with only the thumb and first finger (Fig. 1a).

2   Slowly push the wood of the bow down as far as possible. However hard you press into the string, the thumb can be light and relaxed.

3   Replace the bow on the string a centimetre higher up. Slowly press the wood of the bow down as far as possible. Feel how the thumb has to counter-press a fraction more.

4   Continuing to hold the bow with only the thumb and first finger, press the bow down into the string centimetre by centimetre up the whole length of the bow. Feel all the different degrees of counter-pressure the thumb has to give. Pressing at the point creates the most counter-pressure (Fig. 1b).

5   Using a normal bow hold, press down into the string in every part of the bow, feeling all the different degrees of thumb counter-pressure.

The thumb and second finger

See also About the movement of the bow within the hand, *page 72.*

The thumb and second finger are the centre of the bow hold. The second finger needs to sit very slightly to the left of the thumb (as seen from the player's viewpoint; Fig. 2).

A bow hold with the thumb *between the second and third fingers* can cause tension in the base of the thumb. (Without the bow, hold the hand in bow-hold position. Move the thumb very slowly towards the fourth finger. The closer the thumb gets to the fourth finger the harder the muscle becomes in the base of the thumb.)

The thumb should not be placed *between the first and second fingers* because this gives an unbalanced distribution of the fingers, with three fingers one side of the thumb and one the other side. Another reason is that the first finger would be too near the thumb, causing it to have to work too hard. Any downward pressure from the first finger has a greater effect the further away from the thumb it is.

Fig. 2

 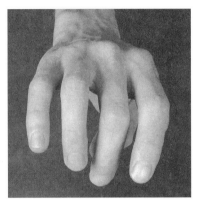 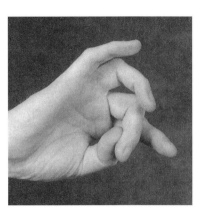

Thumb and second finger relationship

Use a normal bow hold throughout this exercise. Move the tip of the bow up and down using only the fingers, not the hand. To help isolate the finger movement so that the hand itself remains still, hold the right hand with the left hand. Place the thumb on the back of the hand, and the first finger in the palm of the hand.

1   Hold the bow in the upper half (Fig. 3a). Feel the first finger supporting all the weight of the bow.

2   Push down with the first finger, making the heel of the bow move up (Fig. 3b). Notice the fourth finger curving at the same time. Keep the forearm still and use only the finger to move the bow.

3   Release the first finger pressure, letting the heel of the bow move down. Feel the bow moving around the thumb and second finger, like the centre of a seesaw. Repeat the movement several times, in a continuous motion.

4   Repeat with the hand in the middle of the bow, where less weight is pushing into the first finger; at the point-of-balance, where the bow feels evenly balanced; and in the normal bow-hold position, where the fourth finger supports all the weight.

Fig. 3

 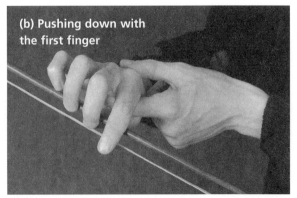

(a) Feel all the weight of the bow in the first finger

(b) Pushing down with the first finger

Holding the right hand with the left hand while doing the exercise

Thumb flexibility

Invisible, unconscious movements of the thumb are an essential part of almost all bowstrokes. A rigid thumb can badly affect the entire bow arm.

1   Playing lightly near the fingerboard, play whole bows on one note. Keep the hand and fingers loose and relaxed.

2   Bend and straighten the thumb ten or more times during each bow (Figs. 4a and 4b). The fingers should curve and straighten at the same time.

3   Repeat while playing between the bridge and the fingerboard, where the bow will be heavier and deeper in the string. Keep the fingers and thumb relaxed and free.

4   Finally, make the movement while playing very heavily near the bridge. The thumb and fingers should remain free even though a lot of weight now has to go into the bow. Keep the right shoulder relaxed.

Repeat on each string. Play double stops as well as single notes.

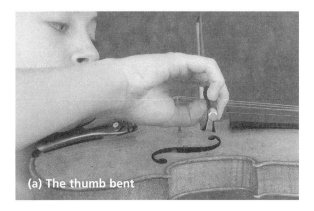 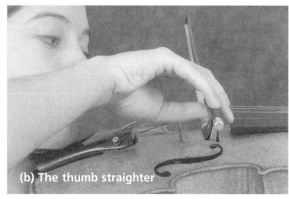

(a) The thumb bent   (b) The thumb straighter

Fig. 4

Balancing with the fourth finger

Playing in the lower half, the fourth finger sits on the bow as on a seesaw, controlling the pressure of the bow in the string. In the upper half the fourth finger balances the first finger, preventing the tone from becoming too pressed.[1] Balancing the bow with the fourth finger is also a major part of all lifted bowings.

Exercise 1

4

Point the bow slightly more towards the left shoulder, as it does during normal playing. Keep the thumb curved and relaxed.

The usual position for the fourth finger is on the *upper, inside edge* of the bow, but in this exercise place it directly on top of the bow. Keep the fourth finger curved all the time.

1   Turn the hand clockwise so that the bow points to the right, and the hair is above the stick (Fig. 5a).

2   Make a fast, anticlockwise movement so that the bow is suddenly returned to its normal position. Make the movement so quickly that there is a 'swishing' noise as the air rushes through the hair.

    Feel all the weight of the bow going into the little finger (Fig. 5b). Relax the thumb.

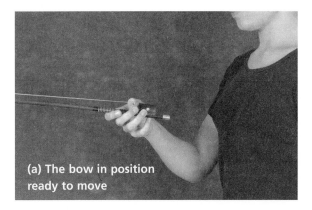 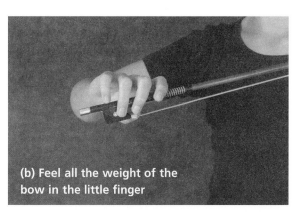

(a) The bow in position ready to move   (b) Feel all the weight of the bow in the little finger

Fig. 5

[1] Some schools say that the fourth finger should be taken off the bow in the upper half; certainly players with short arms often cannot reach the point (with a straight bow) if they do not let the fourth finger come off the bow. If you take the fourth finger off you have to be extra careful not to squash the sound by over-pressing with the first finger.

5

Exercise 2

Point the bow slightly more towards the left shoulder, as it does during normal playing. Keep the thumb curved and relaxed.

1   Hold the bow with only the thumb and fourth finger, just below the point-of-balance[1] (Fig. 6a). Place the fourth finger directly on top of the stick.

2   Move the point of the bow up, by pushing down with the little finger (Fig. 6b), and then let the point down again to the starting point (Fig. 6a). Keep the forearm still and use only the finger to move the bow. Repeat this a few times, in a continuous motion.

3   Place the hand a few centimetres closer to the frog and repeat. Continue, gradually getting closer to the frog, until the hand is in its usual position.

Fig. 6

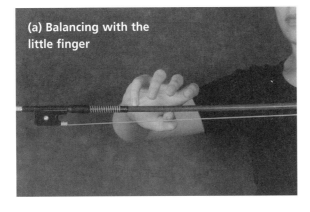

(a) Balancing with the little finger

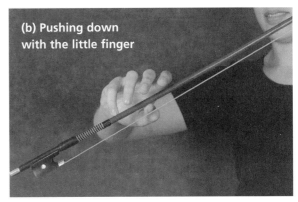

(b) Pushing down with the little finger

Holding the bow without gripping

The fingers must always be *alive* on the bow. Tiny adjustments to the bow hold have to be made all the time, because the conditions of playing are always changing. From note to note, the brain sends millions of subconscious messages to the fingers to change their contact with the bow. These often invisible changes are instinctive reactions to musical feeling and to the changing contacts of the bow with the string, rather than being something that can be taught or learnt. The bow has to be held without undue tension so that the spontaneous adjustments can occur without restriction.[2]

You also have to be able to make larger, deliberate alterations to the bow hand, for instance, when playing **pp** one moment and *martelé* the next.

6

Exercise 1

The fingers hold the bow firmly in strong, forceful playing, even squeezing it at times (for instance, playing a stroke that begins with a sharp bite). Other strokes require more of a bow *balance* than a bow *hold* or bow *grip*.

There is nothing wrong with a strong bow hold when needed, as long as it is always followed by release when no longer needed. To avoid tension, the norm should be a bow balance with a stronger grip when required, rather than the other way round.

[2] 'Our sensitivity diminishes in proportion to the total amount of stimulation. If there are two candles lit in a room, we easily notice the difference in brightness when a third candle is lit. But if there are fifty candles burning, we are unlikely to notice the difference made by a fifty-first. The harder we press on a violin string, the less we can feel it. The louder we play, the less we hear. The more relaxed and ready the muscles are, the more different ways they can move.' Stephen Nachmanovitch: *Free Play – Improvisation in Life and Art* (Los Angeles, 1990), 63.

1   Tilt the bow over, as though playing on the outer edge of the hair. Place the fourth finger on the *upper, inside edge* of the bow. Take the second and third fingers off the bow (Fig. 7a).

Notice the weight of the bow resting on the pad of the first finger and balanced by the fourth finger and thumb. All three support the bow – if any were taken off, the bow would fall. In this position, the bow is balanced in the hand, and does not need to be 'held'.

2   Put the second finger on the frog slightly more to the left of the thumb than usual. Take the first finger off.

Now the bow is balanced by the second and fourth fingers, and by the thumb (Fig. 7b). Feel the weight of the bow resting against the second finger.

3   Put the first and third fingers back on the bow and hold it normally with all the fingers. Find the same feeling of weight and balance in each finger, without gripping the bow with the fingers.

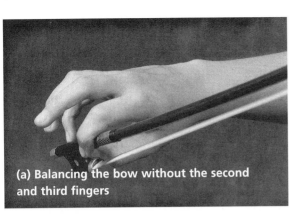

(a) Balancing the bow without the second and third fingers

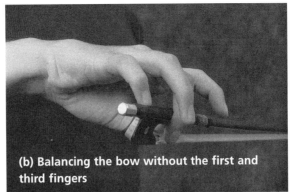

(b) Balancing the bow without the first and third fingers

Fig. 7

Exercise 2

However firmly the fingers hold the bow, they should be able to move freely and flexibly. In this exercise keep the hand quite still, with only the fingers moving. Feel the *pads* of the first and third fingers, the joint nearest the nail of the second finger, and the *tips* of the thumb and fourth finger, on the bow. However firmly they hold the bow, the fingers can move freely, and independently of the hand.

Moving the tip of the bow using only the fingers

1   Hold the bow pointing up vertically.

2   Move the tip of the bow in circles *using only the fingers* (Fig. 8). Hold the bow very firmly, and move the fingers as far as possible. It may be helpful to hold the right hand with the left, to make sure that only the fingers move.

3   Do the same with the bow in playing position.

4   Do the same with the bow pointing to the right, bow hair above the stick.

Exercise 3

● Play several slow, whole bows, *ff*.

● Bowing up and down continuously, move the hand up to the middle of the bow and back again to the heel, using only the fingers to crawl up and down the stick.

It will not be possible to continue crawling up the bow beyond a certain point near the middle, but move up as far as possible. Still play the up-bows to the heel even when your hand is near the middle of the bow. The most difficult part is crawling back down the bow again to the frog.

Fig. 8

Hand balance

At the heel, the first finger contacts the bow closer to the nail joint (Fig. 9a), which makes the hand slightly more vertical on the bow. The fourth finger balances the weight of the bow.

At the point, the first finger contacts the bow closer to the middle joint (Fig. 9b), which makes the hand slightly tilted, i.e., turned away from the fourth finger towards the first finger.

The first finger has two jobs to perform:

1   The part of the first finger on top of the stick injects weight into the string.[1]   Except when playing *f* it touches the stick lightly, and in the lower half sometimes comes a hair's breadth away from the stick.

2   The part of the first finger on the side of the stick helps to keep the bow straight.

Because the contact point on the side of the stick does not change, it feels as though the first finger stays fixed in one position – even though the contact point on top of the stick changes between the heel (nearer the nail joint) and the point (nearer the middle joint).

The fourth finger should stay on the stick in the upper half unless the hand is too small, keeping the hand balanced on the bow and helping to avoid too much first-finger pressure.

The change from more vertical at the heel (Fig. 9a) to more tilted at the point (Fig. 9b) must happen smoothly or the bow will shake somewhere around the middle of a whole down-bow stroke.

[1] The second finger also injects weight into the string. To do this it must be positioned slightly to the left of centre opposite the thumb. (See Fig. 2, page 2.) Sharing the weight between the first and second fingers produces a less pressed, more rounded tone than if you use only the first finger.

Fig. 9

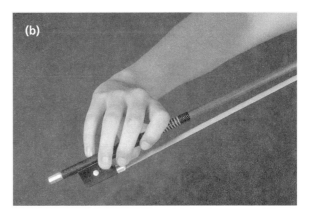

The first finger contacting the bow between the nail joint and the middle joint

Contacting the bow nearer to the middle joint

Play slow, even, *ff*, whole bows near the bridge.

1 Start playing at the heel without the first finger (Fig. 10a). After a few centimetres put the first finger down in its usual place on the stick.

   Continuing down-bow, take off the fourth finger, third finger and second finger in that order. Arrive at the point with only the first finger and thumb on the bow (Fig. 10b).

2 Up-bow: start with only the thumb and first finger; put the second, third and fourth back on the bow in that order; take off the first finger, and arrive at the heel with all the fingers on the bow except the first. Be careful to put the fingers back in their correct shape and position.

3 Do exactly the same, down and up, but without lifting the second finger.

4 The same, but do not lift the third finger either.

5 Start and finish without the first finger as before, but leave all the other fingers on the bow in their usual place.

6 Without lifting any finger, each remaining solidly on the bow, play *f* whole bows with a solid and even tone. Feel the same changes in weight distribution as you play from heel to point and back again.

Fig. 10

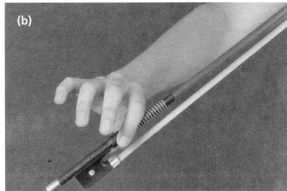

Starting position at the heel

At the end of the first down-bow

10

The give of the hand into the bow

This exercise exaggerates lowering and raising the knuckles.

● For the purposes of the exercise, during the *f* hold the bow firmly and lower the knuckles (Fig. 11a). At the same time curve the thumb and fourth finger.

● During the *p*, release the fingers on the bow and raise the knuckles (Fig. 11b). At the same time let the thumb and fourth finger straighten slightly.

● Play the strokes with an even bow speed and pressure, connecting them to each other seamlessly. Play *subito f* and *subito p*, without any *crescendo* or *diminuendo*.

● Play quarter-length strokes at the heel, middle and point. Repeat using half bows in the lower half, middle, and upper half.

Play two-octave scales in one position across the strings, major or minor, in the following keys:

1 A (1st position) **2** E (5th position) **3** A (8th position)

Lower knuckles ready to begin the down-bow

Higher knuckles ready to begin the up-bow

Fig. 11

Vertical and horizontal finger movement

Exercise 1 – Vertical

- Hold the bow two centimetres above the string at the nut, with exaggeratedly rounded fingers and low knuckles (Fig. 12a).

- Place the bow on the string by straightening the fingers (Fig. 12b), and then lift off back to the starting point by curving the fingers again.

- Keep the arm and hand still, using only the fingers to lower or raise the bow. Repeat the movement up and down several times.

Make sure that the thumb moves freely with the fingers: when the fingers straighten the thumb straightens, and when the fingers curve the thumb curves.

11

The fingers curved ready to place the bow on the string

Placing the bow on the string

Fig. 12

12

Exercise 2 – Horizontal

There is really no such thing as a 'horizontal' finger movement. The fingers are hardly able to move sideways, but when they are placed on the bow so that they lean towards the first finger, rather than vertically, straightening and curving the fingers moves the bow horizontally along the string.

- Play *f*, but using only the fingers to move the bow. Keep the arm and hand as still as possible.
- Curve the fingers to move the bow up, straighten to move down. Figs. 13a and 13c show the fingers curved, ready to straighten for a down-bow. Figs. 13b and 13d show the fingers straighter, ready to curve for an up-bow.
- Use a mirror to see that the bow stays parallel to the bridge.
- Play at the heel, middle and point.

Fig. 13

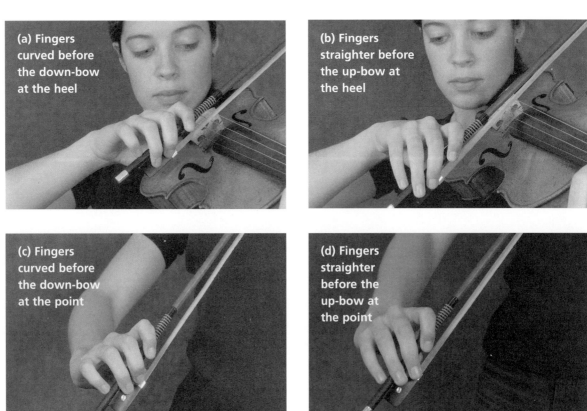

(a) Fingers curved before the down-bow at the heel

(b) Fingers straighter before the up-bow at the heel

(c) Fingers curved before the down-bow at the point

(d) Fingers straighter before the up-bow at the point

(e) Making sure only the fingers move

Making sure only the fingers move

Play a few open strings at the heel, holding the right hand with the left hand (Fig. 13e). Place the thumb in the palm of the hand, and the first finger on the back of the hand. This helps to isolate the finger movement so that the hand itself remains still.

Exercise 3 – Vertical and horizontal combined

Make small circles by combining the flexing movement of the fingers with a small amount of circular hand movement.

Use *as much* finger movement as possible, *as little* hand movement as possible, and no arm movement. Make a sound by touching the string at the bottom of the curve (Fig. 14).

1   Start by holding the bow with curved fingers two centimetres or so above the string. The back of the hand and the fingers should be in a straight line.

2   Lower the bow to the string in a circular movement, straightening the fingers slightly. Play the note, and lift off back to the starting point by curving the fingers.

3   Do this clockwise and anticlockwise, in a continuous motion, at the heel, middle and point.

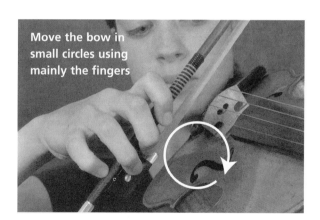

Move the bow in small circles using mainly the fingers

Fig. 14

Changing bow

A little give of the fingers helps the change of bow to be smooth. This exercise exaggerates the give by making it a large, conscious movement of the fingers.[1]

Play short (one eighth of a bow), smooth, sustained strokes at the heel, middle and point.

● Just at the end of each down-bow, while the bow is still moving, smoothly straighten the fingers and thumb. At the same time let the hand move slightly in the same direction as the fingers (i.e., down, producing more of an upward curve at the wrist).

● Just at the end of each up-bow, while the bow is still moving, smoothly curve the fingers and thumb (and lower the knuckles). Move the hand slightly with the fingers (i.e., up, producing less of a curve at the wrist).

Figs. 13a and 13c show the fingers just before the down-bow; 13b and 13d show them just before the up-bow. In reality these finger and hand movements can be so slight as to be invisible, since the tiniest give is enough to make the bow changes smooth.[2]

[1] There is a difference between a give of the fingers and an active finger movement. In reality, finger movements at the bow change should be kept to a minimum, since a 'flick' of the fingers at the change causes the bow speed to increase. Smooth bow changes come more easily from (1) slowing the bow speed, and (2) lightening the bow, just before changing direction. An active finger movement at the heel is often associated with the Carl Flesch school of playing. But Flesch himself said that he introduced the finger action into his teaching method only as a helpful exercise, and had never intended it to become a crucial point of bow technique. 'The finger stroke must only be used in minimal doses because if the change of bow is seen, it will also be heard!' Carl Flesch: *Problems of Tone Production in Violin Playing* (Baden-Baden, 1931), 14.

13

14

[2] Dounis recommended a larger, more visible movement, and called it the 'brush stroke...based on a mental image of the right hand acting like a paint brush, the fingers being the hairs of the paint brush, and the hand the handle.' (Chris A. Costantakos: *Demetrios Constantine Dounis: His Method in Teaching the Violin* (New York, 1988), 76.

15

Bow angle

The fingers help to keep the bow parallel with the bridge. A common error is to try to correct crooked bow strokes by changing what the arm is doing, when the fault really lies with the fingers. This can result in awkward arm movements and tension.

Fig. 15

Using the fingers to alter the angle of the bow

- Hold the bow above the string at the heel. Move the point towards the bridge (Fig. 15a), and away from the bridge (Fig. 15b), using only the fingers.
- To move the point in towards the bridge, pull the first finger in and extend the fourth finger. To move the point out again, pull the little finger in and extend the first finger.
- Keep the heel of the bow above the string.
- Keep the arm and hand still. Place a coin on the back of the hand and make the movements without the coin falling off.

Hand movements

Moving the hand from the wrist, during string crossings, reduces the movement needed by the upper arm and forearm. A little hand movement replaces a lot of arm movement.

16

Exercise 1 – Basic movements

Hold the forearm near the wrist with the left hand.

1   Start with the forearm and hand in a straight line. Then lower the hand from the wrist, below the level of the forearm. This creates a 'high' wrist (Fig. 16a). Return to the straight line again, and repeat several times in a continuous motion.

   Raise the hand above the level of the forearm. This creates a 'low' wrist (Fig. 16b). Return to the straight line again, and repeat several times.

   Keep the forearm parallel with the floor and move only the hand.

2   Move the hand from side to side, keeping the forearm and hand parallel to the floor. Swing the point of the bow towards the shoulder by moving the hand to the left (Fig. 16c), and away again by moving it to the right (Fig. 16d). (Naturally, this movement is never used in actual playing.)

3   Put the vertical and horizontal movements together to make circles. Curve the fingers and thumb as the hand moves up, straighten as the hand moves down. Move the hand only, keeping *the forearm parallel with the floor, and the bow at right angles to the forearm.*

Fig. 16

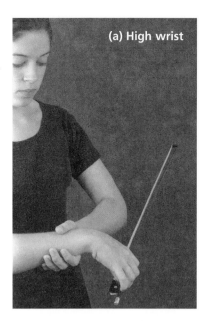

(a) High wrist

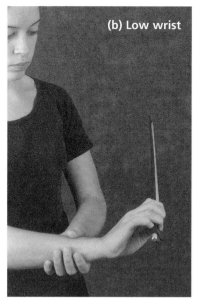

(b) Low wrist

(c) Hand moved to the left

(d) Hand moved to the right

17

Exercise 2

In this exercise, use as little arm movement as possible to cross from one string to another, to exaggerate the hand movement. Mainly use the hand, moving from the wrist, and forearm rotation (see page 15).

- Play only in the upper half.
- In each bar, position the elbow in a middle position so that the hand can reach both outer strings comfortably.
- Use a higher wrist to play a higher string (Fig. 16a), and a lower wrist to play a lower string (Fig. 16b).

Also play Exercise 49 in the upper half, using only the hand to change strings.

18

Exercise 3

As in Exercise 17, use as little upper-arm movement as possible to cross from one string to another, to exaggerate the hand movement. Use a higher wrist to play a higher string (Fig. 16a), and a lower wrist to play a lower string (Fig. 16b). Use plenty of forearm rotation.

1 First play through using ten centimetres of bow in the middle.

2 Then repeat using ten centimetres of bow at the point.

3 Use half bows in the upper half. Now mainly use the arm, with the same hand movement as before but so little that it is hardly visible.

Play the same sequence on the D–A and A–E strings.

Putting weight into the string

When playing _**ff**_, or (for example) playing heavy chords, you use some weight from the upper arm. However, arm weight is often too clumsy for delicate nuances. A finer contact with the string can come from the hand, with the rest of the arm remaining passive. In less powerful playing, or to make subtle changes of colour during a stroke, use the arm to transport the hand and bow along the string, and _move the hand down from the wrist to make the sound._

All the different proportions of arm and hand weight are needed for different strokes and effects: all arm weight, no hand; half arm weight, half hand; all hand, no arm; and all the combinations in between.

19

Using weight from the arm

This exercise requires an assistant:

1 With one hand, support the entire weight of the player's arm at the elbow (Fig. 17a).

2 Put the fingers of your other hand under the wrist, supporting the arm equally with both hands (Fig. 17b).

3 Very slowly remove the fingers supporting the elbow, and gradually transfer all the weight of the arm to the fingers under the wrist. At this point the player must not let the upper arm droop, while still resting the whole weight of the arm into the assistant's supporting fingers (Fig. 17c).

4 Put the fingers of your free hand under the bowing hand, supporting the weight of the arm equally with both hands (Fig. 17d).

5 Very slowly remove the fingers supporting the wrist, and gradually transfer all the weight of the player's arm to your fingers under the bowing hand. The player's wrist must not droop at this point (Fig. 17e).

6 Insert the bow into the player's hand, the player still resting the entire arm weight on the supporting fingers (Figs. 17f and 17g).

Then put the back of your hand under the hair near the heel. The player's arm rests equally on your fingers under the bowing hand, and the back of your other hand under the hair (Fig. 17h).

7   Very slowly remove the fingers supporting the bowing hand, the player gradually resting the entire weight of the arm, through the bow, into the assistant's hand (Fig. 17i).

Fig. 17

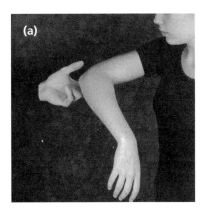

Supporting the entire weight of the arm at the elbow

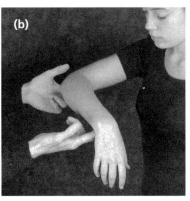

Supporting the weight of the arm equally at the elbow and wrist

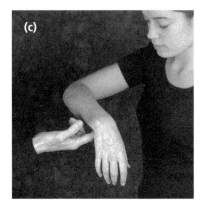

Very slowly remove the left hand, gradually transferring all the weight into the fingers under the wrist

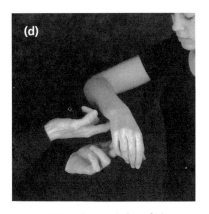

Supporting the weight of the arm equally at the wrist and in the palm of the hand

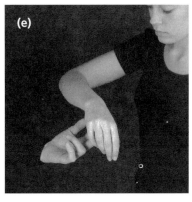

Gradually transfer all the weight into the fingers in the palm of the hand

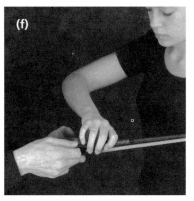

The left hand continues to support the weight as...

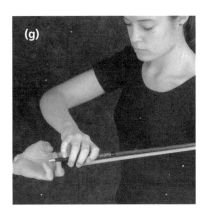

...the right hand inserts the bow into the player's hand

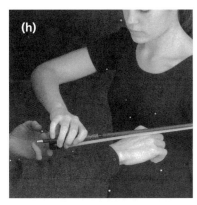

Supporting the weight of the arm equally in the palm of the hand and through the bow

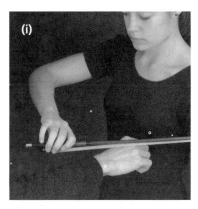

Gradually transfer all the weight into the hand supporting the bow

Right Arm and Hand   13

20

Using weight from the hand

Also see the *Pressure exercise*, Exercise 78.

The movements in this exercise are so slight as to be invisible.

1 Rest the middle of the bow on the string.

Press the wood down to the hair with the hand, in a motion similar to the downward movement that creates a high wrist (Fig. 16a). As a result the wrist will be very slightly more curved upwards. Release the wood again. Do not press the first finger to exert pressure, or turn the hand on to the first finger. Feel the extra pressure from the hand/wrist distributed evenly amongst the fingers.

2 Put the bow on the string a centimetre above the middle and repeat. Do the same, a centimetre higher each time, up to the point.

3 Play the following pattern in the upper half, using only the hand movement to play the stresses. Do not play each note with a fast–slow bow speed: use one even bow speed for the whole bar.

4 Play slow, *f*, down- and up-bow strokes in the upper half, using only the hand movement to sink the hair heavily into the string. Play on each string.

Spreading weight through the hand

Spread bow pressure throughout the bow hand, rather than only pressing into the string with the first finger.

21

Exercise 1

● Play medium-speed, *f* strokes, down-bow and up, with the pad of the fourth finger on the side of the frog (next to the third), like a cello bow hold (Fig. 18). You cannot play to the point holding the bow like this, but play up and down as far as remains comfortable.

● Notice how the weight feels spread across the hand rather than only pressing through the first finger.

● Then find the same feeling while playing with a normal bow hold.

Fig. 18

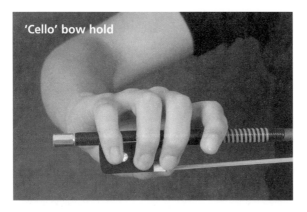

'Cello' bow hold

22

Exercise 2

If the second finger is positioned very slightly to the left of the thumb (as seen from the player's viewpoint), a certain amount of bow pressure can be taken away from the first finger and given to the second.

● Hold the bow without the first finger on the stick, and with the second finger just slightly more to the left of the thumb than usual.

● Play a few long, *ff* notes on each string; or play whole passages in pieces. Feel the second finger helping to produce the sound.

● Repeat with the first finger on the bow. Notice the second finger still taking some of the work away from the first finger, and feel the weight of the whole hand spread evenly over the frog. Pull the third finger in firmly against the frog.

Pull and push

Also see *String tensions*, Exercise 55.

It is significant that we have bow 'strokes', not bow 'presses', and that in French the words for down-bow and up-bow are *tiré* and *poussé* ('pulled' and 'pushed'). The most freely speaking, sweet and resonant tone is produced more by speed of bow than pressure, because then the string is able to vibrate (i.e., swing from side to side) freely.

Play several loud, sustained whole bows on one note.

- **Down-bows:** play without the first finger on the bow.

  Up-bows: play without the fourth finger on the bow.

- *Pull* the down-bows; *push* the up-bows.

- Then feel the same pull and push while playing with a normal bow hold.

Play on each string, using double stops as well as single notes.

Forearm and upper-arm movements

Forearm rotation

A little forearm rotation (the movement used to turn a door handle) can replace a much larger movement of the whole arm.

Exercise 1

Place the bow on the D string at the heel. Then turn the hand clockwise, lifting the bow up and round to the right until it is upside-down (Fig. 19).

Return to the string and repeat several times in a continuous movement.

Turning the bow over using forearm rotation

Fig. 19 24

Exercise 2

25

Play at the extreme heel, with the right elbow positioned level with the middle strings. Move the forearm only. It may be helpful to place the left hand on the right upper arm to help keep it still.

1 At the extreme heel, play a short up-bow on the E string. Stop (Fig. 20a).

2 Move the bow to the G string, using only the hand (forearm) to change levels. Stop (Fig. 20b).

3 Play a short down-bow on the G string. Stop.

4 Return to the E string, using only the forearm. Stop.

5 Move the bow to the G string, and so on several times.

It may be helpful to play the upper string on the outside edge of the hair (tilt the bow towards the fingerboard), and the lower string on the inside edge of the hair (tilt the bow towards the bridge).

(a) The bow ready to play a short up-bow on the E string

(b) Use only the forearm to move the bow to the G string

Fig. 20

26

Exercise 3

Play Exercises 17 and 18 in the *lower third* of the bow.

Play without any hand movement. Cross strings by turning the forearm, and also use a small amount of finger movement (see page 7). Make the string crossings smooth and rounded.

27

Exercise 4

The hand turns towards the first finger (pronation) to give greater pressure into the string.[1] It turns towards the fourth finger (supination) to reduce pressure. A slight supination is an essential element in many off-the-string bowings.[2]

All the movements of the hand in this exercise come from a rotation of the forearm, not the hand itself.

1 Rest the middle of the bow lightly on the string, with the hand in its normal position on the bow.

2 Press the wood of the bow down to the hair by leaning the hand more to the left (pronate): the first and second fingers press the bow down, and the fourth finger straightens slightly (Fig. 21a).

   Release the wood of the bow by leaning the hand slightly to the right (supinate): the fourth finger curves more, and the middle joint of the first finger comes away from the stick (Fig. 21b).

3 Make this from-side-to-side movement several times, in a continuous motion. Do not move the upper arm or elbow. Move the fingers and forearm only, feeling the hand turning around the thumb.

4 Then do the same while keeping the wood of the bow pressed down to the hair all the time, without releasing during the supination. The first and second fingers must now keep pressing down, with the middle joint of the first finger staying on the stick – even though the hand makes exactly the same movement as in (2) and (3) above.

Fig. 21

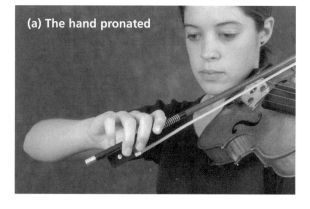
(a) The hand pronated

(b) The hand supinated

Upper-arm movement

28

Exercise 1 – Vertical movement

Play at the extreme tip, using very little bow. For the purposes of the exercise move the *whole* arm from the shoulder.

Play the exercise in two ways:

1 Stop the bow on the string before moving to the next string level: play and stop – move to the next string and stop – play and stop – move to the next string and stop – etc.

2 Play and move all in one action: play and move – play and move – etc.

[1] Increasing the weight of the bow by pressing with the first finger often produces a squashed tone, and should generally be avoided. The feeling of putting more weight into the string should be spread across the fingers. The most direct first-finger pressure is used for biting attacks such as *martelé* and *collé*; but even then it is better if the second finger (positioned slightly in front of the thumb: see Fig. 2, page 2) also helps inject pressure. This gives the bow hand a finer, more sensitive touch and control.

[2] See *About the movement of the bow within the hand,* page 72

Exercise 2 – In and out

Towards the *end of the down-bow* the upper arm pushes *forward* (out). At the *beginning of the up-bow* the upper arm moves *back* (in). Figs. 22a and 22b show the two movements.[1] This exercise exaggerates them, and also helps find the best violin position.

Play in front of a mirror. To see easily if the bow is parallel with the bridge, stand so that the violin is parallel with the mirror.

1   Place the bow on the A string at the point, parallel with the bridge. Angle the violin slightly too far to the left, so that to keep the bow parallel to the bridge the arm has to be straight (Fig. 22c).

2   Play short strokes up-bow and down, in the top quarter of the bow. To keep the bow parallel with the bridge the upper arm has to move in (up-bow), and out (down-bow), much more than usual. Repeat on each string.

3   Now find the correct angle of the violin, where the arm is neither too straight nor too bent at the end of the down-bow. Play the short strokes at the top of the bow again, feeling the same (though smaller) in and out movements as before.

From here to the point the upper arm moves forward ('out')

The upper arm moves back ('in') at the beginning of the up-bow

The violin positioned so that the arm has to be too straight

Fig. 22

About raising the elbow[2]

Some schools of violin playing suggest that the elbow should be on the same level as the bow most of the time. Others suggest that the elbow should be higher in the lower half of the bow (raising during the up-bow, lowering during the down-bow). There are advantages in both methods and many players use a combination of the two, depending on what they are playing.

One advantage of keeping the elbow level with the bow in the lower half is the feeling of the elbow moving *at the same speed as the bow* (in the lowest part of the bow), which gives great control.

Raising the elbow can help to take weight out of the string in the lower half (to 'float' the bow), or it can be used to lever weight *into* the string. It reduces any feeling of being cramped against the side of the body, and produces a wave-like motion which comes from changing the direction of the elbow just before changing bow.

In the upper half, for effortless, sustained, f playing, lever the bow and bow arm into the string by slightly raising the elbow. Leaning into the string by raising the elbow in the upper half is usually so slight that it is hardly visible, although many players need to raise it considerably to find enough power.

[1] In the upper half the upper arm does not always move 'in' and 'out' as described. In many instances it may do the opposite, particularly in fast strokes, moving very slightly back on the down-bow and forward on the up-bow. This gives the feeling of playing with the whole arm, and of powering the strokes from the upper arm even though most of the movement comes from the forearm.

[2] Teaching a beginner, it is usually best to follow the principle of 'one thing at a time'. The student should first learn how to bow with a 'flat' bow arm, the elbow on the same level as the bow at all times. Only once this is established (whether it takes a week, a month or a year), add raising the elbow in the lower half. Once this is established, add raising the elbow in the upper half. Advanced players can practise in the same way: a few minutes with a flat bow arm, a few minutes raising the elbow only in the lower half, and then raising in the upper half.

30

Leading string crossing

The right arm does not have to move all in one piece when crossing from one string level to another. The hand leads when crossing from a lower string to a higher string, and the elbow follows. The elbow leads when crossing from a higher string to a lower string, and the hand follows. This is hardly visible during normal playing, and the exercise exaggerates it by splitting the whole-arm movement into two, separate movements.

First, stop between each movement

Play the note on the upper string – stop – move the elbow to the lower string level – stop – move the hand and forearm to the lower string level – stop, etc.

Then make all the movements continuous

Now play without stopping, so that one movement flows easily into the next. But still exaggerate the timing of the movements by clearly moving first one part of the arm and then the other.

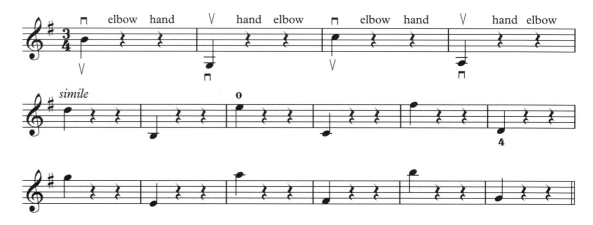

Play in time at a slow tempo (♩ = 60), counting in three:

Bar 1   On count 1 – Play the B with the whole arm on the A string level.

On count 2 – Move the elbow to the G string level, keeping the bow on the A string.

On count 3 – Move the bow to the G string.

Bar 2   On count 1 – Play the G with the whole arm on the G string level.

On count 2 – Move the bow to the A string level, keeping the elbow on the G string level.

On count 3 – Move the elbow to the A string level.

> ### Long, slow sustained bows

Known as 'son filé', this is one of the most important practice methods for bow control and tone production.

31

Exercise 1

● Using whole bows on each string, sustain single notes for as long as possible. Play near the bridge, always aiming for a pure sound even if at times that seems impossible.

● Set the metronome at 60 (i.e., one beat per second). Begin with down- and up-bows lasting 30 seconds, and gradually increase day by day up to 60 seconds or more.

Try to sustain the sound, drawing the bow evenly. The benefits of this work are extraordinary, even if the sound scratches or disappears from time to time because the bow speed is so excessively slow.

32

Exercise 2

● Repeat the bar of rapid sixteenth-notes (semiquavers) for 10, 20, 30 seconds or more. The longer, the louder, and the faster the sixteenth-notes are, the more control is needed to begin the pause note cleanly.

● Play straight from the sixteenth-notes into the pause, beginning it *p* without any hesitation or unevenness in the stroke. Hold the pause 10, 20, 30 seconds or more, sustaining evenly.

Play on each string.

Exercise 3

Playing long, sustained strokes using different lengths of bow, different string crossings and in different positions, there are an infinite number of possibilities of *crescendo, decrescendo* and *sostenuto*. However, since all variations come from the following basic patterns, practice of these alone is sufficient to cover the essentials.

- Play as slowly and as evenly as possible, at about ♪ = 40–60 (the slower the better).
- Stay close to the bridge, rather than going to the fingerboard when playing ***p***.

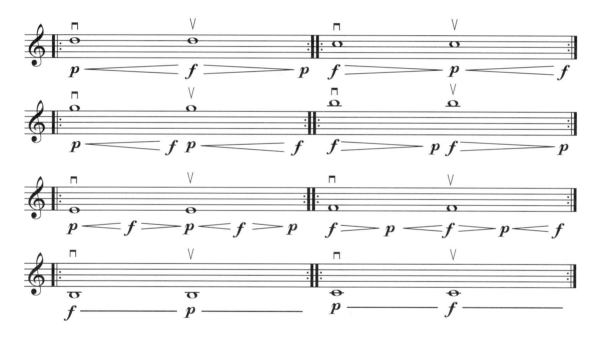

Play on each string.

Exercise 4

Play whole bows on one note with the metronome at 60. *Keep going without stopping throughout the exercise.*

1 Bowing near to the bridge, play 10 beats on the down-bow and 10 on the up. Keep the speed, pressure and distance from the bridge absolutely even.

2 Without stopping, play 12 beats on the next down- and up-bow, and then 14, 16, 18 and 20. Play closer to the bridge as the number increases.

3 Gradually get faster again by reducing the number to 18, 16, etc., down to 10, 8, 6, 4, 3, 2 and 1 bow to a beat. Play further from the bridge as the number decreases, but stay as close as possible.

At each bow speed, feel the exact distance from the bridge that produces the best sound and feeling in the bow. It should feel as though, were you to play a hair's breadth closer to the bridge, the sound would break. 'Ride' the hair against this point like a surfer riding against a wall of water.

35

Exercise 5

Move the bow in the air just above the string, never actually touching it.

- Holding the bow half a centimetre above the string, move as slowly as possible from the heel to the point and back again.
- Relax all the muscles in the bowing arm, and the muscles in the back (between the shoulder blades and on either side of the spine).
- Change the bow hand from heel position to point position gradually and smoothly, the bow moving evenly above the string.
- Breathe normally.

Do the exercise on each string. It feels considerably different on each level.

Bowing parallel to the bridge

About the angle of the violin to the body

Long arms: Point the scroll more to the left. Place the violin lower on the shoulder (i.e., the chin more to the left of the tailpiece).

Short arms: Point the scroll more in front. Place the violin higher on the shoulder (i.e., the chin closer to, or above, the tailpiece).

The more the scroll points to the left (and/or, the lower the violin on the shoulder), the easier it is for the fingers to reach the strings; but the further the right arm has to extend to keep the bow straight at the point.[1]

The more the scroll points to the front (and/or, the higher the violin on the shoulder), the easier it is to keep the bow straight at the point, but the more the left forearm has to twist for the fingers to reach the strings.

At the point, the bowing arm should be neither straight at the elbow nor too bent. By adjusting the direction of the scroll and the height of the violin on the shoulder, every player can find a comfortable playing position. Some teachers recommend that players with very short arms avoid the last two inches of the bow, and/or hold the bow slightly higher up the stick.

36   Fig. 23

Moving the hand along the bow

In this exercise the hand moves along the bow while it rests on the string without moving. Because the bow is parallel with the bridge the arm has no choice but to make exactly the correct movements. This is one of the best exercises because it gives you the *feeling* of drawing a straight bow.

The exercise requires an assistant[2] who rests the bow on the string at the point, holding it exactly parallel to the bridge (Fig. 23). Use only the screw of the bow to hold it, to leave as much room as possible for the player's hand.

The arm naturally performs the right movements for a straight bow

- Position the violin so that at the end of the down-bow the arm is neither straight at the elbow nor too bent.
- The player lightly runs his or her hand up and down the bow, which remains stationary. Begin slowly but later make the movement faster.
- Keep the hand in bow-hold shape wherever it is on the bow, letting it change naturally from its shape when playing at the heel, to its shape when playing at the point.[3]
- Begin with a flat bow arm, i.e., keep the elbow approximately level with the stick in all parts of the bow. Then add any other movements, if (for example) you normally raise the elbow in the lower half.
- The assistant should hold the bow on each string, and at different distances from the bridge, always keeping the bow parallel to the bridge.

Fig. 24 shows the different movements of the arm in each part of the bow.

[1] Imagine that the violin and the bow were joined together as one solid piece of wood. The point of the bow is joined to the violin between the bridge and the fingerboard, and the bow is fixed parallel to the bridge. With your chin staying in one place on the chin rest, move the scroll of the violin to the left: the frog of the bow moves further away from you. Move the scroll to the right: the frog of the bow moves back, closer to you. Now keep the scroll in one position and move the chin-rest end of the violin to the right, so that your chin is very much to the left of the tailpiece. The frog of the bow again moves forward. Keeping the scroll in the same place, move the violin to the left, so that your chin is above the tailpiece: the frog of the bow moves back, closer to you.

[2] If help is not available, it is possible to rest the frog of the bow on the music stand

[3] See *Hand balance*, page 5

Heel: only the upper arm moves, with little or no forearm

Point-of-balance: some upper-arm and some forearm movement

Square: only forearm, the best place to play short, fast sixteenth-notes (semiquavers)

Fig. 24

Between the square and the point: mainly forearm, with some forwards (down-bow) and backwards (up-bow) movement of the upper arm

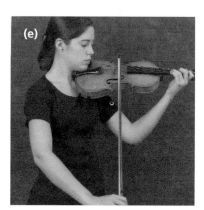

Point: some forearm and more forwards and backwards movements of the upper arm

Dividing the bow into four parts

37

The idea is to play quarter-length strokes in each part of the bow, and then half bows, three-quarter bows and whole bows, keeping the bow parallel with the bridge throughout.

- Play in front of a mirror, holding the instrument parallel to the mirror.
- Play four smooth strokes to a note, using, for example, a two-octave scale in broken thirds. Begin quickly, and play more slowly as you use more bow.

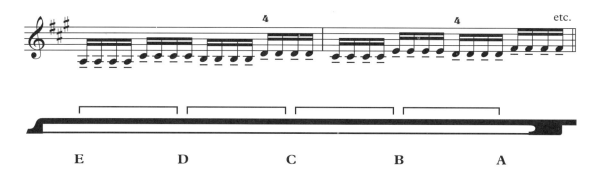

E   D   C   B   A

1 First play medium-speed strokes, bowing from **A** to **B**, from **B** to **C**, from **C** to **D**, and from **D** to **E**.
2 Then play slightly slower strokes, bowing from **A** to **C**, from **B** to **D**, and from **C** to **E**.
3 Bow from **A** to **D**, and from **B** to **E**.
4 Whole bows.

38

Dividing the bow into two parts

First practise the stroke from the *heel to the square*,[1] and then from the *square to the point*. The aim of the exercise is to use the arm, hand and fingers in such a way that the bow stays parallel to the bridge however fast each stroke.

Repeat each bar several times, playing in the following three areas of the bow:

1 From the heel to the square.

2 From the square to the point.

3 Whole bows, from the heel to the point.

- Play each stroke as fast as possible, so that you cannot correct the angle of the bow during the stroke. This is one of the few occasions when tone quality is not important – just move the bow along the string as a physical action. If the bow is parallel to the bridge the end of the stroke will be at exactly the same distance from the bridge as the beginning of the stroke.

- Before playing each stroke, check in the mirror to see that the bow is exactly parallel with the bridge. During the stroke, the bow should move as straight as an arrow. Keep the elbow approximately level with the bow.

- At the end of each stroke, pause with the bow on the string and see whether it is still straight with the bridge. If not, decide what caused it to deviate: the movement of the upper arm? of the forearm? fingers changing the angle of the bow? wrist tight? violin position?

Then straighten the bow, play the next stroke, see whether the bow is parallel to the bridge, and so on.

39

Bowing at an angle

See also *Changing soundpoint,* Exercise 67; *Speed exercise moving across soundpoints,* Exercise 72.

To draw a straight bow, the bow must be exactly parallel to the bridge. When the bow is not parallel it slides across the strings as it moves down or up. The greater the angle to the bridge, the faster it slides.[2]

Fig. 25a shows the bow angled in.[3] During the down-bow, the bow moves towards the fingerboard. During the up-bow, it moves towards the bridge. Fig. 25b shows the bow angled out. During the down-bow, the bow moves towards the bridge. During the up-bow, it moves towards the fingerboard.

You can angle the bow deliberately to move further from, or closer to, the bridge. In (a), angling the bow in makes the hair automatically move towards the fingerboard. In (b), angling the bow out makes the hair automatically move towards the bridge.[4]

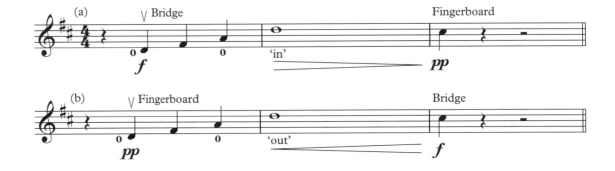

[1] 'Square' is the name Galamian used for the place in the bow where there is a right angle between the bow and the forearm, the forearm and the upper arm, and between an imaginary line drawn from the shoulder to the bow. Longer-armed players have the square higher up the bow, above the middle. Shorter-armed players have it lower down in the bow, directly at the middle. The square is the only place where the forearm can move alone, without the upper arm moving as well. This area is really only a couple of centimetres long. Add a few centimetres above and below this area to play longer strokes, so that the upper arm is still only used to the smallest extent. This is often the best place to play short, fast sixteenth-notes (semiquavers), without having to use the much larger apparatus of the upper arm.

[2] Although the norm should be a straight bow, different tone colours can be found by deliberately drawing the bow slightly crookedly to the bridge, while at the same time forcing the bow not to travel towards or away from the bridge.

[3] 'In' and 'out' refer to the position of the frog of the bow, not the point. When the bow is angled 'in' the frog is brought closer in to the body.

[4] Of course you can also move to the fingerboard while keeping the bow straight, and it is possible to diminuendo with the bow staying quite near the bridge.

You can also angle the bow to help stay near the bridge in f passages. Angle it only very slightly:

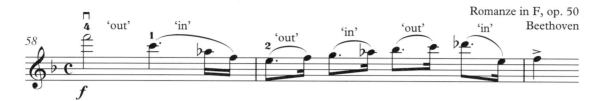

The bow angled in   **The bow angled out**

Fig. 25

Practising angled bowing increases your ability to make instantaneous adjustments while playing, improving bowing technique in general. The bow ends up straighter and is easier to correct the moment it goes off course:

Bow angled in

1 Place the bow on the string at the heel, near the bridge. Angle the bow in. Do not angle the bow too much or it will slide across the strings too quickly.

2 Play a whole bow to the point, medium speed. As the bow moves it will drift closer and closer to the fingerboard. *Do not try* to make this happen – let the bow drift automatically because of its angle. Keep the sound even and smooth. Begin with a lot of pressure, and decrease the pressure as the bow drifts to the fingerboard.

3 Having arrived at the point leave the angle the same – i.e., the heel is further back than the point.

4 Play a whole bow back to the heel. Let the bow drift away from the fingerboard back to the starting place. Increase the pressure during the stroke.

Bow angled out

1 Place the bow on the string at the heel, near the fingerboard. Angle the bow out.

2 Play a whole bow to the point. As the bow moves it will drift closer and closer to the bridge. Begin with hardly any pressure, and increase the pressure as the bow drifts to the bridge.

3 Having arrived at the point leave the angle the same – i.e., the heel is further forward than the point.

4 Play a whole bow back to the heel. Let the bow drift away from the bridge back to the starting place. Decrease the pressure during the stroke.

Using half bows instead of whole bows, repeat both angles in the middle of the bow, and in the lower and upper halves. Always playing with a pure tone, increase or decrease the angle to drift across the strings at different speeds.

40

Fast whole bows in the air

In a well-developed bow arm the whole-bow stroke feels like one single action, not a series of smaller movements joined together. In this exercise the bow is moved in the air, to help develop the feeling of one movement more easily.

Use a mirror to check that the bow remains parallel to the bridge.

1 Play a very small stroke at the heel. Stop on the string and wait.

2 Make a sudden, fast movement in the air to the other end of the bow, and place the bow on the string. Stop and wait.

3 Play a very small stroke at the point and leave the bow on the string. Wait.

4 Make a sudden, fast movement in the air to the heel, and place the bow on the string. Wait.

Move the bow through the air as fast as possible, as straight as an arrow, without wobbling in the air or losing its parallel line with the bridge.

During the movement the hand must change from heel position (fingers slightly more vertical, fourth finger curved), to point position (fingers slightly more tilted to the left, fourth finger straighter). See Figs. 9a and 9b, page 6.

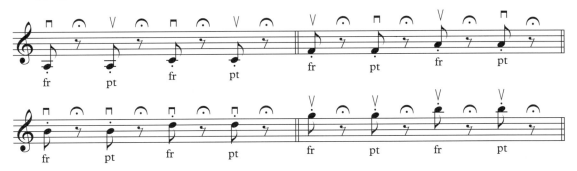

5 Then play without stopping between the stroke and the movement.

Play the short stroke at the heel, and in the same movement move above the string at great speed to the point. Pause. Play and move to the heel. Pause, and so on.

41

Fast, short strokes moving up the bow

A simple test of whether the bow stroke is straight or not is to play fast thirty-second-notes (demisemiquavers) with separate bows. The soundpoint[1] changes on each stroke if the bow is not parallel to the bridge, because you cannot correct the bow during a stroke. Watch the point of the bow to see that its movement is straight up and down with no sideways movements.

Using very little bow, play fast thirty-second-notes on one note at the heel, ♩ = 66.

• Without stopping, gradually move the bow up to the point, and down again to the heel.

• Do the same with strokes about ten centimetres long (♩ = 60) and then about twenty centimetres (♩ = 50).

Keep the bow in good contact with the string, with a clean sound. Watch the bow in a mirror, and make sure that it stays exactly parallel to the bridge. Use the fingers as well as the hand to control the direction of the bow (see *Bow angle*, Exercise 15). Play on each string.

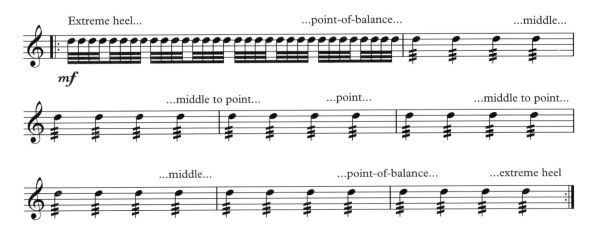

[1] See *Soundpoints*, page 41

Pivoting and string crossing

Seven levels of the bow

Level 1   G string   **Level 4**   D–A double stop   **Level 6**   A–E double stop

Level 2   G–D double stop   **Level 5**   A string   **Level 7**   E string

Level 3   D string

Exercise 1 – Single strings

42

Play the theme using the nine bowing variations. Play at slow, medium and fast speeds.

Theme

Nine bowing variations

Start each variation beginning up-bow as well as down-bow.

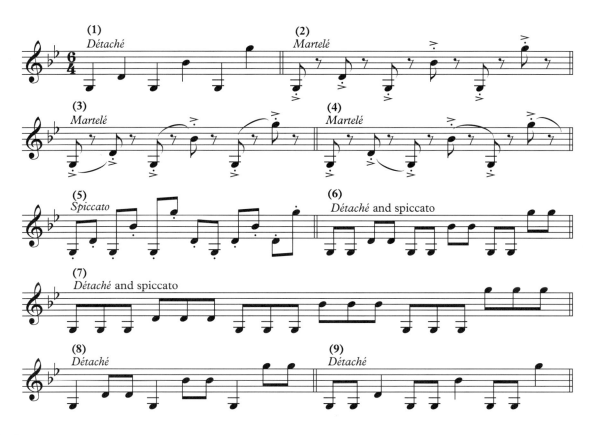

Strokes

Martelé: Begin each stroke with a firm bite. Leave the bow on the string throughout. Notice the different parts of the bow hair that catch the different strings.[1]

1   Quarter-length strokes at the heel, middle and point.

2   Half-length strokes in the lower half, middle, and upper half.

[1] For example, play a down-bow on the G string, and stop the bow on the string. Notice the exact part of the hair that touches the G string where the bow has stopped. Leaving the bow on the string, pivot over to the E string and stop the bow on the string. The place on the hair that now contacts the E string is a few centimetres lower down the hair than the hair that finished on the G string.

Détaché: Play a slow, smooth *détaché*, *f*, sustaining the sound fully. Connect the strokes well, joining one stroke to another solidly.

1 Quarter-length strokes at the heel, middle and point.

2 Half-length strokes in the lower half, middle, and upper half.

Spiccato: Use three different spiccato strokes:

1 Just below the middle: fast, light, short, low strokes.

2 At the point-of-balance: medium strokes.

3 Near the heel: slow, heavy, long, high strokes.

Exercise 2 – All levels

This continuous study includes every crossing from any level to any other. Play the same strokes as in Exercise 42. Play at slow, medium and fast speeds.

Practice method: balancing double stops

The perfect balance of the bow playing two strings at once (i.e., the best weight distribution), is rarely even. Normally one string will need slightly more weight than the other, depending on the relative thickness of each string, and the lengths of each string. (A perfect fifth creates the same string lengths, an octave creates different string lengths.)

A useful practice method to balance the bow perfectly on each string is to tremolo the bow across the strings:

Find how to play the tremolo very fast and perfectly evenly, each note sounding clearly. Afterwards the double stop will feel more evenly balanced.

Practise double-stop scales by playing each interval with a tremolo before playing it as a normal double stop.

Pivoting

See also Exercises 124–5 for *Smooth pivoting* in chord playing.

Pivoting, the movement around the string that takes the bow from one string to another, is one of the most important elements of bowing. The bow moves around the string while moving along as an up- or down-bow.

In the examples, ◄— means pivot to the next lower string, —► means pivot to the next highest string. In both cases pivot during the note before the string crossing.

42 Etudes ou caprices, no. 29
Kreutzer

'Allemanda' from Partita in D minor, BWV 1004
J. S. Bach

Pivoting is an example of technical timing that is earlier than the musical timing.[1] The pivoting movement has to be timed so that the first note on the new string sounds as if there had been no string crossing.

You can see clearly how smooth or sudden the pivot is by standing with the violin at right angles to a mirror.

Exercise 1

Play whole bows, pivoting several times during each stroke without touching an adjacent string.

- Pivot while the bow is moving along the string. Pivot two, four and eight times in each stroke, making it sound like normal playing on one string without pivoting. The example below shows four pivots on each string.

  On the **G string**, pivot to the left until the hair almost touches the rim of the violin; pivot to the right until almost touching the D string.

  On the **E string**, pivot to the right until the hair almost touches the rim of the violin; pivot to the left until almost touching the A string.

  On the **D and A strings**, pivot between the adjacent strings as far as possible without touching them.

- In the upper half, moving the hand from the wrist reduces the amount of arm movement needed.

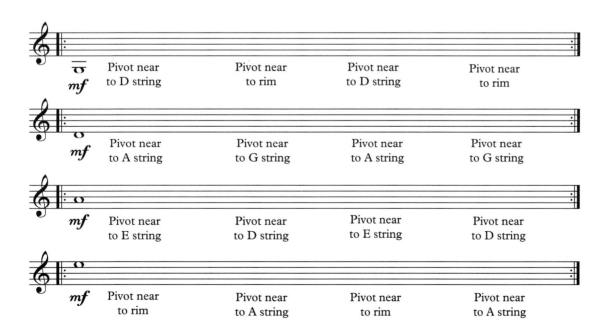

44

[1] Musical timing is *when* you want the note to sound; technical timing is sometimes at the same moment as the note sounding, and sometimes *before* the sound. Other obvious examples of early technical timing are finger preparation, biting the string before strokes such as *martelé*, and shifting. See Ivan Galamian: *Principles Of Violin Playing And Teaching* (New Jersey, 1962).

45

Exercise 2

This passage should sound as though one player is sustaining smooth and even whole-notes (semibreves), while another is playing short, smooth eighth-notes (quavers) on each beat.

1 Use half bows in the lower half, middle, and upper half.

2 Use whole bows.

46

Exercise 3

When legato string crossings are not smooth enough, it is usually because the string crossing is too late. The bow should pivot across to the new string *while* playing the note before the string crossing, not *after* playing it.

This exercise uses double stops to force the string crossing to be too early. The double stop is gradually shortened, making the pivot happen later and later, until finally reaching a normal and very smooth string crossing.

● Play half-length strokes in the lower half, middle, and upper half.

● Although pivoting later and later, continue to make the movement rounded and smooth by pivoting *while* playing the first note, gradually bringing the hair nearer and nearer to the new string.

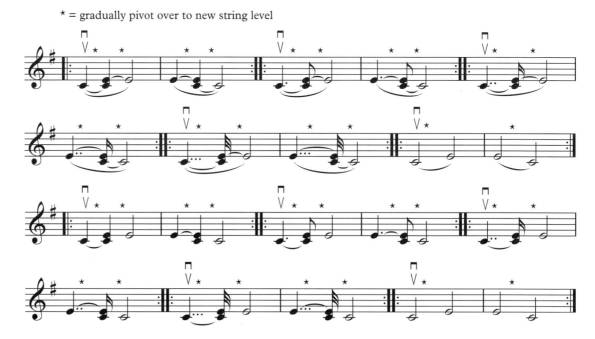

Repeat on the D–A and A–E strings.

Exercise 4

- In (1) and (2), keep the whole-note (semibreve) sustained evenly while pivoting to and from the quarter-note (crotchet). Accent the quarter-note without disturbing the whole-note.

- In (3) and (4), play the whole-note *f*. Begin the half-note (minim) *p* and make a *crescendo*. This forces the pivot to be slow and measured.

- In (5) and (6), play the whole-note *p* and the half-note *f*. Do not let the pivot, or the *f* half-note, disturb the whole-note.

- Continue the examples up the scale.

Also play these patterns on double stops in high positions for the different feel of the strings.

48

Exercise 5

Sustain the whole-notes (semibreves) evenly. Keep the bow close enough to the two strings so that the pivoting movement does not have to be too large.

1 Use half bows in the lower half, middle, and upper half.

2 Use whole bows.

49

Exercise 6

Keep the bow deep in the string, with the hair close to both strings. Make each bar sound the same as if playing with a normal fingering, either on one string or across the strings.

1 Use half bows in the lower half, middle, and upper half.

2 Use whole bows.

Hold fingers down on the string for as long as possible.

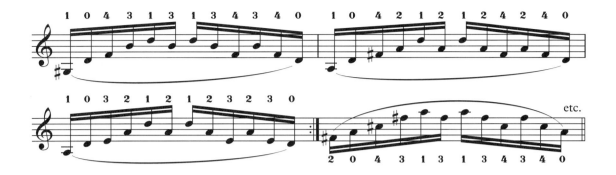

Curves on one string

There is no bow stroke on the violin that moves in an exactly straight line. Even simple down- and up-bows on one string move in curves. The curved bow stroke is the same as a pivoting movement. These exercises make the curves much larger than normal.

Exercise 1

50

- Sustain the tied notes solidly, so that they sound like one continuous note.
- During the tied notes, pivot towards the next double stop smoothly and evenly. Pivot as far as possible without actually touching the next double stop, so that to play it (on the new bow) you only have to pivot a fraction further.
- Begin with quarter-length bows near the heel; in the middle of the bow; and at the point. Then use half-length bows in the lower half, middle, and upper half.

51

Exercise 2

1 First play the notes equally. Notice the size of the bow movement from the first pair of strings to the second pair.

2 Repeating the bar continuously, very gradually reduce the distance of the bow movement from the first double stop to the second, so that you play the outer strings more and more quietly.

3 Continue to reduce the movement until the bow only barely touches the outer strings, and then does not touch them at all. The x-notes in the last bar of the example indicate the bow moving towards the outer strings without touching them.

- Begin with quarter-length bows near the heel; in the middle of the bow; and at the point. Then use half-length bows in the lower half, middle, and upper half.

- Repeat on the G–D–A strings.

- Also play on the G string, using the rim of the violin as an extra 'string'. Play a 'double stop' made up of the rim and the G string, and play normally on the G and D strings for the other side of the movement.

- Similarly on the E string, use the rim as an extra string. Play a 'double stop' made up of the rim and the E string, and play normally on the E and A strings for the other side of the movement.

52

Accented string crossing

Play through the double-stop sequence using the string crossing variations that follow.

- Patterns 1–2: Play half bows in the lower half, middle, and upper half. Then play whole bows.

- Patterns 3–6: Play at the heel, middle and point with separate bows. Also slur in pairs.

- Begin each pattern up-bow as well as down-bow.

Scale string crossing

An effective way to make string crossings smooth and rounded is to play them as a double stop (Example 1). Bumpy string crossings come from changing from one string to another too late; playing the crossing as a double stop remedies this by doing the opposite – changing string level too early. All smooth string-crossing passages can be practised like this.

Another effective practice technique is to leave out the left hand, and just play the bowing pattern on open strings. Example 2 shows Example 1 played without the left hand.

Every scale or run produces its own pattern when reduced to open strings. The study below covers every possibility, including slurs across two, three and four notes.

- Begin with quarter-length bows near the heel; in the middle of the bow; and at the point. Then use half-length bows in the lower half, middle, and upper half.

    In each case first play the whole study beginning down-bow, and then beginning up-bow.

- Tempo: slow, medium and fast.

Keep the bow deep in the string, sustaining each stroke firmly and joining it to the next without any break. Play all the tied notes solidly and evenly.

Tone Production

part b

General contact exercises

About the tilt and the angle of the violin to the floor

The flatter the violin is held, the more comfortable it is to play on the E string. There is a feeling of the bow resting on the E string, which supports it. The more tilted the violin is, the more there is a feeling of having to hold the bow *against* the E string. This is a common cause of poor tone production on the E string.

However, the flatter the violin is held, the more uncomfortable it is to play on the G string. The right upper arm has to be held unnaturally high, and the left upper arm may have to be pulled in too far to the right for the fourth finger to reach the G string easily enough. This is a common cause of tension.

Therefore, the best possible tilt of the violin is one where the E string gives sufficient support to the bow, while at the same time the right arm and fourth finger can easily reach the G string. In certain passages it is possible to tilt the violin less when playing on the E string, and more when playing on the G string.

When the body of the violin is held parallel to the floor, the neck of the violin slopes down away from the bridge. Therefore, for the strings to be horizontal the scroll of the violin must be slightly raised. It is often better, particularly in high positions, to play with the strings sloping down *towards* the bridge, which helps the bow keep a good point of contact not too far from the bridge. This means that the scroll has to be raised considerably. Many violinists (and particularly violists, because of the viola's extra length and heaviness) play with the scroll of the instrument too low, which means that the bow has to sit on a sharp downward slope.

Bow tensions

54

A major factor in using the bow is the springiness of the wood and hair. A violinist does not so much play with the bow itself, as with this force *in* the bow. The feeling of playing in the lower half is different from playing in the upper half, because the amount of 'give' in the hair and the wood changes.

At the heel, the hair gives and the wood of the bow is rigid.

At the point, the wood gives and the hair is rigid.

In the middle, both the hair and the wood give equally.

See Figs. 1a and 1b, page 1, which show the hair bending when the bow is pressed down at the heel, and the wood bending (in the middle of the bow) when the bow is pressed down at the point.

The passage from the Brahms Violin Concerto shown below is played with a broad *détaché* in the upper half, but the player feels the give of the wood in the middle of the bow. It is difficult to play such strokes just by feeling the contact of the hair with the string.

Violin Concerto in D, op. 77, mov. I
Brahms

The opposite is true of this passage from *Zigeunerweisen*. Here, the sixteenth-notes (semiquavers) are played deep in the string in the lower half, with a tiny amount of bow. The player plays into the hair, which *remains 'bent' throughout the four notes*. It is difficult to play the passage by feeling anything in the wood of the bow.

Zigeunerweisen, op. 20
Sarasate

1 Rest the bow on the string at the heel, near to the first finger.

Press the hair into the string heavily, without moving along the string. The wood of the bow remains rigid while the hair gives completely. No amount of pressure alters the curve of the bow, while the hair 'bends' where it touches the string.

2 Do the same near the point, pressing the hair down into the string heavily.

The hair is now completely rigid, while the wood gives easily in the middle of the bow. No amount of pressure will 'bend' the hair where it touches the string.

3 Press down in the middle of the bow, where both wood and hair give equally.

4 Still without playing, press down many times, a centimetre or so apart, up and down the whole bow. Notice all the different amounts of give in the hair and wood.

5 Playing *f* on one note, play short down- and up-bows at the heel, in the middle and at the point. Notice the different feel of the wood and hair at each place in the bow.

6 Play whole bows on each string, playing heavily into the stick and the hair. Feel the same changing proportions of give in the different areas of the bow.

String tensions

55

The friction of the bow pulls and pushes the string from side to side. A magnified, slow-motion film of a bow stroke would show that during the down-bow the hair 'catches' the string and pulls it to the right. The further the bow pulls or 'bends' the string, the more the tension of the string increases until the tension is such that the string suddenly snaps back. The hair instantly catches the string again, and the 'catch, pull, snap-back, catch' repeats an infinite number of times. The up-bow pushes the string to the left until the tension is such that the string snaps back. If the bow is drawn too quickly or lightly there is a whistling sound because the hair skids over the surface of the string without catching it. Too much pressure produces a torn, scraped sound because the string cannot move freely from side to side underneath the hair.

Fig. 26

The bow pulling the string sideways on the down-bow: the string is just at the point where it will snap back

In this exercise the hair catches, pulls and releases the string once at a time, which produces a 'click' sound. This 'click' is the sound at the very beginning of strokes such as *collé*, *martelé*, or sharply accented strokes.

1 Without moving the bow along the string, grip the string with the hair by pressing heavily. At the same time begin to pull the string to the right as slowly as possible (Fig. 26).

2 Gradually increase the tension of the string by pulling it more, fraction by fraction, until the tension is such that the string suddenly snaps back with a sharp 'click'.

3 Do not release the bow when the string snaps back, so that the bow catches the string again, resulting in a continuous catch–pull–click–catch, pull–click–catch, pull–click–catch, pull–click–catch, etc. Do this at about one click per second.

4 Do the same on the up-bow by pushing the string to the left.

There should be no sound other than one single click at a time. Practise at the heel, middle and point, at different distances from the bridge, on each string.

Resonance

A very short, resonant note, such as third finger D on the A string, rings on after the end of the note. The same note played longer should ring *during* the note, as well as after the note stops. Tone production is always enhanced when the player listens as much to the background resonance as to the principal sound.

Exercise 1

56

This is a very simple but effective exercise. Pluck the string well to make a full, rounded note, and listen to the ring. Suzuki calls this ring the 'true sound of the string'. Then listen for the same ring in the sound while playing the note with the bow.

Exercise 2

57

1 Without vibrato, play a very short stroke at the heel (bar 1). Lift the bow immediately (indicated by '∥') and listen to the sound ringing on for a few seconds afterwards. Find how to play the note so that it has the longest possible ring. Make sure that the D is perfectly in tune with the open D.

2 Play longer and longer strokes (bars 2–5). Listen to the ring *during* the note as well as after it has ended (bars 4–5).

3 Changing bow direction (bars 6–8), join the end of one stroke solidly into the beginning of the next without any break or disturbance to the note, and then lift off: listen to the background ring *during the bow change*.

4 Play continuous strokes without lifting the bow (bar 9). Listen to the three different sounds that make up the tone: the actual note you are playing, the surface noise of the hair on the string, and the continuous, background ring.

Using any fingered G, D, A or E, play the exercise on different soundpoints,[1] on each string, in various positions.

Exercise 3

58

1 Play several strokes in one bow, lifting the bow a little *off the string* between each stroke. Listen to the continuous background ring, both during the strokes and between the strokes.

2 Play the same figure with the bow firmly *on the string* all the time, stopping the bow on the string between each stroke. Listen to the background ring during the strokes, and while the bow has stopped on the string between the strokes.

3 Do the same on each soundpoint, even near the bridge where it is difficult to catch the string because the string is so hard, and at the fingerboard where it is difficult to catch the string because it is so soft.

[1] See *Soundpoints*, page 41

59

Exercise 4

This exercise is very good for improving listening, and greatly increases richness of tone. Listen to the resonance of 'dead' notes (i.e., A♭) as well as 'live' notes (i.e., G, D, A, E).[1]

1   Play the first note with emphasis, lift the bow, and listen to the ring.

2   Play the first two notes smoothly connected, with an emphasis on the second. Hear the ring during the first note, and after the second note.

3   Play the first three notes smoothly connected, with an emphasis on the third. Hear the ring during the first and second note, and after the third. Stop on the fourth, fifth notes, etc., up the scale.

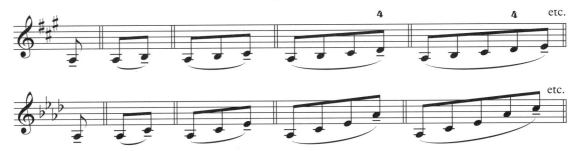

First play without vibrato, aiming for maximum resonance with the bow only. Then use vibrato, particularly vibrating the last note as though the vibrato will make the resonance last longer.

Play on each string in low, middle and high positions. This is also a good practice technique for passages from the general repertoire.

60

Bow tilt

The tilt of the bow has to be altered frequently. More hair is used for the strongest, thickest and deepest tone, less hair for playing more *p* or *dolce*. Lifted strokes respond differently with different amounts of hair, and in the lowest quarter of the bow, many strokes work more easily with slightly tilted hair.

● The exercise alternates flat hair and tilted hair (wood tilted towards the fingerboard). Roll the bow between the fingers to adjust the amount of hair, and use a little hand movement if that feels more comfortable.

● Play continuous whole bows, up and down, on one note. The tone will be richer and thicker during the full hair, but should remain even and strong throughout.

● First play the exercise on soundpoint 2, then on 3 and 4.

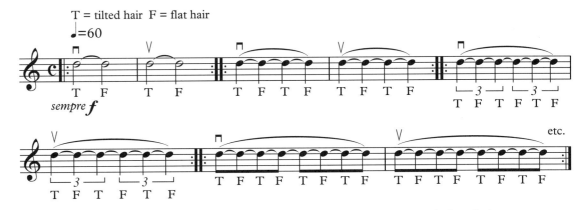

1   Play one tilted–flat combination in a bow (bars 1–2), dividing the bow exactly into halves:

Down-bow   Lower half tilted, upper half flat

Up-bow   Upper half tilted, lower half flat.

2   Play two in a bow (bars 3–4), dividing into exact quarters.

3   Play three, four, six, and eight tilted–flat combinations in one bow. The example shows as far as four in each bow.

4   Repeat the exercise the other way round. Begin with full hair:

Down-bow   Lower half flat, upper half tilted

Up-bow   Upper half flat, lower half tilted, etc.

Use various notes, in different positions, on each string. Play double stops as well as single notes.

[1] If you think that you cannot hear any resonance in a 'dead' note, imagine how it would sound if the body of the violin, instead of being an empty resonating box, were filled solid. Then, since a note such as A♭ really would be 'dead', what you are hearing normally is in fact resonance – just not as much as from 'live' notes.

True legato

Sometimes you have to use a slight portato instead of true legato, for projection or clarity, or for musical reasons. But ordinarily the strokes should be entirely smooth, and the vertical finger actions should not affect the horizontal bow stroke.

Exercise 1

61

1 Play whole bows on the open string, very evenly and solidly.

2 Still play the open string, and silently finger the adjacent string (written as x-notes). Move the fingers with a fast and decisive action, and with vibrato. Keep the feeling (and sound) of the evenness of the bow playing the open string.

3 Bow and finger together on the same string. The bowing should remain just as even and solid as before.

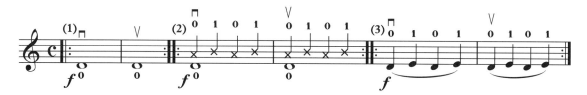

Apply the same method to all the two-note fingering possibilities: 01, 02, 03, 04; 12, 13, 14; 23, 24; 34.

Also play on the other strings, and in low, middle and high positions.

Practice method

The exercise improves technique overall, but it can also be applied as an ordinary part of learning or practising any legato passage. In the example from Brahms, finger the notes normally on the E and A strings, but bow on the open A and D strings. Or play it the other way round, fingering on the A string while bowing on the E string. In the Grieg, bow the open G with deep sonority while fingering silently on the D string. The strokes on the open strings should sound legato, undisturbed by the silent fingering on the other strings.

Sonata no. 3 in D minor, op. 108, mov. I
Brahms

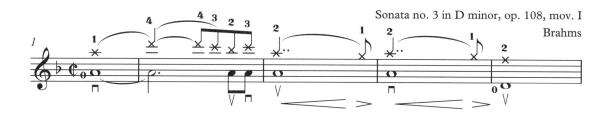

Sonata in C minor, op. 45, mov. I
Grieg

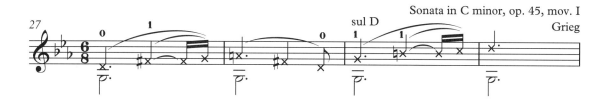

This type of practice also gives good results with the bow kept on one string, even though in the actual passage it crosses from string to string:

Chanson de matin, op. 15, no. 2
Elgar

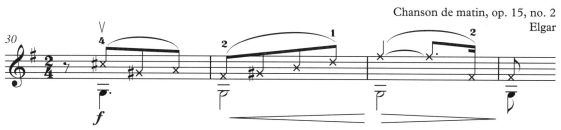

Tone Production   39

62

Exercise 2

- Sustain the open G throughout while running the fingers up and down whole scales.
- Feel the smoothness and evenness of the bow, completely undisturbed by the finger action.
- Then play the scale normally, feeling the same evenness in the bow.

Finger the x-notes silently while bowing the open G string

Also play the scales in Exercise 226, bowing on one string while fingering another.

63

Attacks

Strokes can be started from above the string or from on the string. They can begin (1) with a sharp attack, or (2) with the same sound as the rest of the stroke; or (3) they can begin imperceptibly, so that the first millimetre is *pp*, the second millimetre is *p*, the third *mp*, and so on. This gives an immediate but very smooth beginning to a note.

Play repeated half-notes (minims) on one note, alternating down- and up-bows, separated by a rest.

First play in the lower half, then in the middle, and then in the upper half. In each area of the bow, begin each stroke as follows, playing several of each type before changing to the next:

1 Smooth, imperceptible beginning to each note, placing the bow on the string before playing the stroke.

2 Smooth, imperceptible beginning, starting from above the string. Experiment with different angles of descent, from smooth (like a plane approaching a runway) to almost vertical. Experiment with different speeds of descent, from slow to very fast.

3 Clear, articulated beginning, starting on the string. The very beginning of the stroke should sound exactly the same as the sound that follows.

4 Clear, articulated beginning, starting from above the string. Experiment with different speeds and angles of descent.

5 'Bite' the beginning of the stroke, like a *martelé*, placing the bow on the string before beginning the stroke.

6 Bite the beginning of the stroke, starting from above the string. This is one of the most powerful attacks.

Play on each string, and in different positions – each attack has to be slightly different depending on the thickness and length of each string. Also play double stops on each pair of strings with the same six attacks.

Soundpoints

Flesch and Galamian, amongst others, divided the area between the bridge and the fingerboard (known as the point-of-contact), into five 'soundpoints'. Flesch called them 'at the Bridge', 'Neighbourhood of bridge; that is between Bridge and central point', 'at the central point', 'Neighbourhood of Fingerboard; that is between Fingerboard and central point', 'at the Fingerboard'.[1]

Fig. 27a shows the five soundpoints in 1st position. Since the height and slope of the bridge varies from instrument to instrument, the exact place for each soundpoint may be different.

When exercises using all five soundpoints are played in high positions, the soundpoints have to be squeezed closer and closer to the bridge as the left hand plays higher and higher up the string. Fig. 27b shows the five soundpoints in 9th position.

Naming the soundpoints is useful in teaching, making it possible to call out 'Three', 'Two', and so on while the student is playing.

In low positions, the G and D strings are too thick and hard to respond easily when the bow is very close to the bridge. Near the fingerboard, the A and E strings are too soft to be able to take more than minimum pressure. (Four-string chords sound better when the lower strings are bowed further from the bridge, and the upper strings closer to the bridge.) Nevertheless, wherever possible play the exercises at every distance from the bridge.

Do not use open strings when playing tone exercises on one note, since they ring easily anyway. Begin with resonant notes such as third finger D on the A string, and then 'dead' notes such as second finger C♯.

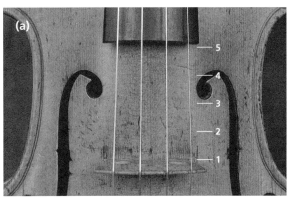
The five soundpoints in 1st position

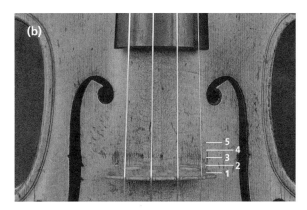
The five soundpoints in 9th position

Fig. 27

Practice method

Normally the bow plays on different soundpoints from note to note, and from phrase to phrase. To experiment with the proportions of speed and pressure, keep the bow on only one soundpoint at a time. All the soundpoints referred to in this exercise are from Fig. 27a.

- Begin on soundpoint 5. Use fast, light strokes. By finding exactly the right speed and pressure, make the strings vibrate as widely as possible, with a ringing, resonant tone.

- Repeat the phrase or passage playing only on soundpoint 4. Although still fast and light, the bow will now need to be slightly slower and heavier. Find exactly the right speed and pressure to make the strings vibrate as widely as possible.

- Repeat on soundpoint 3. By now the bow pressure will be significantly heavier than it was on soundpoint 5, and the speed of bow slower – either use less bow or slow down the tempo. Find exactly the right speed and pressure to make the strings vibrate as widely as possible.

- Repeat on soundpoint 2. Now the bow pressure will have to be considerable, and the bow speed much slower. Play at a slower tempo. Sink the bow heavily into the strings, feeling the different 'give' of the hair and wood of the bow.[2] Find exactly the right speed and pressure to make the strings vibrate as widely as possible.

- If possible, repeat on soundpoint 1. Play the phrase or passage at a very slow tempo. The bow speed will have to be extremely slow, and the bow pressure extremely heavy. Find exactly the right speed and pressure to make the strings vibrate as widely as possible.

[1] Carl Flesch: *Problems of Tone Production in Violin Playing* (Baden-Baden, 1931), 18

[2] See *Bow tensions*, page 35

64

Soundpoint exercise: whole bows

In low positions the string is hard and inflexible near the bridge, and the bow has to be drawn slowly and heavily. Near the fingerboard the string gives to the slightest pressure, and the bow has to be drawn quickly and lightly. Enough pressure has to be used to engage the string, but too much pressure constricts the side-to-side movement of the string and chokes the sound. For a pure tone, pressure is always *only as much as necessary for the bow speed.*

1   Draw continuous whole bows up and down on soundpoint 5. Play without vibrato.

Try more and less pressure, and faster and slower bow speed, to find which combination of speed and pressure makes the string vibrate the widest. Watch the string vibrate as well as listening. Only a little extra pressure may make the string vibrate less, or just a little faster bow may let it vibrate more, etc.

2   When you are sure the speed and pressure are exactly right, i.e., the vibration of the string is at its widest, add a little vibrato. Listen to the resonance of the violin.

3   Start again on soundpoint 4 without vibrato. Find the right balance of speed and pressure to make the string vibrate to its maximum, and then add vibrato. Do the same on soundpoints 3, 2 and 1. Each time the bow is placed nearer to the bridge, use a slower bow with more pressure.

To stay on one soundpoint the bow must be exactly parallel to the bridge. The sound should be entirely pure and resonant all the time. Notice how the slightest excess pressure makes the width of the string vibration narrower.

Play notes on each string in low, middle and high positions, where you have to squeeze the soundpoints closer to the bridge. Also play double stops.

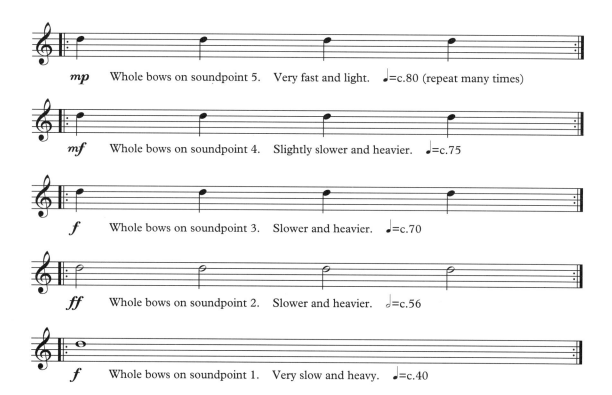

Soundpoint exercise: short bows

1 Play without vibrato. Begin at the point on soundpoint 5, using ten or twelve centimetres of bow. Play sixteen or thirty-two strokes or more, moving the bow quickly and lightly.

As in Exercise 64, watch the string vibrate as well as listening. Notice how the slightest excess pressure makes the string vibrate less, or how just a little less pressure (or more bow) may make it vibrate more.

2 Staying at the point and without stopping the strokes, move to soundpoint 4 and again stay there until you find the combination of speed and pressure that makes the string vibrate the widest.

3 Do the same on soundpoints 3, 2 and 1, and then 2, 3, 4 and 5 again. The speed will have to be very slow on soundpoint 1, and the pressure very heavy. *Do not stop the strokes as you change soundpoint.*

4 Repeat the whole routine using ten or twelve centimetres in the middle of the bow, then again near the heel.

5 Repeat the whole routine using twenty-five centimetres of bow in the upper half, at the middle, and in the lower half.

Play notes on each string in low, middle and high positions. In high positions squeeze the soundpoints closer to the bridge. (See Fig. 27b.) Also play double stops.

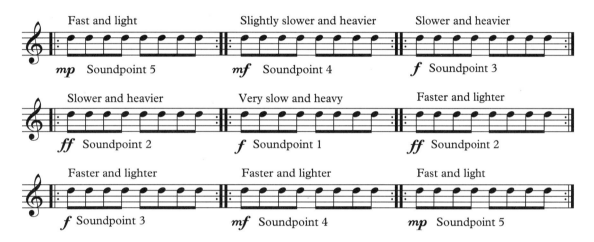

Soundpoint exercise: changing the length of bow

66

Play two bows to a beat. Begin at ♩ = 56, and gradually increase up to about 75.

1 Play in the middle of the bow on soundpoint 5. Using very short, sustained strokes, find the balance of speed and pressure that makes the string vibrate as widely as possible.

2 Gradually lengthen the strokes until you use the whole bow. Keep the sound pure and unforced – increase the pressure as necessary to balance the steadily increasing bow speed.

3 Gradually shorten the strokes again until arriving back in the middle of the bow.

4 Without stopping the repeated short strokes in the middle of the bow, move on to soundpoint 4 and repeat the exercise. Do the same on soundpoints 3 and 2.

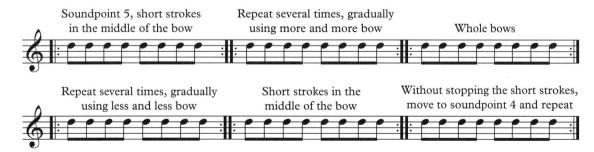

As the strokes get longer you may reach a point where the bowing feels awkward and the tone is uneven. Relax whichever parts of the arm, hand or fingers have a resistance that interferes with a natural, fluent arm movement.

Play notes on each string in low, middle and high positions. In high positions squeeze the soundpoints closer to the bridge. (See Fig. 27b.) Also play double stops.

67

Changing soundpoint

Also see *Bowing at an angle*, Exercise 39.

- Play whole bows down and up on one continuous note. Play without vibrato.

- During the whole bow strokes, move towards and away from the bridge. Begin with one fingerboard–bridge–fingerboard in each down- and up-bow, and then two in each bow, three and so on. The sound should remain pure and resonant while the bow moves across the soundpoints.

Fingerboard–bridge–fingerboard once in each bow

Down-bow Heel = soundpoint 5, middle = soundpoint 1, point = soundpoint 5.

Up-bow   Point = soundpoint 5, middle = soundpoint 1, heel = soundpoint 5.

1 Place the bow on soundpoint 5, at the heel. Angle the bow 'out' (Fig. 28a). While playing from the heel to the middle of the bow, move to the bridge (Fig. 28b). Do not try to change soundpoint – let the bow drift because of the angle to the bridge.

2 Arriving at the bridge in the middle of the bow, angle the bow 'in' (Fig. 28c) *without stopping the bow,* and continue the down-bow while drifting back to soundpoint 5 again (Fig. 28d).

3 Having arrived back at the fingerboard at the end of the down-bow, keep the bow angled 'in' (Fig. 28d). Then play from the point to the middle of the bow, letting the bow drift towards the bridge (Fig. 28c).

4 Arriving at the bridge in the middle of the bow, angle the bow 'out' (Fig. 28b) *without stopping the bow,* and continue the up-bow while drifting back to soundpoint 5 again (Fig. 28a).

The speed pattern on both down- and up-bow is *fast–slow–fast,* and the pressure pattern *light–heavy–light.*

Tilt the bow more on soundpoint 5, and play flat hair on soundpoint 2–1.

Fig. 28

The bow angled out

The bow angled out

The bow angled in

The bow angled in

Fingerboard–bridge–fingerboard twice and more in each bow

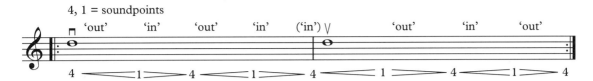

- Place the bow on soundpoint 4, at the heel. Use a quarter of the down-bow to reach the bridge; change the angle of the bow without stopping the down-bow; drift back to soundpoint 4 by the middle of the bow; change the angle of the bow; then do the same in the upper half. Repeat on the up-bow.

- Then move towards and away from the bridge three times, four times, etc., up to about eight. With each increase in number start nearer the bridge, ending up playing only on soundpoint 2–1.

Play on each string in low and middle positions. Also play double stops.

Alternative

Play the exercise with a straight bow, using the arm to move towards and away from the bridge.

Different soundpoints, same speed

68

The faster the bow moves across the string, the more pressure is needed to catch the string. Fast bows near the fingerboard need less pressure because the string is so soft; fast bows near the bridge need great pressure because the string is so hard. This exercise highlights the pressure differences by keeping the same speed while changing the soundpoint.

Play this exercise with a metronome to ensure that the speed of bow does not change. (The length of bow must also stay the same for the bow speed not to change.)

1 Without vibrato, play whole bows on soundpoint 5. Find the balance of speed and pressure that makes the string vibrate as widely as possible, as in Exercise 64.

2 Then, *without changing the speed of bow* (or length of bow), move to soundpoint 4. Increase the pressure. Stay on soundpoint 4, adjusting the pressure until the string vibrates as widely as possible.

3 Repeat on soundpoint 3, still without changing the speed or length of bow, and then on soundpoint 2.

4 Having moved as far into the bridge as possible, move out again, decreasing the pressure on each soundpoint, back to the fingerboard.

Play notes on each string in low, middle and high positions. In high positions you have to squeeze the soundpoints closer to the bridge. (See Fig. 27b.)

69

Different soundpoints, same pressure

Normally when you move towards or away from the bridge you have to change the pressure to keep the speed/pressure/soundpoint balance correct. However, you can keep the pressure the same (or almost the same) if the speed of bow is altered instead.

1 Without vibrato, play on soundpoint 1 in the middle of the bow, using centimetre-long bows. Find the balance of speed and pressure, for that length of bow and soundpoint, that makes the string vibrate the widest.

2 Then *without changing the pressure,* move to soundpoint 2. Increase the bow speed by using more bow. Stay on soundpoint 2, adjusting the speed (i.e., length of bow) until the string again vibrates as widely as possible.

3 Move to soundpoint 3, using as much bow as necessary to keep the sound from breaking, but still without changing the pressure. Repeat on around soundpoint 3–4, using whole bows.

4 Having moved as far towards the fingerboard as possible, move in towards the bridge again, now using less bow on each soundpoint, back to soundpoint 1. Use exactly the same pressure on each soundpoint, changing only the bow speed (length) to keep the sound pure.

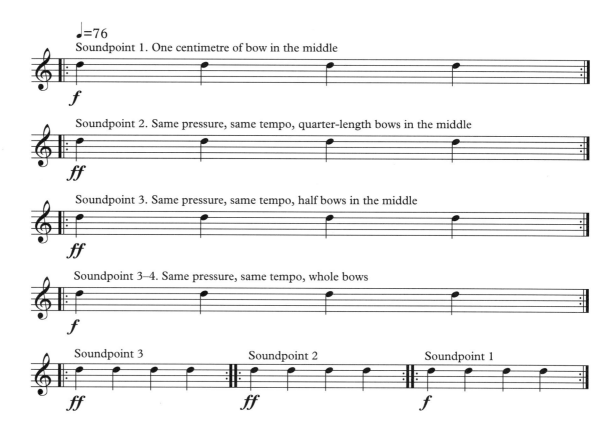

Play notes on each string in low, middle and high positions. In high positions squeeze the soundpoints closer to the bridge. (See Fig. 27b.)

70

Rhythms on each soundpoint

Play a variety of bowing and rhythm patterns on each soundpoint. Play the groups faster near the fingerboard, slower near the bridge. Whatever the dynamic, soundpoint or length of bow, play with maximum resonance and a completely pure tone.

1 Start on soundpoint 5. Play the rhythm pattern several times, experimenting with speed and pressure until the string vibrates as widely as possible on each note, the sound is pure, and the violin resonates.

2 When the speed and pressure are both perfect, move the bow to soundpoint 4 and again find the right speed and pressure to make the string vibrate as widely as possible. Do the same on soundpoints 3, 2 and 1, and then work back again through 2, 3, 4 and 5.

Then continue in reverse through soundpoints 2, 3, 4 and 5.

Use quarter-length bows at the point, in the middle and at the heel. Also use more bow – half bows for the quarter-notes (crotchets) – playing in the upper half, middle, and lower half.

Start each variation up-bow as well as down-bow.

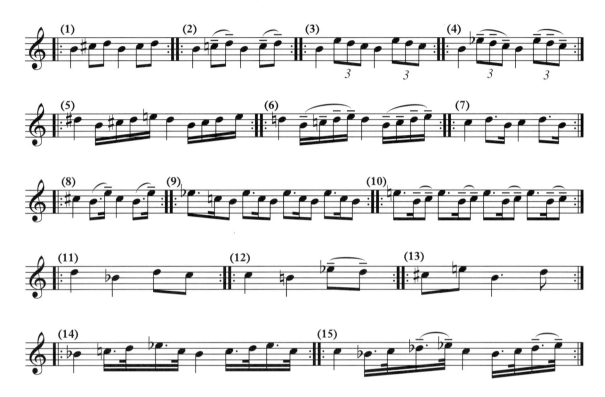

Other positions

Play the same notes on the other strings in various octaves:

In high positions squeeze the soundpoints closer to the bridge. (See Fig. 27b.)

Also use other notes and other bowing patterns. This is the sort of exercise where even a small amount of work produces long-lasting results. But always be sure that the sound really is pure before moving to the next soundpoint.

Bow speed

Every shade of tone colour is available through the different degrees of speed, pressure and distance from the bridge. Proportions of more pressure to less speed are used for more closed, darker or denser tone colours. But for the most open, freely speaking, resonant sound, tone production is based on speed of bow, not pressure.

71

Speed exercise

This exercise uses fast–slow strokes – strokes that begin quickly and then are almost immediately slow, with no silence between the fast and the slow parts of the stroke. The aim is to make the string vibrate widely during the fast part of the stroke, using speed rather than pressure to make the notes speak.

Watch the string vibrating as well as listening closely to the sound. Find the balance of speed and pressure that makes the string vibrate as widely as possible during the fast part of each stroke.

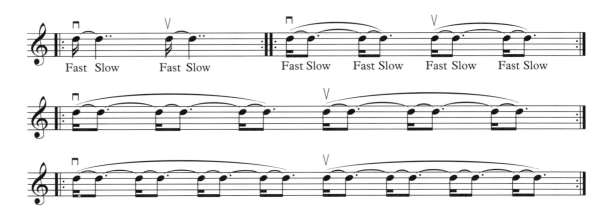

1   Begin with one fast–slow in a bow. Play without vibrato, about a centimetre from the bridge.

2   Use more bow and more pressure for the fast part of the stroke, less bow and less pressure for the slow part. However, use as little extra pressure as possible during the fast part of the stroke: only as much as necessary to keep in good contact with the string – 'float' the bow along the string horizontally, rather than digging in vertically.

3   Then divide the bow into two halves, playing one fast–slow in the lower half, and one in the upper. Do not try to play a fast and *then* a slow bow – each fast–slow is one action, not two.

4   Then play three fast–slow divisions in each bow, 4, 6, 8, 9, 12, 16, 20, 24, 28 and 32. The example above shows up to 4 fast–slows in a bow. From 12 onwards, play and count in groups of four. The exercise sounds like a series of throbs within one unbroken, continuous note.

Listen to the continuous background ring.[1]

Also play midway between the fingerboard and the bridge, and at the fingerboard. Play notes on each string in different positions, and also double stops.

Tempo

The more fast–slows there are in a bow, the faster the tempo. For example, play the first bar of the exercise (one fast–slow in each bow) at about ♩ = 52. Two fast–slows in each bow: ♩ = 52, one fast–slow on each quarter-note (crotchet) beat. Twelve fast–slows: 63, four on each metronome beat. Thirty-two: 76, four on each metronome beat.

Variation

This helps to keep the flow of the bow steady and even.

●   Before playing the first fast–slow, and before each new stage of the exercise, play sustained, even whole bows, down and up.

●   Play on soundpoint 2, at about the tempo that you will use for the fast–slow strokes.

●   Then play the fast–slows, keeping the same feeling of the bow and arm travelling smoothly and evenly.

[1] See *Resonance*, page 37

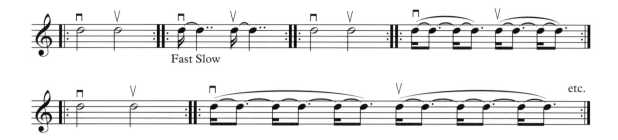

Speed exercise moving across soundpoints

Exercise 1

Play 8 and 16 fast–slows in each bow. Adjust the speeds and pressures to suit each soundpoint, so that the sound remains entirely pure and even throughout – use very little bow when playing near the bridge.

5, 4, 3, 2, 1 = soundpoints

The oblique strokes are only to make the exercise visually clearer. Play so that the sound is continuous.

1 Once into the bridge and out again in each bow. One fast–slow on each soundpoint.

2 Once into the bridge and out again in each bow. Two fast–slows on each soundpoint.

3 Twice into the bridge and out again in each bow. One fast–slow on each soundpoint.

4 Twice into the bridge and out again in each bow. Two fast–slows on each soundpoint.

Play on each string.

Variation

Reverse the order: begin and end near soundpoint 1, moving away from the bridge and back again. This requires great control of the bow near the bridge.

73

Exercise 2

Play the speed exercise while moving between the fingerboard and the bridge. The examples show up to three fast–slows in a bow, but continue through 4, 6, 8, 9, 12, 16, 20, 24, 28, 32.

- **Down-bow**   *p*–crescendo–*f*

  Up-bow   *f*–diminuendo–*p*

- Angle the bow slightly 'out' throughout the exercise.[1]

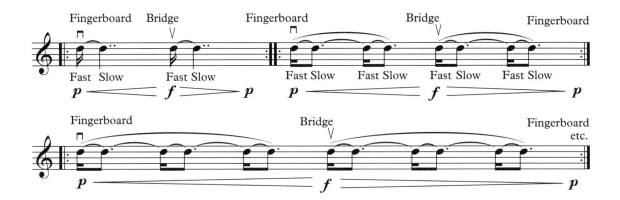

- **Down-bow**   *f*–diminuendo–*p*

  Up-bow   *p*–crescendo–*f*

- Angle the bow slightly 'in' throughout the exercise.

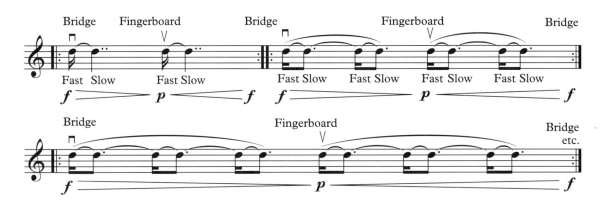

Play on each string.

74

Speed exercise using broken thirds

The best balance of speed, pressure and soundpoint to produce the fullest tone depends on the length of string that the hair is playing on; this changes from note to note. The best balance also changes from string to string because of each different string thickness and tension. Scales in broken thirds, in different octaves, provide ideal material to experiment with all the different responses of the string to the bow hair.

Play two-octave scales in one position across the strings, major or minor, in the following keys:

    1   A (1st position)   **2**   E (5th position)   **3**   A (8th position)

The following example shows the speed exercise through 1, 2, 3 and 4 fast–slows to a bow. Continue in the same way with 6, 8 and 12 to a bow. (Continuing further, with 16 and 24 fast–slows to a bow, is a good exercise for staccato.)

[1] See Fig, 25, page 23

Uneven bow speeds

Exercise 1

75

H – heel   P.O.B. – point-of-balance   M – middle   Pt – point   UH – upper half   WB – whole bow

'Two thirds/one third/two thirds' is a bow division for groups of three strokes, used for travelling to a higher or lower place in the bow without playing accents.

In the following examples, no. 1 shows how you can start at the heel and finish at the point using ⅔–⅓ –⅔. Using this bow division makes it easier to play evenly, without accenting any one note. Nos. 2 and 3 show how using more bow on one note, to travel between the heel and the point, may cause an unwanted accent.

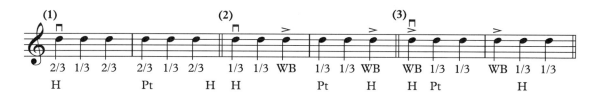

In the example from Bach, the ⅔–⅓–⅔ is played between the middle of the upper half, and the point-of-balance. In the Sibelius, the ⅔–⅓–⅔ is played over the whole bow from heel to point. In either case, the bow division ⅓–⅓–⅔, or ⅔–⅓–⅓, could easily produce an unwanted accent.

'Allemanda' from Partita in D minor, BWV 1004
J. S. Bach

Violin Concerto in D minor, op. 47, mov. I
Sibelius

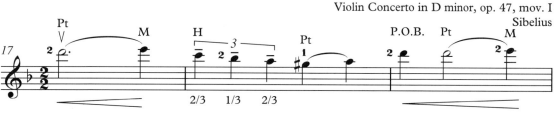

Play the following passage so that it sounds as even as if you were using the same length of bow on each note.

- Whole bows. The first bar begins at the heel, the second bar at the point, the third bar at the heel, and so on.

- Half bows. Use the same distribution in the lower half, middle, and upper half.

Sustain each stroke evenly, joining it to the next stroke without a break. Play *f*, keeping the bow deep in the string throughout, and also *p*.

76

Exercise 2

Play Kreutzer Etude no. 2 (or a similar study) with short, evenly sustained strokes.

- Gradually move up and down the whole length of the bow without any unevenness in the tone. Make it sound as if you were playing normally in one place on the bow.

42 Etudes ou caprices, no. 2
Kreutzer

- Do the same while playing dotted rhythms:

Exercise 3

For the purposes of the exercise, use the same length of bow on each down- and up-bow – do not use more bow for a longer note and less bow for a shorter note. This means that (for example) the quarter-notes (crotchets) have double the bow speed of the half-notes (minims). By varying the pressure and, if necessary, the soundpoint, play with a *completely even sound and even volume,* without accenting the faster-moving strokes more than the slower strokes.

Play in the following areas of the bow:

1 Quarter bows. Play at the heel, in the middle and at the point.

2 Half bows. Play in the lower half, middle, and upper half.

3 Whole bows.

Bow pressure

There is a certain proportion of pressure to speed which causes the string to vibrate the most (i.e., causes it to swing the furthest from side to side under the hair). How heavy the bow must be to do this depends on the distance from the bridge, but it is the amount of pressure where a fraction more would reduce the freedom of the string swinging from side to side. Production of the lightest, most open and singing tone is based more on speed of bow than pressure, because the string is able to swing freely under the bow hair. Darker and richer colours come from greater proportions of pressure in relation to the speed.

78

Pressure exercise

Leopold Mozart was one of the first to teach this exercise.[1] In recent times it has been a central practice technique taught by Capet and his pupil Galamian. Cellists know it as the 'Casals exercise'. Dounis applied a variation of the exercise to pieces. (See page 55.)

The exercise uses strokes that change from loud, in the first part of the stroke, to soft in the second part. The aim is to find a rich and resonant tone; and to associate that tone with the sensations of 'give' and resistance in the bow, bow hair and string that go with the tone.

- Play whole bows on one note, without vibrato.

- Play one *f*–*p* on the down-bow, and one on the up-bow. Then play *f*–*p* twice in each bow, then 3, 4, 6, 8, 9, 12, 16, 20, 24, 28, 32 times. The example below shows up to four in a bow.

- Use the *arm* to transport the bow up and down; use the *hand* to make each *f*.

- During the *f*, play as loudly as possible without forcing. Listen to the pitch: it should not flatten because of too much pressure. To avoid squashing the tone, use a little more bow speed (i.e., a little more bow) for the *f* than for the *p*.

- Play *subito f* and *subito p*, without *crescendi* or *diminuendi*. Do not have any break in the sound between the *f* and the *p*.

- Playing *f*–*p* once or twice in a bow, play the *f* nearer the bridge and the *p* slightly further from the bridge. From three *f*–*p*s onwards, play on soundpoint 2 without changing soundpoint.

- In the first stages of the exercise, the *f* and the *p* are two separate actions. From about four *f*–*p*s onwards, let each *f*–*p* become one action, i.e., *f*-release. The exercise then sounds like a series of 'throbs' within a continuous sound. *Listen to the continuous background ring.*[2]

- Up to about three *f*–*p*s, use a flatter hair in the *f* and more tilted in the *p*. From then on use three-quarters of the hair throughout.

- Also play without the first finger on the bow.

Play notes on each string in low, middle and high positions: the shorter the string length, the less pressure the string can take.[3]

Also play double stops.

Tempo

The more *f*–*p*s there are in a bow, the faster the tempo. For example, play the first bar of the exercise (one *f*–*p* in each bow) at about ♩ = 60 (two beats *f*, two beats *p*). Two *f*–*p*s in each bow: ♩ = 60 (one beat *f*, one beat *p*). Twelve *f*–*p*s: 52 (four on each metronome beat). Thirty-two: 76 (four on each metronome beat).

[1] '...loudness, alternating with softness, can obviously be performed four, five, and six times [and] often even more in one stroke. One learns through practice of this...to apply strength and weakness in all parts of the bow...By diligent practice of the division of the stroke one becomes dexterous in the control of the bow, and through control one achieves purity of tone.'
Leopold Mozart: *A Treatise On The Fundamental Principles Of Violin Playing* (Augsburg, 1756; Eng. trans. Editha Knocker, Oxford, 1948), 99.

[2] See *Resonance*, page 37

[3] See *Pressure and length of string*, page 57

Variation

This helps to keep a steady flow of the bow during the heavy–light pressure changes.

- Before playing the first *f–p*, and before each new stage of the exercise, play sustained, even whole bows, down and up.
- Play on soundpoint 2, at about the tempo that you will use for the fast–slow strokes.
- Then play the *f–p*, without losing the feeling of the bow travelling smoothly and evenly.

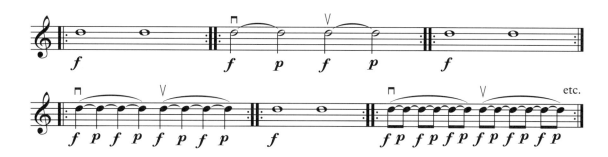

Practice method

Playing legato passages with portato accents was a practice method taught by Dounis. Draw the bow as in the exercise, playing deep-into-the-string accents within the legato stroke. Vary the number of 'throbs' per note according to the time of the passage in question. Use the soundpoint that permits the maximum depth of hair–string contact, feeling all the give and resistance of the bow, bow hair and string. Then find the same deep-but-unforced contact when playing the passage normally.

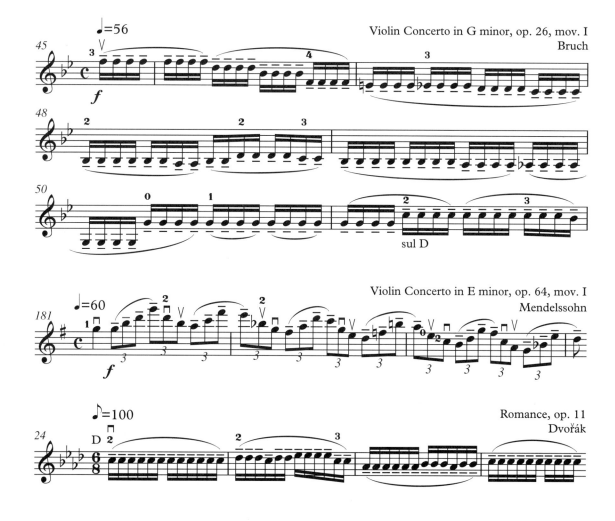

79

Pressure exercise moving across soundpoints

Play 8 and 16 **_f_–_p_**s in each bow. Find the right speeds and pressures for each soundpoint, so that the sound remains entirely pure and even throughout – use very little bow when the bow is near the bridge, and near the fingerboard play **_p_–_pp_** rather than **_f_–_p_**.

5, 4, 3, 2, 1 = soundpoints.

The oblique strokes are only to make the exercise visually clearer. Play so that the sound is continuous.

1 Once into the bridge and out again in each bow. One **_f_–_p_** on each soundpoint.

2 Once into the bridge and out again in each bow. Two **_f_–_p_**s on each soundpoint.

3 Twice into the bridge and out again in each bow. One **_f_–_p_** on each soundpoint.

4 Twice into the bridge and out again in each bow. Two **_f_–_p_**s on each soundpoint.

Play notes on each string in different positions. Also play double stops.

Variation

Start the other way round: begin near soundpoint 1, move towards 5 and then back to 1. This requires great control of the bow near the bridge.

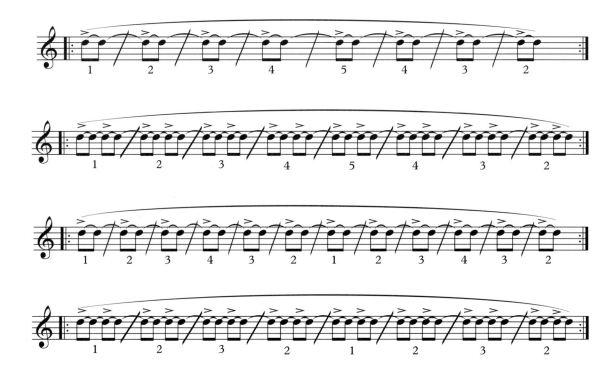

Pressure exercise using scales

The best balance of speed, pressure and soundpoint to produce the fullest tone depends on the length, thickness and tension of each string. Play the pressure exercise using two-octave scales in one position across the strings, major or minor, in the following keys:

1 A (1st position)   **2** E (5th position)   **3** A (8th position)

Pressure and length of string

Three principles of tone production:

1 Closer to the bridge, more weight.

2 The higher the fingers play up the string (the shorter the string), the nearer the bow plays to the bridge.

3 The shorter the string, the less pressure it can take from the bow.

The third principle overrules the first. The bow plays *heavily* near the bridge in low positions. The bow plays *lightly* near the bridge in high positions.

In the examples below, the top E in the Wieniawski and the top B in the Kreisler must be played surprisingly gently near the bridge if they are to sound pure and stay in tune. After the top B the open E must be played much more powerfully.

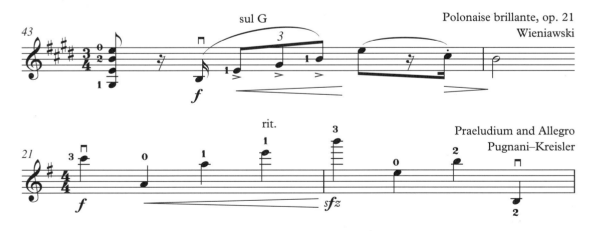

Intonation difficulties in high double stops are often blamed on the left hand, when in fact the bow pressure is the cause. Just a little excess pressure at the top of the A string causes the notes to go flat.

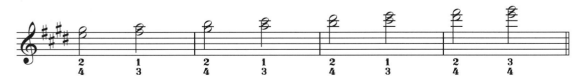

81

Exercise 1

In this exercise, play every open string heavily; play the stopped notes more and more lightly as they get higher.

1 **Play only on soundpoint 4.**

Play all the eighth-notes (quavers) *mf*.

Begin the quarter-notes (crotchets) *mf*, and play them more and more lightly as they get higher, reaching *ppp* at the top.

2 **Play only on soundpoint 3.**

Play all the eighth-notes *f*.

Begin the quarter-notes *f* and play them more and more lightly until reaching *pp* at the top.

3 **Play only on soundpoint 2.**

Play all the eighth-notes *ff*, moving the bow slowly and heavily.

Begin the quarter-notes *ff* and play them more and more lightly until reaching *mp* at the top.

4 **Change the soundpoint throughout.**

Play every note *f*.

Move nearer to the bridge to play each quarter-note; play all the eighth-notes on soundpoint 4.

Play the first few quarter-notes on soundpoint 2–3. As they get higher, play them nearer and nearer to the bridge, until the last three or four are played very close to the bridge (eighth-notes on soundpoint 4, quarter-notes on soundpoint 1).

Play the same sequence on each string.

82

Exercise 2

5, 4, 3, 2, 1 = approximate soundpoints

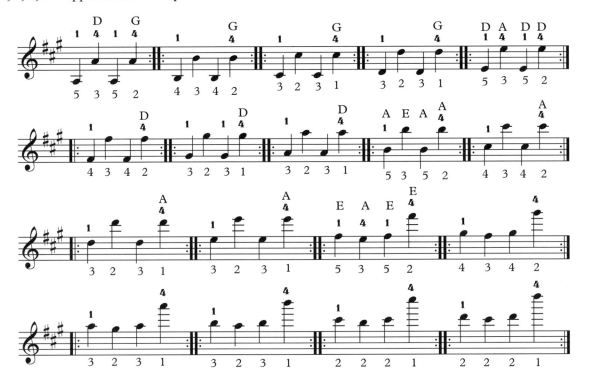

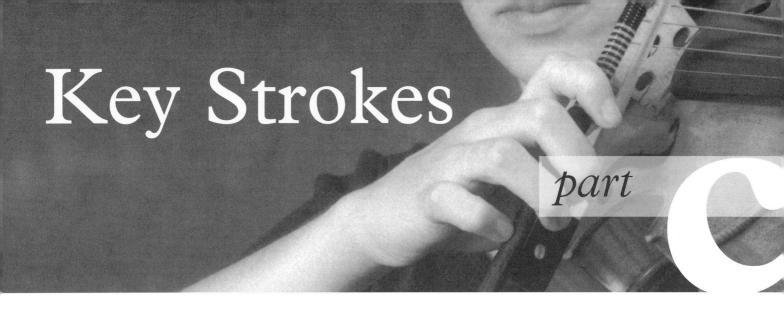

Key Strokes

part

Détaché

Simple *détaché*: Simple *détaché* is smooth and even, each note joined to the next without a break. It is a foundation for all other strokes, because the speed and pressure is entirely even from the beginning of the stroke to the end.

Accented *détaché*: Simple *détaché* becomes accented *détaché* when the even speed and pressure changes to fast–slow and heavy–light. When accented *détaché* begins with a bite it becomes *martelé*.

83

Even speed and pressure

The bow speed and pressure of simple *détaché* should be even. When the bow is drawn unevenly, the changes of speed and pressure may be extremely slight, and may even be unnoticeable to many listeners. The aim of this exercise is to gain the feeling of an even stroke, where the speed and pressure does not change, by first *deliberately* changing the speed and pressure.

- For the sake of clarity, the variations below are written out using different note values to show the different parts of the stroke; but each bar should basically sound like continuous, smooth, simple *détaché* strokes on one note:

♩=60–80   etc.

- Repeating each bar several times, first play the speed and pressure patterns in the upper half, at the middle, and in the lower half, using quarter-length strokes. Then play whole bows.

- Make the speed or pressure changes so slight that they are only just noticeable, playing each stroke *almost* evenly.

Speed changes

F = Very slightly faster bow speed   S = Very slightly slower bow speed

F S   F S   S   F S   F   F S   F FS   F   S   F S   S   F S   Even speed

Pressure changes

Play only the slightest *crecendo* and *diminuendo*

>   >   <   <   >< ><   <> < >   Even pressure

Be sure to make only the very slightest speed or pressure changes, as though you do not want anyone to notice that the strokes are not in fact even.

Be particularly careful in the last centimetre of each bowstroke. For example, the speed pattern in the first bar should not become 'fast–slow–fast' instead of 'fast–slow'. The first pressure pattern should not become 'heavy–light–heavy' instead of 'heavy–light'.

Repeat on each string.

Smooth connections

Exercise 1

84

How to stop the bow well is not only relevant to ending notes, but is also a part of connecting strokes smoothly. Dorothy DeLay calls this exercise 'parking the bow', like bringing a car to a halt. Stop the car gently and smoothly, without a jolt; do not slow down too early, or drift on past the place where you wanted to stop.

The notes in the example below sound like one, unbroken half-note (minim). The tied sixteenth-note (semiquaver) represents the *last centimetre* of the stroke.

1 Play repeated down- and up-bows on one note, separated by silence. Play *mf*–*f*, using about a quarter of the bow, moving the bow at a medium speed. Move the bow evenly, without speed or pressure changes.

- In the *last centimetre* of each stroke, slow down and come to a gentle halt: get slower, slower, slower, and stop, all in the space of about a centimetre or less. The stopping must not be sudden, nor take too long, and must be entirely even. Leave the bow on the string.

- Play in the upper half, at the middle, and in the lower half.

2 Play the same strokes as before, but very gradually make the silence between the notes shorter and shorter. Finally join the strokes, still 'parking the bow' in the last centimetre of each stroke, but now playing a continuous, even and smooth *détaché*.

Repeat on each string.

Exercise 2[1]

85

There is no such thing as a completely inaudible bow change. Four quarter-note (crotchet) D's played with separate bows will never sound like a whole-note (semibreve) D. But if the connection of the strokes is solid and even enough, and the note changes at the same time as the bow, you can give an illusion of one, unbroken sound.[2]

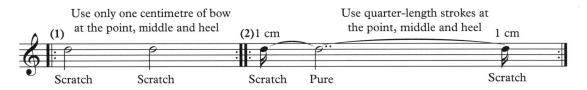

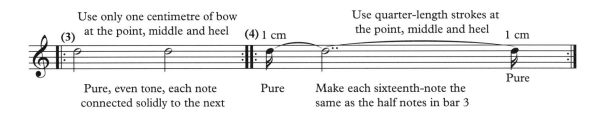

[1] There are exercises which I have hesitated to include in this collection, either because they may seem odd or because they are too difficult to represent well enough on paper. This is one such exercise; however, it is very effective.

[2] At a party once, Joseph Silverstein came up to Dorothy DeLay and said: 'You know, Dotty, I've just spent the last forty years trying to master the inaudible bow change, and I've only just realised that it does not exist!'

Play each stage at the point, middle and heel. Play on each string, using double stops as well as single notes.

1 *Use only one centimetre of bow*, playing up and down as slowly as possible. Press the wood of the bow down slightly too far, without releasing, to make an even, sustained sound of scratch.

2 Play ordinary quarter-length, *f* strokes. Scratch the last centimetre of each stroke, and the first centimetre of the next stroke, joining them together evenly.

Going from the ordinary stroke into the scratched last centimetre should be smooth, the one flowing into the other. Do this simply by slowing the bow down without changing the f pressure. Overpress and scratch evenly, without release.

3 *Use only one centimetre of bow.* Play slowly and loudly but do not overpress. Solidly connect the end of each bow to the beginning of the next, without any release of pressure, so that there is no break or *diminuendo* between the strokes.

4 Play quarter-lengths, with a full and evenly sustained tone. End and begin each stroke with one of the not-scratched, centimetre-long bows from stage 3. Join the strokes solidly, without a break or *diminuendo*.

Simple *détaché* to *martelé*

86

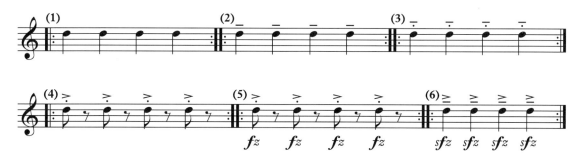

Play strokes on one note, on each string, at ♩ = 80–92. Play stages 1–7 without stopping.

1 Start with simple *détaché*: smooth, even, each stroke connected to the next without a break.

2 Gradually increase the bow speed and pressure at the beginning of each stroke, so that little by little the simple *détaché* becomes accented *détaché*.

3 Once the accented *détaché* is strong, begin to stop the bow at the end of each stroke. Gradually make the strokes shorter, with a longer and longer silence between them.

4 During the pause between each stroke, begin to grip the string silently with the bow. Gradually grip more and more firmly, so that the strokes begin with a greater and greater bite and change into short *martelé* (see page 63).

5 Once the stroke has changed into short *martelé*, begin to lengthen the strokes so that the *martelé* becomes more and more sustained.

6 Finally arrive at sustained *martelé*. Begin each stroke with a strong bite, with great pressure and speed in the first quarter of the stroke. Then sustain the sound with a slower bow, remaining f to the end. There should be the smallest space between each stroke, just enough time to catch the string again to make the next bite.

7 Gradually change the strokes back to short *martelé*, accented *détaché* and finally simple *détaché*.

First play with quarter-length strokes at the point, then in the middle of the bow, and at the heel. Repeat with half length strokes in the upper half, middle, and lower half.

Repeat on each string.

Portato

87

- Play Kreutzer Etude no. 8 (or a similar study), as follows, making the portato strokes in bars 2 and 4 sound identical to the *détaché* strokes in bars 1 and 3.

- Play at a medium tempo in the upper half, middle, and lower half.

Collé

Galamian described this stroke as a 'pizzicato' with the bow. Although it is normally a lower-half stroke, regularly playing *collé* in all parts of the bow greatly improves tone production in general.

One *collé* stroke:

1   Place the bow on the string at about the point-of-balance. Curve the fingers and lower the knuckles (Fig. 29a). 'Catch' the string.[1]

2   Make the down-bow stroke by straightening the fingers quickly, and at the same time lift the bow off with the arm so that the note rings (Fig. 29b). The single 'click' at the beginning of the stroke must not be a scratch: release the pressure as soon as the stroke begins.

3   Place the bow back on the string with the fingers straighter and the knuckles higher (Fig. 29c), and 'catch' the string.

4   Make the up-bow stroke by curving the fingers quickly. Release the pressure as soon as the stroke begins, and lift off with the arm (Fig. 29d).

Fig. 29

(a) Curved fingers, lower knuckles, ready for the down-bow

(b) Straighter fingers just after the down-bow

(c) Straighter fingers just before the up-bow

(d) Curved fingers just after the up-bow

88

Warm-up exercise

Play continuous *collés* on one note, lifting the bow off after each stroke.

● Start at the heel. Play each stroke a centimetre higher up the bow than the last, gradually working up the bow to the point. Then work back down to the heel again.

● First play all up-bows, then all down-bows, and then alternate up and down.

● Play on each string, in low, middle and high positions.

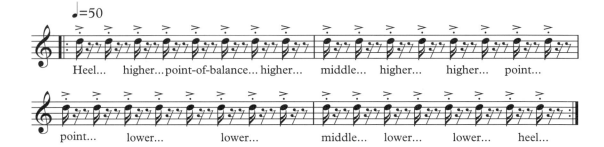

♩=50

Heel...   higher...point-of-balance... higher...   middle...   higher...   higher...   point...

point...   lower...   lower...   middle...   lower...   lower...   heel...

Martelé

Violin Concerto no. 2 in D minor, op. 22, mov. I
Wieniawski

188 sul G
at the point

f *marcato e rubato*

Martelé strokes are played with heavy–light bow pressure and fast–slow bow speed, beginning with a 'bite'.

Short *martelé*: Short, quick stroke ending with silence.

Sustained *martelé*: After the initial attack the bow speed is slower, and the pressure more sustained, with hardly any separation between the strokes – just enough time to catch the string again ready for the next stroke.

Catching the string

Play in all parts of the bow.

89

1 Before playing each note, stop the bow on the string. Press the bow down heavily to grip the string hard with the hair. Pull and push the string from side to side (shown as an x-note in the example). This should be entirely silent – do not let the string snap back.[1]

2 Having moved the string from side to side a few times, stop the bow on the string *without releasing the pressure*. Then play the *martelé* stroke.

The tension of the strings increases as the string length gets shorter, making the 'catch' of the strings different. Play this exercise using two-octave scales in broken thirds, in one position across the strings, major or minor, in the following keys:

    1 A (1st position)   **2** E (5th position)   **3** A (8th position)

Finger action

90

In *martelé*, the fingers straighten slightly on the down-bow and flex on the up-bow. For the purposes of the exercise, exaggerate this movement greatly. Fig. 30a shows the hand just before the down-bow, and Fig. 30b just before the up-bow.

(a) Setting the hand for the down-bow *martelé*

(b) Setting the hand for the up-bow *martelé*

Fig. 30

[1] See *String tensions*, page 36

- Play the first bar using only the fingers, *with no arm movement*. Straighten the fingers to make the down-bow, and curve (flatten the knuckles more) to make the up-bow.
- Then make the strokes with the same finger action, but with a fast–slow arm movement as well.

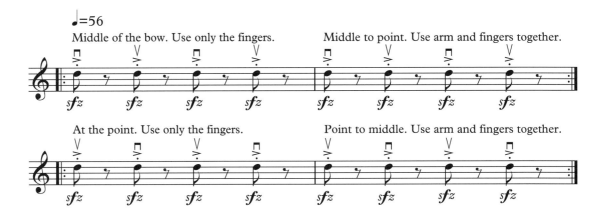

Repeat on each string.

91 **Bow hold**

Play continuous *martelé* strokes on one note in the upper half, with a pause between each stroke.

1 **Placing the first finger further from the thumb**

If the first finger is too near to the thumb, there is not enough leverage. If it is too far away from the thumb, there can be tension in the base of the first finger and in the base of the thumb.

- Begin with the first finger very close to the second finger. After every four strokes or so, move the first finger slightly higher up the bow, away from the second finger. Find the place where the first finger has maximum effect with the least tension. You may find the bow hold more balanced if you place the second finger very slightly higher up the bow than the thumb.

2 **Turning the hand more on to the first finger**

If the hand does not lean enough into the bow, there is not enough power in the *martelé*. If it leans too much, the tone is too pressed and squashed.

- Begin with the fingers quite vertical on the bow. After every four strokes or so, lean slightly more on to the bow (pronate). Find the angle where the hand has maximum effect with the purest tone.

3 **Lowering the knuckles**

If the knuckles are too high, there is not enough power in the *martelé*. If they are too low (a straight line from the back of the hand across the fingers), the hand can become tense.

- Begin with the knuckles quite high. After every four strokes or so, lower them a little more. Find the position of the knuckles where the hand has maximum effect with the greatest ease.

Practise on each string: because of the different string tensions and thicknesses, each string feels considerably different.

Staccato

Introduction et rondo capriccioso, op. 28
Saint-Saëns

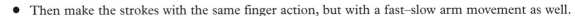

Many violinists have their own way of playing staccato. As long as it works well it does not matter how you do it. But the best staccatos often appear to be some combination of the following factors:

The impulse comes from the forearm, with a relaxed upper arm, and you *let* the fingers (and hand) move. In other words, a *passive* movement of the fingers helps to make each note. The hand and fingers play each staccato note, the arm simply transporting the hand like the beam of a crane.

The finger movement is a slight curving and straightening *and* a slight supination and pronation. (See Exercise 27.) The fingers curve and supinate, at the same time, to play the note; then straighten and pronate to prepare for the next note.

Another approach is to keep the fingers solid on the bow and make each note with the forearm or whole arm. Either way the arm can be loose or stiff. However, although solid finger, stiff-arm staccatos can be very fast and brilliant, they may sound too pressed and harsh.

Up-bow: (1) Play on the outer edge of the hair; (2) higher elbow; (3) angle the point of the bow slightly towards the fingerboard; (4) lean the hand slightly towards the fourth finger.

Down-bow: (1) Inner edge of hair; (2) lower elbow; (3) angle the point of the bow slightly towards the bridge; (4) lean the hand slightly more on to the first finger.

It often helps if you take the second and fourth fingers off the bow: holding the bow with only the first and third fingers (and thumb), pull in tightly against the frog with the third finger during the staccato.

In staccato you have to use enough pressure, playing into the elastic spring of the bow, bow hair and string, that the bow naturally bounces out of the string (without leaving the string), after each stroke. Play deep into the string (bend the wood of the bow down towards the hair), so that the bow springs naturally.

Curves

92

Rapid, anticlockwise forearm rotation is an important arm movement in the staccato. The bow stroke that plays each staccato note is curved, and is played *around* the string, not as a straight line *along* the string. The angle of the pressure for each note *curves* into the string rather than pushing down vertically. Watch the point of the bow while playing a staccato run: the point makes little 'dipping' movements up and down.

Continue the following examples up to twenty, thirty or more strokes in one bow.

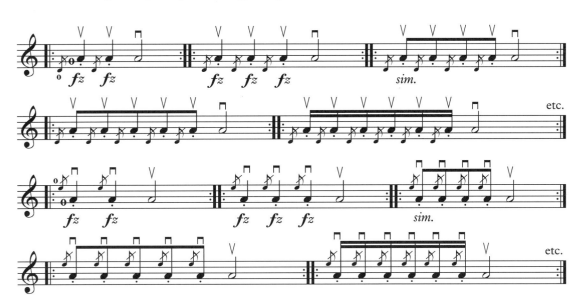

- Play in the upper half. Begin the up-bow staccatos near the point, the down-bow staccatos near the middle.
- Touch the grace note as lightly and as briefly as possible. Begin every *fz* with a bite. (Leave the bow on the string after each *fz*.)
- When there are only a few strokes in each bow, make larger movements between the two strings. As more and more strokes are added, gradually play with the bow nearer and nearer the level of the two strings, until almost playing a double stop. *Whatever the number of strokes in a bow, use as little bow as possible.*

Play on the G–D and A–E strings.

Alternative

To keep the curved movement small, play the grace note as a double stop throughout the exercise:

Based on *martelé*

Solid staccato is like a series of rapid *martelé* strokes all in one bow.[1]

- When there are only a few strokes in each bow, make very heavy bites at the beginning of each staccato by catching the string heavily, and immediately play the rest of the stroke piano. As more and more strokes are added, gradually play with a smaller and smaller bite.

- Play with the same curved stroke as in the previous exercise.

- Feel how the stick wants to bounce out of the string after each attack, even when there are many strokes all in one bow and the bite has become very slight.

Play on each string.

String crossings

String crossings can spoil an otherwise good staccato. This exercise covers all the possibilities in the same way as Exercise 53.

- Play with a metronome, beginning slowly at ♩ = 60 and gradually increasing to ♩ =120.

- Play up- and down-bow, in the upper half throughout.

- Play with a strong rhythmic pulse, practising with a strong accent at the beginning of every group of four notes. Later, feel the accents without sounding them.

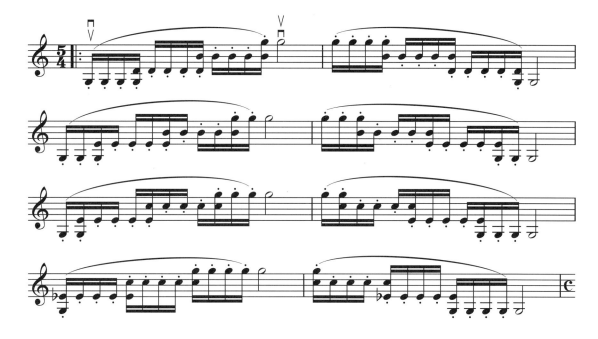

[1] See *Martelé*, page 63. *Martelé* is an example of a technique that has a speed limit: beyond a certain speed it is impossible to catch the string before each stroke. The obvious, instinctive solution is to join the strokes together in one bow, which is then called staccato. Other examples of speed limits are spiccato, which beyond a certain speed turns into *sautillé*; and the action of raising and dropping fingers individually, which turns into 'blocks' (see page 139)

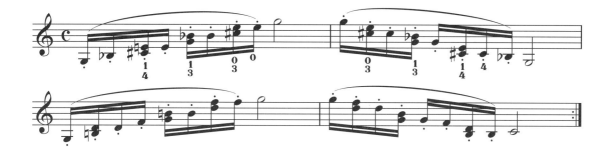

Practice method

Practise all string crossings in staccato runs as double stops, as in the exercise.

Violin Concerto no. 2 in D minor, op. 22, mov. I
Wieniawski

Note: Before playing staccato, always first practise the runs with ordinary slurred legato, to make sure that the left hand is even. Then add the staccato. The same applies to this practice method.

Tremolo exercises

95

- Play a fast tremolo at the point, using one centimetre of bow, f. Use the arm, or use the hand and fingers, or a combination of all three, to make the stroke.

- Gradually begin to 'catch' the string with the up-bows (★). This causes the bow to begin to move away from the point, moving in a staccato towards the middle. Let it turn into a proper staccato, and play to the middle of the bow.

- Play the tremolo in the middle of the bow to begin the down-bow staccato, and then move in a staccato to the point.

Do the same, using a very fast dotted rhythm instead of a tremolo. Grip the string firmly.

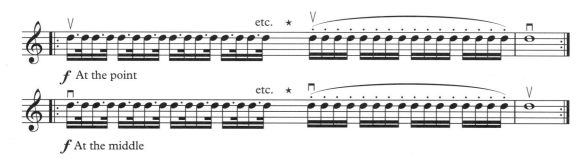

Play on each string.

96

Scales

Play two-octave scales, ascending and descending. Angle the bow 'in' for the up-bow staccato, and play on the outer edge of the hair. Angle the bow 'out' for the down-bow staccato, playing on the inner edge of the hair. (See Fig. 25, page 23.)

- Use as little bow as possible, in the upper half.
- Begin the rhythm patterns as slowly as necessary, and gradually speed up until they are very fast.
- At the slower speeds make all the elements of the stroke larger: a deep bite at the beginning of the stroke, a big 'hooking' movement as the bow goes from biting the string to releasing, a visible movement along the string to make each note. As the speed gets faster, each of these elements has to get smaller.

Example

Rhythm patterns

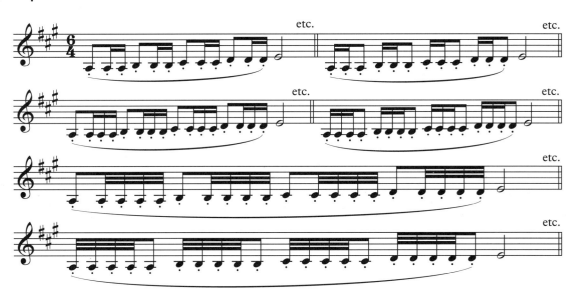

Alternative

Play the same rhythms without pausing on the half-note (minim), using continuous down- and up-bow staccatos:

Kreutzer Etude no. 4

A traditional practice method for staccato uses Kreutzer no. 4:

- Play the whole study through, first with one staccato to a note, then two, three and four.

- Play the first note of a staccato run with an extra strong accent, which 'kicks' the run off. This is musically undesirable in most cases, but is a useful practice method.

- First play with a slight pause (marked by the comma), and use that time to grip the string with the hair. After the comma, play the staccato fast, beginning with a sharp accent. It does not matter if the comma distorts the rhythm slightly. Later, play without the comma.

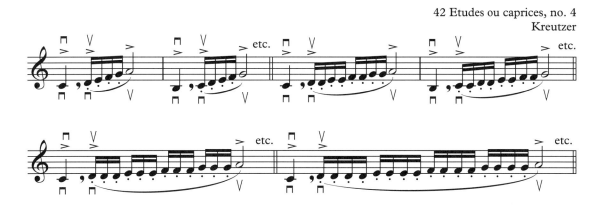

42 Etudes ou caprices, no. 4
Kreutzer

About *collé*-spiccato

Also see *Collé*, page 62.

The energy of a spiccato is increased or decreased by altering the speed of the spiccato stroke itself (which is not to be confused with the tempo of the notes). The least energy comes from an even stroke, with the same speed of bow before and after touching the string, the hair catching the string at the bottom of the curve. The most energy comes from a spiccato stroke that begins close to the string, and then moves very quickly, catching the string hard and suddenly, throwing the stroke out like a pizzicato. This is very similar to *collé*, except that in a true *collé* the stroke begins on the string. Examples:

Sinfonia concertante, K364, mov. I
Mozart

Violin Concerto in A, K219, mov. I
Mozart

Practice method

Play each stroke on the same part of the hair near the point-of-balance, without travelling along the bow.

Violin Concerto in D, K218, mov. I
Mozart

The spiccato stroke can be approached as follows: starting from high above the violin, make large semicircles with the bow, just catching the string at the very bottom of the curve. Make progressively smaller and smaller semicircles, moving along the string a little longer each time, until the semicircles are very small and produce a clean spiccato.

98

Natural bounce

The bow wants to bounce. The idea that playing on the string is easy, and lifted bowings are more difficult, is not correct – rather it is the other way round. To sustain the sound requires *doing*, i.e., pushing against the springiness of the wood of the bow, bow hair and string. Lifted bowings require *letting*, i.e., not resisting the natural bounce of the bow out of the string.

1   Moving the arm as if playing short up- and down-bows, play continuous bounced strokes on one string. Hold the bow with *the thumb and second finger only*. Do not try to make the bow bounce – let it bounce by itself.

2   Put the third and fourth fingers on the bow, without the natural bounce of the bow diminishing.

3   Finally, add the first finger. Feel how the pad of the first finger, on the side of the bow, helps keep the bow straight, while the part of the first finger on top of the bow does not prevent the bow from bouncing freely and naturally.[1]

Play as high as the middle, and as low as the point-of-balance, on each string.

Proportions

All the different types of spiccato strokes are achieved by using different proportions of the vertical and the horizontal movements of the bow. The higher the bounce and the less movement along the string, the shorter and crisper the spiccato becomes. The lower the bounce and the more movement along the string, the longer and more rounded the spiccato.

99

Exercise 1 – Height and length

Play continuous strokes on one note.

1   Playing between the point-of-balance and the middle, tap the bow vertically up and down on the string (the same arm movement as turning a door handle). This does not make any real sound.

2   Begin to add length to the vertical movement. Do this so gradually that the stroke changes imperceptibly. As more and more length is added, the stroke gradually changes into a clean spiccato.

3   Continue to add length so that the spiccato becomes more and more rounded ('long spiccato'). After a while the hair begins to stay on the string while the wood of the bow continues to bounce. Let this finally develop into a 'short *détaché*', the hair staying on the string all the time without the wood of the bow bouncing.

4   Gradually shorten the stroke and begin to let the wood of the bow 'bounce' again while the hair stays on the string.

Continue to shorten the stroke until the hair leaves the string, ending up back at the vertical tapping.

5   Do the same in reverse: start *détaché* on the string, shorten the strokes until tapping vertically, and then lengthen again back on to the string.

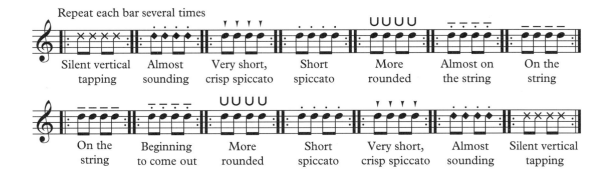

[1] See *About the movement of the bow within the hand,* page 72

Play on each string and in different positions, to include various string tensions.

Exercise 2 – Area of bow

Play continuous spiccato strokes on one note.

1 Begin a couple of centimetres below the middle, playing light, fast strokes. Keep the bow close to the string.

2 Without stopping the strokes, slowly move lower down the bow. Gradually make the strokes slower and longer, with larger and larger curves.

3 Having arrived about ten centimetres from the frog, playing long, slow, heavy strokes, begin to move back up the bow again to the middle.

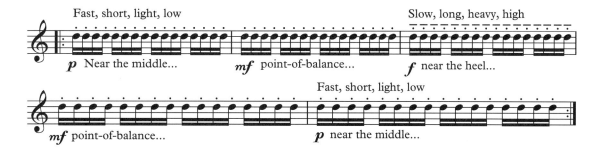

Play on each string and in different positions, to include various string tensions.

Exercise 3 – Soundpoints

The string is soft near the fingerboard, and hard near the bridge. The best proportions of height to length are different for each soundpoint because of the different string tensions.

Spiccato nearer the *fingerboard*: shorter, lighter, faster.

Spiccato nearer the *bridge*: longer, heavier, slower.

1 Play spiccato on one note on soundpoint 4. First play at the middle of the bow (short, low and fast), then at the point-of-balance (medium), and finally near the heel (long, high and slow).

Adjust the speed, height, length and pressure, so that each stroke has a round, clean sound at each place on the bow.

2 Repeat on soundpoints 3 and 2.

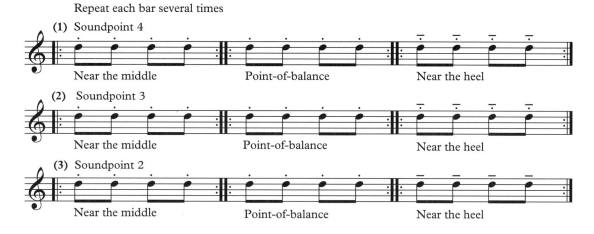

Play on each string and in different positions: the various tensions and thicknesses of string make a considerable difference.

Alternative

Stay in the middle of the bow and play eight or sixteen spiccato strokes on soundpoint 5, then on 4, 3, 2, 3, 4 and 5 again. Then do the same while playing at the point-of-balance; and then the same at the heel.

102

Exercise 4 – Bow tilt

The best proportions of height to length change according to how much hair is used. In this exercise, experiment with all the different tilts of the bow, from full hair to playing on the very edge of the hair.

- Just below the middle of the bow, play continuous spiccato strokes on one note. Begin with the bow tilted on the outer edge of the hair, playing the spiccato on 'one hair'.

- Staying just below the middle, without stopping the strokes, gradually use more and more hair until it is flat on the string; then gradually tilt the bow on to the outer edge again.

- Do the same at the point-of-balance and near the heel. Adjust the speed, height, length and pressure so that the stroke is always resonant and pure.

Repeat each bar several times

Very tilted | Getting less tilted | Almost flat | Flat hair | Almost flat | Getting more tilted | Very tilted

Play on each string.

103

String crossing

This is like *Scale string crossing*, page 33. For other string crossings see Exercises 114, 115, 117, 119, 120.

- Play quickly near the middle of the bow (low spiccato); at a medium speed at the point-of-balance; slowly near the heel (high spiccato).

- For the smoothest string crossings (not as a rule, but in this exercise), move the upper arm across the strings continuously, without stopping on each individual string level.

[Springing bowings]

In slow spiccato (which is a 'thrown' stroke[1]), you can control each individual stroke. Faster, you control it in pairs, the first being 'active' and the second 'passive', like a rebound. Spiccato has a definite speed limit after which it turns into *sautillé*, which is a springing bowing. Springing bowings, which are usually too fast to control individually, come from *letting* the strokes happen rather than from *making* them happen.

About the movement of the bow within the hand

During springing bowings (sometimes also in spiccato and in certain fast string crossings), the frog makes tiny pivoting movements exactly like a seesaw, turning around where the thumb and second finger hold the bow. Because the pivot of this 'seesaw', the thumb and second finger, is so near the end of the bow (rather than being in the middle as in a real seesaw), a very small movement at the frog produces a much larger movement at the point.

[1] 'In the thrown stroke the player is *active*, the bow *passive*; *I* throw the bow. In the springing stroke the player is *passive*, only watching over what the bow does; the bow is *active*, since, in consequence of its elasticity in the region of its balancing point, it *must* spring of itself, when not held down on the string by force. The type of stroke to be chosen depends on the tempo: in a *slow* tempo the bow must be *thrown*, in a *rapid* one it *springs* of itself.' Carl Flesch: *The Art of Violin Playing* (New York, 1924), 73.

These tiny pivoting movements are made possible by the first finger being very light on the stick, and often coming a hair's breadth away from the top of the stick. The fourth finger helps by flexing slightly. Many difficulties in bowing come from a stiff bow hold which prevents these movements of the bow from happening naturally. In particular, the base joint of the first finger must be relaxed.

To see the movement clearly:

1   Hold a pencil with the left hand, and put the right hand on the pencil in bow-hold position. Take off all the fingers except the thumb and second finger (Fig. 31a).

2   Move the pencil up and down with the left hand, without moving the right hand (Fig. 31b).

3   Do the same with all the fingers on the pencil in a normal bow hold.

Keep the hand still while moving the pencil with the left hand. Do not allow too much movement in the fourth finger: let it curve only slightly more as the tip of the pencil is moved down, and slightly less as it is moved up.

As the tip of the pencil is moved down, let the part of the first finger that is on top of the pencil come away from it slightly.

4   Do the same using the bow.

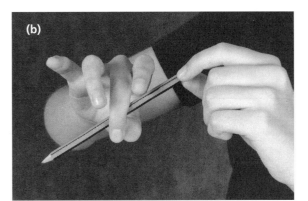

Fig. 31

Pencil at two angles relative to the hand

Sautillé

Violin Concerto no. 2 in D minor, op. 22, mov. III
Wieniawski

In *sautillé* the wood of the bow bounces without the hair leaving the string (although at times it can). It has to be played in a particular place on the bow, usually somewhere around the middle, where the stick has the greatest natural bounce.

To find a *sautillé*, play continuous thirty-second-notes (demisemiquavers) on one note, ♩ = 80–92:

• Begin with a short, rapid *détaché*. Gradually use less and less bow and pressure until the wood of the bow begins to bounce with the hair staying on the string.

• *Use flat hair.* Make the stroke mainly with the hand (moving from the wrist), with only a little forearm movement.

• Turn the hand in to the bow (pronate), and allow little passive or sympathetic movements in the wrist and fingers, which must be loose.

104

Exercise 1

In *sautillé* the bow plays around the string in a slightly curved motion. Watch the point move in a circle during the stroke. This exercise exaggerates that circle.

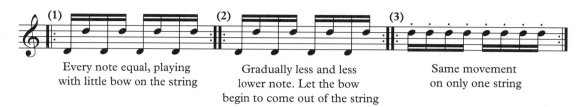

Every note equal, playing with little bow on the string

Gradually less and less lower note. Let the bow begin to come out of the string

Same movement on only one string

1 Playing around the middle, wherever the bow bounces most easily, repeat this pattern many times.

2 Gradually make a smaller and smaller circle until the bow no longer touches the D string.

3 Finally make a very small 'circle' on the A string, with the hair staying on the string and the wood of the bow bouncing.

Repeat on the G–D and A–E strings.

105

Exercise 2

Each *sautillé*, successful or unsuccessful, comes from a certain combination of movements. The key factor is the size of the movements relative to each other. What the best proportions of different movements are (of the arm, hand and fingers) depends on how much hair is used, how near the bow is to the bridge, and the thickness of the strings. In this exercise, the individual movements are performed separately, and are then put together in the completed stroke.

Play continuous *sautillé* strokes on one note. Play the exercise on each string.

1 First play the *sautillé* moving only the *forearm*, keeping the wrist and fingers firm.

2 Then play using only the *hand*, moving it rapidly from the wrist. Keep the arm still.

3 Then play rapid sixteenth-notes (semiquavers) on the string, using only a *rapid finger movement*. (This will hardly produce a proper sixteenth-note stroke.) Keep the arm and hand still.

4 Then play the *sautillé* using the forearm, hand and fingers together, feeling all three moving at the same time. (Note that the finger movement is now a 'sympathetic' movement, not an active finger movement.)

106

Exercise 3

Play continuous *sautillé* strokes on one note. Play the exercise on each string.

● Play with only the thumb and first finger on the bow. Feel how the bow is able to move freely, unrestricted by the hand.

● Repeat with a normal bow hold, making sure that the stroke feels just as free as when holding the bow with only the thumb and first finger.

Ricochet

Violin Concerto no. 1 in D, op. 6, mov. III
Paganini

To play a *ricochet,* which is like bouncing a ball, drop the bow from 2–3 centimetres above the string, at the same time simply pulling or pushing the bow. After the initial impact the bow bounces naturally.

● **Nearer the point**   Faster, lower bounce, lighter, less bow.
   Nearer the middle   Slower, higher bounce, heavier, more bow.

● The less bow you use, the lower and faster the bounce. The more bow, the higher and slower the bounce.

¹ See About the movement of the bow within the hand, page 72

As well as playing with a normal bow hold, it may be helpful to play these exercises without the first finger on the bow, feeling how the bow springs naturally and has a movement *within* the hand.¹

Exercise 1

Play the following patterns one at a time, in the upper half, repeating each bar several times. The idea is to get as much substance and as much ring as possible by trying different combinations of height, length and pressure.

- First play each pattern at the extreme point. Experiment with the length of bow, height and speed of bounce, weight, and tilt of the hair, to find the purest possible tone.

- Then play it a little lower down the bow, finding the new length and height, etc. for the purest tone. Gradually work down to the middle, and back up again to the point, changing the proportions throughout.

Example

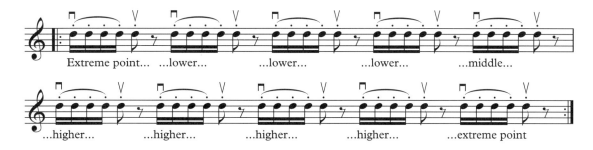

Extreme point...   ...lower...   ...lower...   ...lower...   ...middle...

...higher...   ...higher...   ...higher...   ...higher...   ...extreme point

Patterns

Play on each string.

Exercise 2

- Play the same patterns as Exercise 107, using simple scales.
- Play slow, medium and fast.

Examples

Exercise 3

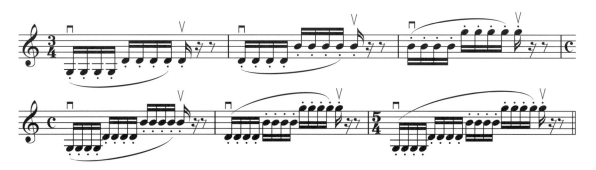

Springing arpeggios

Violin Concerto in E minor, op. 64, mov. I
Mendelssohn

It is possible to play this stroke at many different speeds. The more it is under control, the more slowly it can be played. As in all lifted bowings, the main proportions to adjust are the ratio of height of bounce to length of stroke: the slower it is, the more bow; the more bow, the higher the bounce.

110

Exercise 1

Here, the impulse for the bounce comes from a small 'whipping' movement of the fingers and hand. At the end of the up-bow, just before the down-bow, the fingers straighten slightly and the wrist is slightly raised. At the same moment as beginning the down-bow, the wrist comes down again quickly and the fingers flex. This makes the hair hit the string at a slight angle and causes the bow to bounce. *This finger, hand and wrist movement can be so slight as to be practically invisible.*

- To start the down-bow make this movement, in the middle of the bow, at the end of the held G. After the attack simply pull the bow, letting the bow bounce once, twice, and so on.

- To change from down-bow to up-bow, simply change direction after the fourth bounced down-bow and let the bow bounce the other way.

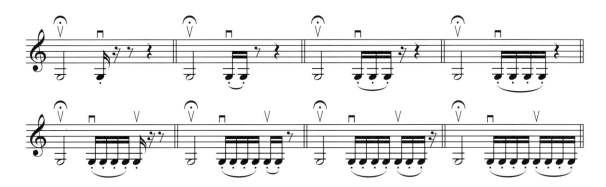

111

Exercise 2

- First play this exercise without the first finger on the bow, feeling how the bow bounces naturally even if the second finger and thumb squeeze the bow to try to prevent it from bouncing. Then ensure that the first finger, when it is on the bow, does not reduce this natural bounce.

- Use full hair, the wood of the bow directly above the hair.

- Try different areas of the bow to find the place where it bounces the most (somewhere around, or just above, the middle of the bow).

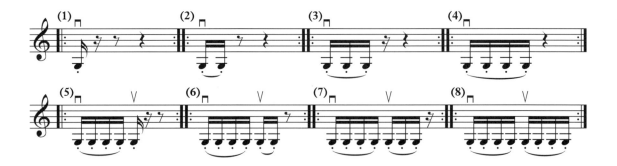

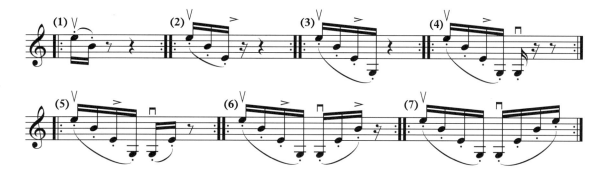

Bar 1　　Drop the bow on to the string in a curved motion, letting it bounce back out naturally.

Bars 2–4　　After dropping the bow on to the string, pull it smoothly so that the next notes 'play themselves'.

Bars 5–7　　Change direction from down to up smoothly, so that the notes are played with machine-like regularity.

Bar 8　　Repeat continuously, using a slight 'kick' on the first down-bow to keep the momentum going (as in Exercise 110).

Bars 9–15　　Move the elbow very smoothly and evenly across the different string levels. Notice how each string has its own particular part of the hair (i.e., the hair that plays the D string is a little lower in the bow than the hair that plays the G string).

Slightly accent the marked notes to avoid any feeling of playing the first three notes as a triplet.

Also play bars 9–15 in reverse

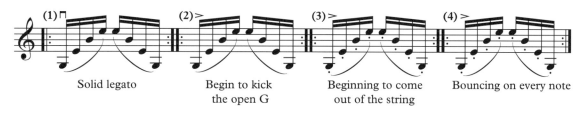

Exercise 3

（112）

Solid legato　　Begin to kick the open G　　Beginning to come out of the string　　Bouncing on every note

Bar 1　　Keep the bow deep in the string and evenly sustained.

Bars 2–3　　Begin to give a slight kick to the first down-bow so that the bow wants to leave the string. Repeat the pattern continuously, gradually letting the bow come out of the string more. The deeper the bow plays into the string, the more springiness there is to play with.

Bar 4　　Repeat the bar continuously, the bow bouncing from string to string.

It is often helpful to give a slight kick to the first note of the up-bow as well as to the first note of the down-bow.

Key bowing patterns

The number of bowing variations is infinite, so it is clearly not possible to practise every single one. The bowings here are the most basic patterns from which others are derived. If these are mastered, all other combinations deriving from the basic patterns are made easier. There are also a few difficult combinations of basic patterns that frequently occur.

Tempo

Bowings cannot be considered to be completely mastered until it is possible to play them extremely fast. Playing any pattern, always work towards pushing your comfortable upper speed limit more and more. The speed limit will vary according to which part of the bow is used. For instance, most patterns will have to be played more slowly at the heel. Even if a particular pattern feels awkward in a certain place in the bow, and would not normally be played there, it is still important to practise it there to improve overall control.[1]

How much bow

How much bow to use depends on the tempo. Use a lot of bow at slower speeds, and very little bow at faster speeds; but at each tempo *always use as much bow as possible.*

Metronome

It is very helpful to play these exercises with the metronome. Start at a comfortable tempo, and gradually speed up. Work each bowing pattern until (1) it can be played very fast, (2) the sound is entirely pure whatever the speed, (3) the rhythm is even, and (4) it feels easy.

113

Exercise 1

- Play at the heel, middle and point. Keep the bow solidly sustained in the string.
- Also play around the point-of-balance, using half-bounced strokes (the wood of the bow bounces but the hair does not leave the string).

Bowing patterns

[1] Different proportions between the lower and upper half:

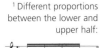

Played near the frog: the heel of the bow makes small movements; the point makes large movements. Played near the point: the heel makes large movements; the point makes small movements.

Also, the hand and forearm can take part in string crossings in the upper half (see *Hand movements*, page 10). In the lower half the hand movement is mainly replaced by forearm rotation (see page 15).

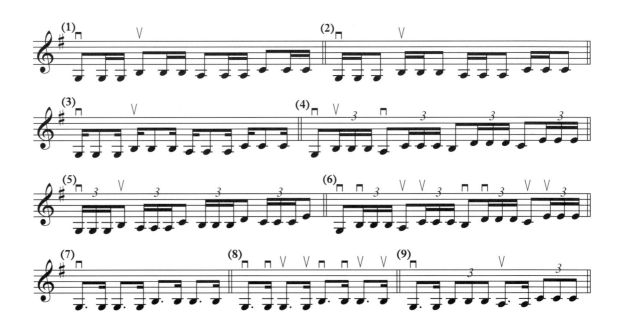

Exercise 2

● Play each pattern five times, using the chord sequence.

● Play at the heel, middle and point using short strokes. Play in the lower half, middle, and upper half using half-length strokes. Play deeply into the string, sustaining the sound evenly.

● Begin each pattern up-bow as well as down-bow.

● Also play patterns 1–5 spiccato (or *sautillé* at the faster speeds).

114

115

Exercise 3

- Play each pattern four times, using the chord sequence.
- Play at the heel, middle and point using short strokes. Play in the lower half, middle, and upper half using half-length strokes. Play deeply into the string, sustaining the sound evenly.
- Also play spiccato (or *sautillé* at the faster speeds).
- Begin each pattern up-bow as well as down-bow.

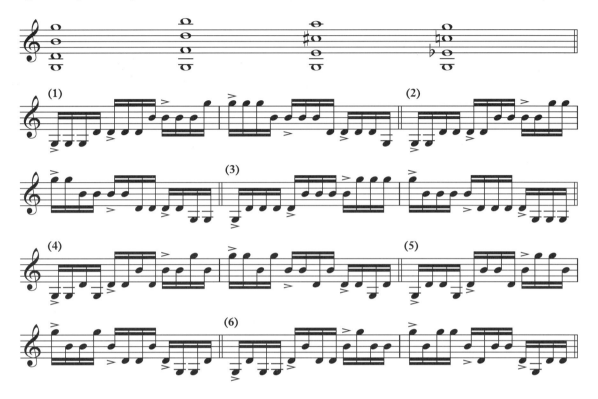

116

Exercise 4

- Play at the heel, middle and point.
- Begin each pattern down-bow, keeping the bow smoothly sustained and playing deeply into the string.

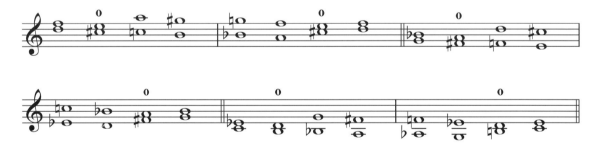

Example

Bowing patterns

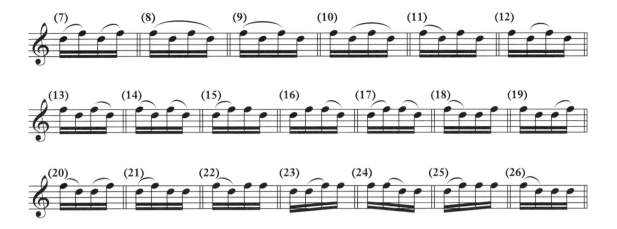

Exercise 5

● Play at the heel, middle and point. Keep the bow smoothly sustained, playing deeply into the string.

● Begin each pattern up-bow as well as down-bow.

● Also play patterns 5–10 spiccato.

117

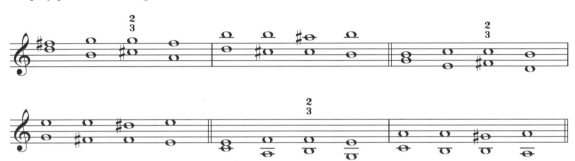

Example

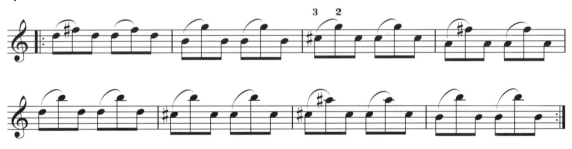

Bowing patterns

118

Exercise 6

- Play each pattern four times, using each chord from the sequence.
- Play at the heel, middle and point. Keep the bow smoothly sustained, playing deeply into the string.
- Begin each pattern up-bow as well as down-bow.

119

Exercise 7

- Play at the heel, middle and point. Keep the bow smoothly sustained, playing deeply into the string.
- Begin each pattern up-bow as well as down-bow.
- Also play patterns 4, 8 and 12 spiccato (or *sautillé* at the faster speeds).

Example

Bowing patterns

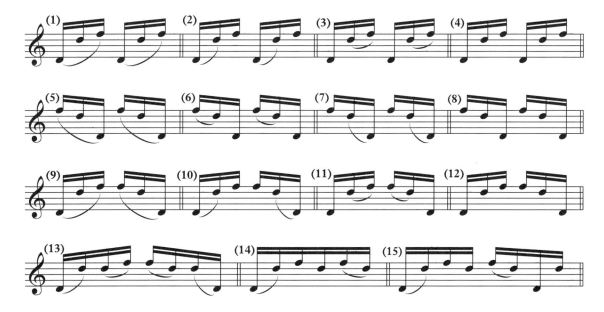

Exercise 8

120

- Play at the heel, middle and point.
- Begin each pattern down-bow, keeping the bow smoothly sustained and playing deeply into the string.
- Also play patterns 1, 7, 13 and 19 spiccato (or *sautillé* at the faster speeds).

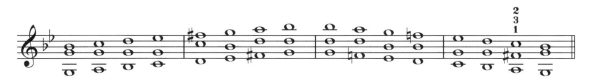

Example

Bowing patterns

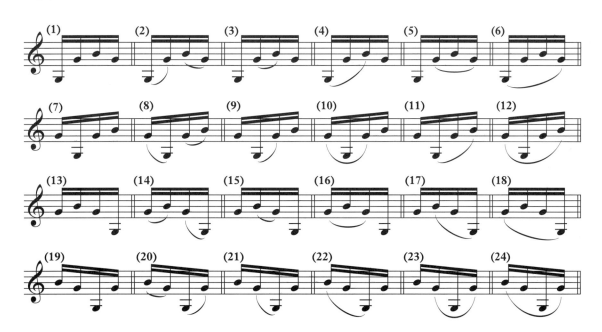

121

Exercise 9

- Play each pattern four times, using the chord sequence.

- Play at the heel, middle and point using short strokes. Play in the lower half, middle half and upper half using half-length strokes. Play deeply into the string, sustaining the sound evenly.

- Begin each pattern up-bow as well as down-bow.

122

Exercise 10 – Kreutzer Etude no. 2

Playing Kreutzer no. 2 (or a similar study) with bowing variations is one of the key technique-building methods practised by countless violinists through the generations. Most editions of Kreutzer studies include a number of variations. Galamian[1] gives over sixty bowing patterns as well as different rhythms; Massart[2] provides 150 bowing patterns.

The benefits of playing just a few patterns, as given here, are dramatic, yet are often overlooked just because they seem so familiar and apparently ordinary.

42 Etudes ou caprices, no. 2
Kreutzer

[1] International Edition

[2] L. Massart: *L'art de travailler les Etudes de Kreutzer* (Bibliothèque-Leduc)

- Play the study with each pattern three times – in the lower quarter, at the middle, and in the upper quarter.
- Begin each bowing pattern up-bow as well as down-bow.
- Keep the bow deep in the string throughout. Sustain each stroke solidly and connect each note to the next seamlessly.

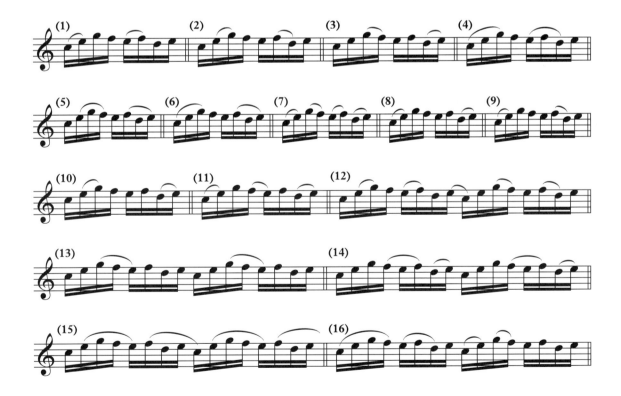

Chords

About timing finger placement in chords

One of the single most important parts of successful chord playing is to place the fingers on the string quickly enough, in time before the bow moves. In any rapid series of chords, the key to correct timing is to place the next chord as the final action of playing the previous chord. In other words:

Play the first chord – instantly place the fingers ready for the next chord. (Play–place, play–place),

instead of

Place the fingers – play; place the next fingers – play, and so on. (Place–play, place–play.)

123

Voicing

Using the chord sequence above, sound all three strings at the same time to play a short but clear sixteenth-note (semiquaver) chord. Quickly release the bow, and sustain the tied note (or notes) without a break in the sound. In other words, the tied notes should sound like half-notes (minims):

Example

Play the chord sequence in the following six ways:

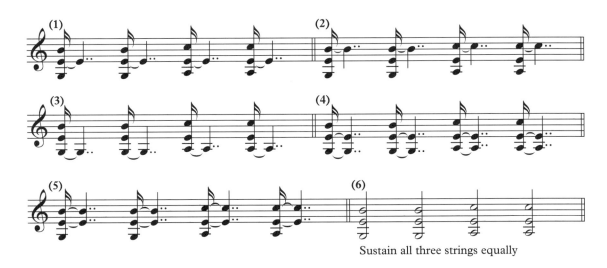

Sustain all three strings equally

- Throughout, play as close to the bridge as possible – just as far away as necessary to catch all three strings at once.

- To begin each chord, place the bow on the middle string of the chord. Press the middle string down until the bow hair catches the outer strings of the chord.

Feel how, at the heel, the hair gives and catches the three strings; while at the point the wood of the bow gives in the middle of the bow, the hair remaining rigid.[1]

Smooth pivoting

Also see *Pivoting*, page 27.

Exercise 1

Play the chord sequence in the following five ways:

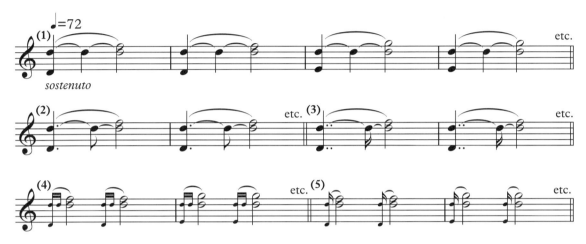

Exercise 2

Play the chord sequence in the following eight ways:

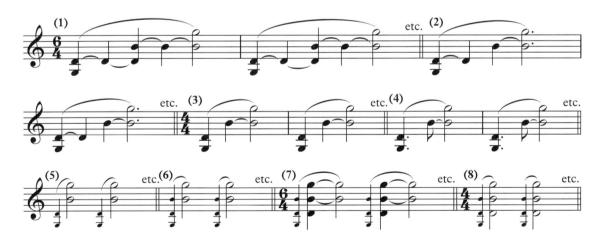

Gradually increasing length

Throughout the exercise, hold the wood of the bow down towards the hair without release. Play as close to the bridge as possible, but as far away as necessary to catch all three strings at once.

1　Place the bow on the string near the heel (**A** in the illustration below). Press the middle of the three strings down until the bow hair catches the outer strings of the chord. Choose a soundpoint where this is possible.

Play the three strings exactly like a triple-stopped *collé*.[1] Think of the stroke as being like a pizzicato. Listen to the chord ring after the stroke.[2]

Repeat at the point-of-balance (**B**), middle (**C**), between the middle and the point (**D**), and near the point (**E**).

2　Starting near the heel again (press the middle string down until the bow has caught all three strings), play the chord slightly longer, e.g., three centimetres long. Repeat as before in the other places on the bow.

3　Repeat with quarter bows (**A–B**, **B–C**, etc.), and then half bows (**A–C**, **B–D**, etc.). Finally play whole bows, sustaining all three strings evenly from the beginning to the end of the chord.

126

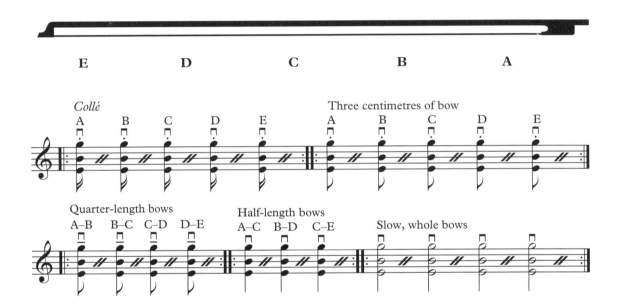

Repeat using up-bows, starting near the point:

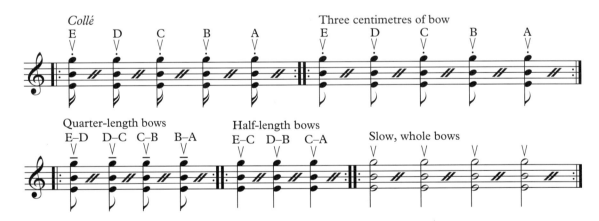

Also use a similar chord on the G–D–A strings.

[1] See *Collé*, page 62

[2] See *Resonance*, page 37

Left Hand

part d

Reducing thumb counter-pressure

The thumb provides counter-pressure against the neck, sideways and upwards. To play freely and without tension, counter-pressure must always be *only as much as necessary and as little as possible*. See also *Finger pressure*, page 103, since the less finger pressure there is, the less counter-pressure is necessary.

Positioning the thumb

127

Heifetz's teacher, Leopold Auer: place the thumb directly opposite the second finger playing F♮ on the D string. Galamian: between the first and second fingers, or opposite the first. Flesch, Ševcík: opposite the first finger playing E on the D string. Suzuki: between the first finger playing E on the D string, and the nut.

Whatever the main thumb position:

1   Use the thumb lightly, without squeezing the neck of the violin between the thumb and the fingers.

2   Like the fingers, the thumb has three main joints. It does not begin at the point where it appears to join on to the hand, but has its base joint (the 'ball' of the thumb) near the wrist. Trying to use only the upper two joints of the thumb, without the base joint also taking part, causes stiffness which can affect the entire hand. Keep the space open between the base of the thumb and the first finger, without squeezing together (Fig. 32).

3   The thumb does not stay in one fixed position, but constantly changes with the actions of the fingers and hand. The changes are sometimes obvious, sometimes so slight as to be invisible, but however big or small are rarely made consciously.

To find a natural position for the thumb in 1st position, drop the hand to the side and relax it completely. First without the violin, and then with the violin, quickly raise the hand into playing position. If the hand and arm are completely relaxed, whatever position the thumb naturally arrives at is the correct position for that particular hand. This is the position that the thumb departs from, and returns to, as it moves around on the violin neck.

Fig. 32

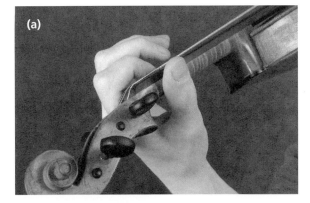

Note the space between the base of the thumb and the first finger

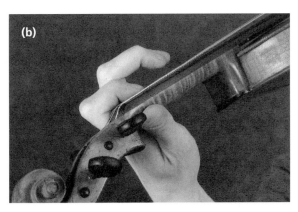

Thumb squeezing

128

Warm-up exercise

To stop squeezing the neck too hard between the thumb and the fingers, play this fingering pattern (which includes every possible combination of any two fingers) without the thumb touching the neck. Capture the feeling of the thumb's independence from the fingers, and then find the same feeling with the thumb in its usual position.

- Play with the thumb well forward, somewhere opposite the third finger, and about a centimetre away from the neck (Fig. 33). Keep the side of the first finger lightly touching the neck.

- Playing with the metronome, first play in eighth-notes (quavers), then sixteenth-notes (semiquavers) and thirty-second-notes (demisemiquavers).

- For the purposes of the exercise, 'hang' the arm from the fingers, using arm weight to stop the notes. Relax the entire weight of the head into the chin rest to hold the violin firmly. Or rest the scroll against the wall.

Example

On different occasions play through the sequence with different tone–semitone spacings between the fingers:

Play the same sequence on each string.

Fig. 33

Practice method

Play phrases, whole passages, or whole movements without the thumb on the neck, as in the exercise. Rest the scroll against the wall to avoid having to press on the chin rest for long periods.

Taking the thumb off the neck to avoid squeezing

Thumb independence

129

- Move the thumb backwards and forwards as shown in the first three bars. Begin with the thumb far forward, somewhere opposite the third finger, and move it back between the first finger and the nut.
- Change direction with the thumb at the same time as changing direction with the bow. That is, if the thumb is moving towards the bridge, and you are on an up-bow, start moving the thumb towards the scroll when you change to the down-bow. This ensures that the thumb is always moving when raising or lowering a finger. Do not momentarily stop moving the thumb as the finger is dropped or raised.

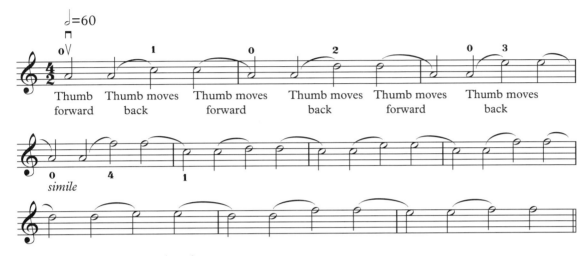

Play the same sequence on each string.

Rolling fingers into the string

130

'Rolling' fingers into the string is the same as the movement of the fingertip in vibrato. (See Fig. 54, page 219.)

Fingers are often rolled rather than 'pressed' into the string, especially the first note after a rest. Rolling automatically stops the string enough without pressing, and the least thumb counter-pressure is needed. (Place the palm of your hand flat on a table-top, relaxing the weight of the arm into the hand. Now slightly roll the hand from one side to another: feel how the side of the hand presses into the table more.)

Play a two-octave scale of A major in first position, with a pause between each note.

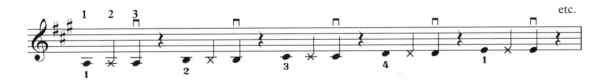

1   Silently place the note in tune, with the finger in its normal, rounded shape (Fig. 34a).

2   Then roll the finger back on to the pad, away from the tip and lowering the pitch (Fig. 34b). At the same time release the string, so that the finger rests on the string as lightly as if to play a harmonic (written as an x-note). Completely relax the thumb.

3   Roll forward on the pad of the finger. As the finger rolls, the string will automatically be pressed down towards the fingerboard, without much counter-pressure from the thumb.

Roll until the tip of the finger is on the right pitch, and then play this note pizzicato.

Feel how relaxed the thumb is. There may be a feeling of it sliding upwards a little, as the finger goes down, but it hardly has to press against the neck at all.

4   Repeat, playing the note with the bow instead of pizzicato. Play the in-tune note only, without a slide – make sure the bow stroke begins at exactly the same moment as the finger arrives at the in-tune note.

Fig. 34

(a)

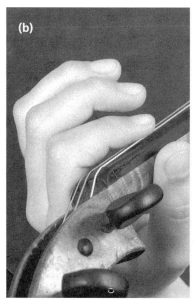

(b)

The finger in its normal position before rolling back

The finger rolled back: note that the string is no longer held down

131 Upward counter-pressure

A slight upward feeling in the thumb, to counter the downward finger movement, reduces sideways thumb counter-pressure.

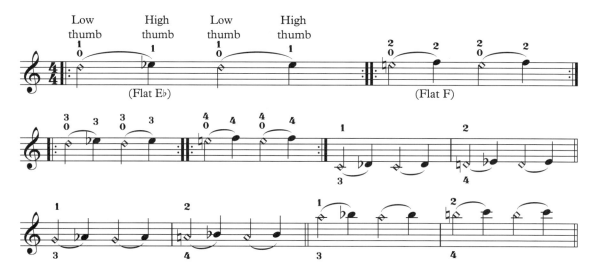

First make sure that the thumb and the side of the first finger are touching the neck as lightly as a feather.

1 Rest the tip of the thumb on the neck, below the level of the fingerboard. Rest the fingertip on the string ready to play the harmonic (Fig. 35a).

   While playing the harmonic, slide the thumb upwards and slightly back (i.e., diagonally upwards), until it is sticking up above the fingerboard (Fig. 35b). Let the thumb movement help the finger stop the string enough to lose the harmonic and sound the stopped note. In other words, actually press the finger down as little as possible – try to make it feel almost as if the sliding movement of the thumb is enough to stop the string.

   Move the fingertip diagonally down into the string, rather than vertically down. Play a very flat E♭ just above the D, and a very flat F just above the E.

2 Place the thumb in its normal playing position, with the fingertip ready to play the harmonic. Play the exercise again but only move the thumb diagonally upwards the smallest amount, just enough to be visible. More finger action is now necessary to stop the string.

3 Repeat with the thumb again in its normal position, but without moving it on the neck. Even though the thumb does not visibly move, feel the same movement in the thumb as the finger moves from the harmonic to the stopped note.

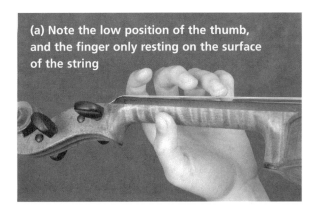

(a) Note the low position of the thumb, and the finger only resting on the surface of the string

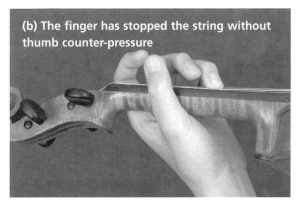

(b) The finger has stopped the string without thumb counter-pressure

Fig. 35

Widening at the base joints

About fingertip placement and base joints

The part of the fingertip that touches the string affects the angle of the base joints to the fingerboard. If you place all the fingers on the left side of the fingertip (Fig. 36a), the base joints take too steep an angle to the fingerboard (Fig. 36b). This angle of the base joints also makes the wrist curve out too much, and the elbow to pull in too far to the right, both of which can cause tension in the hand and upper arm.

Equally, placing the fingers too much on the right side of the fingertips, to keep the base joints parallel with the fingerboard, can cause tension (Fig. 36c). The most natural angle of the base joints varies with each player (Fig. 36d).

The fingertip also affects whether or not the fingers touch each other. For example, if the first finger is placed on the left side of the tip, and the second finger is placed on the right side of the tip (Fig. 36e), there will be a space between the fingers. If both fingers are placed on the left side, they will squeeze together (Fig. 36f).

Fig. 36

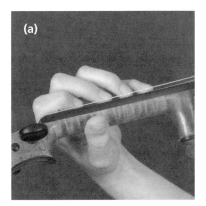

(a)

Fingers all placed on the left of the fingertip

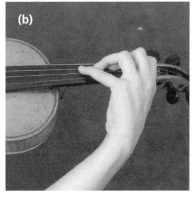

(b)

Note the steep angle of the base joints to the fingerboard

(c)

Base joints forced to be unnaturally parallel with the fingerboard

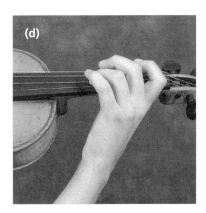

(d)

Unforced, natural angle

(e)

The fingertip placement opens a space between the first and second fingers

(f)

The fingertip placement causes the first and second fingers to squeeze together

132

Fingertip placement

In this exercise, the finger lifts from, and drops on to, one note, each time using a different part of the fingertip to play the note. At the same time another finger is held down on the string, always on the same part of its tip. The pitch of the note should stay the same, whichever part of the tip plays it.

'Left, middle, right' indicates the part of the fingertip that should touch the string (as seen by the player).

- Ascending: keep the *lower finger* on the *left* side of the tip (not as a rule, but in this exercise).
- Descending: always place the *upper finger* on the *right* side of the tip (not as a rule, but in this exercise).

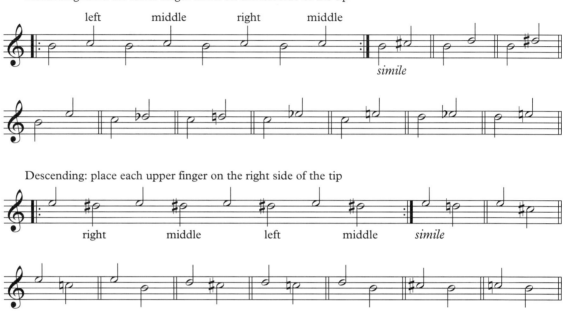

Play on each string.

Relaxation

After each bar, take the hand away from the violin and relax it completely. If there is any feeling of strain in the hand and thumb do the exercise without the bow, while resting the scroll against the wall.

With your right hand, help the held-down finger stay in position. If it is a lower finger (Fig. 37a), gently hold it in place leaning towards the scroll; hold an upper finger (Fig. 37b) so that it leans a little towards the bridge. Keep the space open between the base of the thumb and the first finger. (See Fig. 32, page 89.)

Fig. 37

Gently hold a lower finger back while placing an upper finger at different angles

Gently hold an upper finger forward while placing a lower finger at different angles

Contrary motion

- In the following three exercises, leave out any bars that are impossible to reach if your hand really is too small.

- Move both fingers at the same time, in contrary motion, to change from one double stop to the next. Keep the hand still while moving the fingers.

- Where possible find the part of the fingertip that opens the base joint the widest (Fig. 38).

- Widen the fingers at the base joint. Be careful not to strain – continually relax the hand completely, and never force. Keep the space open between the base of the thumb and the first finger. (See Fig. 32.)

Fig. 38

Note the fingertip placement of the first and fourth fingers, causing the hand to widen at the base joints

The fingertip placement has caused the fingers to squeeze together

Exercise 1

133

It may be helpful to play this (and the following exercise) *pp* at first, to encourage the hand and fingers to be very loose and relaxed. Then play more and more loudly, while keeping the same relaxation in the left hand.

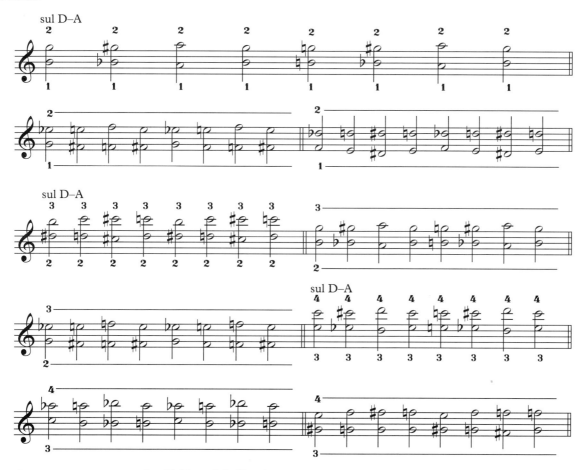

Play the same sequence on the G–D and A–E strings.

134

Exercise 2

As well as for widening the hand, this is also a good exercise for fingered octaves. Keep the fingers as upright on the string as possible, to make the fingers widen at the base joint as much as possible.

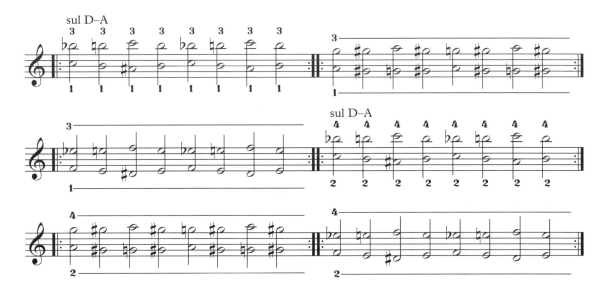

135

Exercise 3

- In each bar, hold the second finger down – written as whole-notes (semibreves) – without sounding it.
- In the second bar of each line, move both fingers at once, in contrary motion. Allow the space between the base of the first and second fingers to open as the first finger moves back.

Play the same sequence on the G–D and A–E strings.

136

Sliding exercise

- Hold down the whole-note (semibreve) without playing it, and slide the other fingers up and down. Widen the fingers at the base joint.
- The hand must feel soft and relaxed throughout – do not overpress with the held-down finger while sliding the other finger. If some of the suggested notes are impossible for your size of hand, simply move the finger as far as you can.
- For the purposes of the exercise, if the whole-note is a lower finger, position it more on the *left* side of the tip, with the sliding finger touching the string more on the *right* side.

  If the whole-note is a higher finger, position it more on the *right* side of the tip, with the sliding finger touching the string more on the *left* side.
- Position the thumb well forward, and relaxed at the base joint. Do not overpress.
- Keep the elbow in its normal position while sliding the finger up or down – do not pull it further to the right than usual.

Extensions

See also *Extensions*, page 140.

See also *Extensions*, page 140.

- Hold the whole-note (semibreve) down without playing it, and play only the eighth-notes (quavers). If your hand is too small, leave any bars that are too difficult to reach.

- Continually relax the hand and never force the muscles. Where possible find the part of the fingertip that opens the base joint the widest.

- Keep the hand and forearm in a straight line, or slightly giving inwards (Fig. 39).

Rhythm variations

Repeat on the G–D and A–E strings.

Pushing the wrist out reduces
the reach of the fingers

Hand and forearm in a straight line

Fig. 39

Left Hand   97

Hand position

In low positions the hand has to be placed differently according to the size of the hand.

Large hands can be based on the first or second finger, with the third and fourth fingers still able to reach their notes easily. On the E string, place large hands with the middle joint (approximately) of the first finger touching, or behind, the nut (Fig. 40a).

Small hands need to be based more on the second finger, with the first finger reaching down a little to its notes, and the third and fourth fingers reaching up to theirs. On the E string, place small hands higher up the fingerboard than large hands, with a small distance between the first finger and the nut (Fig. 40b). Touch the side of the neck with the first finger between the middle joint and the base joint (approximately).

To reach the G string the hand has to be brought much higher over the fingerboard (Figs. 40c and 40d). It is important not to leave the base joints in a position suitable only for the upper strings (Figs. 40a and 40b), forcing you to stretch forward with the fingers to reach the lower strings. Keep the fingers curved and bring the base joints closer to the lower string (Figs. 40c and 40d).

Reaching back from the fourth finger: Large hands or small, it is important that you bring the fingers over the notes by spreading the hand – i.e., widening at the base joints (Fig. 40e) – rather than stretching up from a position only favouring the first finger (Fig. 40f). It is extremely beneficial, even for large hands, to practise basing the hand *entirely* on the upper fingers and reaching back to the lower notes, as in the following exercises.

Fig. 40

Large hand positioned
for the E string

Small hand positioned
for the E string

Large hand positioned
for the G string

Small hand positioned
for the G string

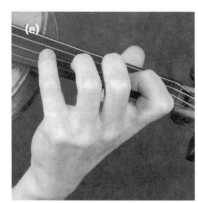

Reaching back from
the fourth finger

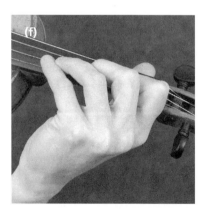

Stretching up from
the first finger

Reaching back from the fourth finger

As well as helping to reach back from the fourth finger, these exercises are also good for keeping the fingers above the strings, instead of pulling them back too far away from the fingerboard.

Exercise 1

138

If the notes in the last two bars are impossible for your size of hand, simply move the finger as far as you can.

In each bar balance the hand on the fourth finger. For the purposes of the exercise make sure of the following:

1 Place the fourth finger more on its tip than its pad, keeping it in a rounded shape. It is most important (in this exercise) not to change the shape or angle of the fourth finger as you use the third finger.

2 Reach back with the third finger by widening at the base joints between the third and fourth fingers. Keep the base joint of the fourth finger close to the level of the fingerboard (or even a little below if the fingers are long).

3 Keep the thumb opposite the second finger (not as a rule, but in this exercise).

4 Keep the entire hand soft and relaxed, playing with a loose vibrato. (Do not clamp the hand against the shoulder of the violin.)

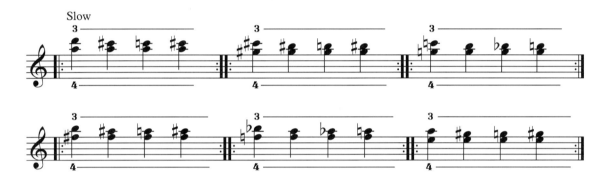

Also play on the G–D and D–A strings.

Exercise 2

139

Hold the fourth finger down without playing it. Position the hand to favour the fourth finger.

Rhythm variations

Also play on the G–D and A–E strings.

140

Exercise 3

Balance the hand on the fourth finger as in Exercise 138. Keep it curved throughout, with the tip of the finger on the string not the pad.

- In the first bar, do not change the shape or angle of the fourth finger as you extend back with the other fingers.

- At the end of the first bar the balance of the hand should still be on the fourth finger, with a wide space between each finger at the base joint. Keep this hand shape as you play the ascending notes in the second bar.

Also play on the G–D and A–E strings.

141

Exercise 4

In these Ševčík-type patterns, hold the fourth finger down on the string without playing it. Position the hand to favour the fourth finger, so that it is curved, relaxed and comfortable.

- The more the *tip* of the finger touches the string, the more curved the finger is; the more of the pad touches the string, the straighter it is.

Play each bar in quarter-notes (crotchets), eighth-notes (quavers) and sixteenth-notes (semiquavers), playing with the metronome at ♩ = 60–72.

- At each speed, drop fingers on to the string *as late as possible*, (the finger action should be *fast* rather than *heavy*). Lift off as late as possible.

- Wherever possible, lightly hold fingers down on the string.

- Also play the patterns on the D string, holding the fourth finger on the G string, and similarly on the E string, holding the fourth finger on the A string.

- If the hand becomes tense in this or the following exercise, stop and rest. When beginning again, lean the scroll against the wall and play without the thumb on the neck. Keep the thumb well forward (whether on or off the neck), approximately opposite the second finger.

Exercise 5

142

Silent exercise without the bow, tapping the fingers in time with the metronome.

1 Put the fingers of each chord on the string one at a time in the order 4–3–2–1 (whatever strings the fingers are on).

Position the hand to favour the fourth finger, so that it is curved, relaxed and comfortable. Then reach each lower finger back, widening the hand at the base joints.[1]

2 Lightly hold down the whole-notes (semibreves) while moving each finger in turn. Move in quarter-notes (crotchets), eighth-notes (quavers) and sixteenth-notes (semiquavers), as shown in the example.

Move the fingers from the base joint, not from the middle joint. Keep the back of the hand and forearm in a straight line.

Keep the thumb, hand, wrist and arm as relaxed as you can, despite the awkward stretches. Maintain an alive, buoyant feeling in the arm.

[1] See *Widening at the base joints,* page 93

143

Positioning the hand for thirds

For playing thirds, the hand position is based more on the third and fourth fingers than usual, the lower fingers reaching back. If the hand is based on the first and second fingers it is more difficult for the upper fingers to reach, and the hand can become tense (Fig. 41).

Fig. 41

Hand position based on the third finger

Hand position based on the first finger

While being an excellent exercise for thirds, this also helps to find a more balanced hand position in general. Play slowly, without keeping to any particular pulse.

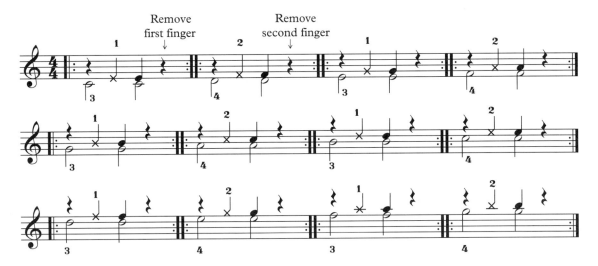

1   Place the third finger on the string. Position the hand to favour the third finger so that it is rounded and relaxed, without having to stretch up to the note.

Keep the space open between the base of the thumb and the first finger. (See Fig. 32, page 89.)

2   While playing the third finger, silently place the first finger (written as an x-note) *without altering the shape of the third finger* – play the double stop – take the first finger off again, leaving the third finger on the string in its rounded shape.

3   Place the fourth finger on the string, and then remove the third. Position the hand to favour the fourth finger, so that the tip is on the string and the finger is rounded and relaxed.

4   Reach back with the second finger *without altering the shape of the fourth finger* – play the double stop – take the second finger off again, leaving the fourth finger on the string in its rounded shape.

5   Shift up to the new third finger, and continue in the same way.

Fingered octaves

Practise fingered octaves in exactly the same way – a key practice technique.[1]

- Small or medium hands may not be able to keep the fourth finger rounded, but keep it as rounded as possible.
- Keep the space open between the base of the thumb and the first finger. (See Fig. 32.) For practice purposes, position the thumb well forward, at a middle point between the two fingers.

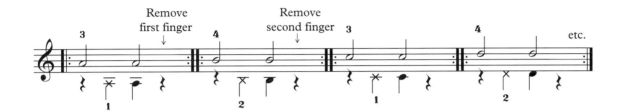

Finger pressure

The body works as a whole: tension in one area creates tension in other areas. If the fingers and thumb overpress, the base joints and the palm of the hand become tight. If the hand is tight the wrist tightens. If the wrist tightens the upper arm tightens, if the upper arm tightens the neck and shoulders tighten, and so on.

As the fingers stop the string:

- The thumb counter-presses against the neck of the violin as much as necessary but as little as possible.
- They press the string just enough to produce a clean note, without pressing further.
- The base joints remain relaxed.
- The fingers above the string remain relaxed.
- They do not squeeze sideways against each other.
- The wrist remains relaxed.
- The upper arm does not pull in too far to the right.
- The violin is not squeezed too hard between the shoulder and the chin.

Finger independence

144

The amount of space between each finger varies from player to player, some having clear space between their fingers, others not being able to avoid some touching. What is important is that there be no active sideways pressing against another finger as part of stopping a note (Fig. 42a).

In this exercise, slowly stop the string with each finger in turn, while checking all the areas mentioned above for unnecessary involvement or tension.

1. As if playing harmonics, place all the fingers lightly on the surface of the string without pressing.
2. Slowly push the first finger down to the fingerboard, without any movement in any other finger or in the hand or wrist. Slowly release the string up to the 'harmonic' level again. Make sure the finger that is pressed down does not lean sideways against an adjacent finger (Fig. 42b). Do the same with each finger, the other three fingers always resting lightly on the string. React hardly at all with the thumb as the finger stops the string.

Play the same patterns on each string, using all the tone–semitone groups given below.

Place all the fingers in each bar on the string together

[1] Basing the hand position on the upper finger should not be confused with tuning the two notes of the octave. If an octave is not quite in tune, it will sound more in tune if the lower note is played louder than the upper note.

Fig. 42

(a) Squeezing the fingers together while playing with the second finger

(b) Keep the space between the fingers while stopping each note one at a time

Minimum pressure

The right amount of finger pressure is the same everywhere on the fingerboard: *as much as necessary but as little as possible*. This is one of the single most important aspects of left-hand technique. A great ease comes into the hand when the fingers are light, and sensitive to the elastic give of the string. The left hand feels the give of the string while the right hand feels the give of the bow, bow hair and string.

The hand can become tense if the player's mental picture is one of 'dropping fingers = press the string to the fingerboard'. It may be that the string does touch the fingerboard, especially in low positions, or it may not; but the main sensation should remain one of playing on the 'bounciness' of the string, the finger 'bending' the string just enough for the note to sound properly.

145

Exercise 1

1 Drop the finger quickly and lightly, and then instantly release the string to the harmonic.

2 'Slowly change' means press the finger down very slowly to change from the harmonic to the stopped note. In other words, while playing the harmonic push the finger down gradually, feeling for the right amount of pressure needed to stop the note well. First the harmonic will 'break', and neither it nor the stopped note will sound properly. Then a fraction more pressure will stop it cleanly. Do not stop it more than this.

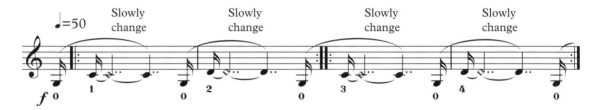

Play f throughout, near to the bridge,[1] feeling the bow heavy in the string while the left hand and fingers feel light. Play the sixteenth-notes (semiquavers) clearly, however quickly you release to the harmonic.

Completely relax the base joints and the thumb during the open string, and as the string is released to the harmonic. *Keep that relaxation as the finger goes back down into the string to stop the note.*

Also play on the other strings, using the equivalent harmonics.

Alternative

● Drop the finger quickly and lightly to play the harmonic. Then instantly stop the string just enough to play the stopped note, feeling for the exact amount of pressure needed. Keep the hand and finger as relaxed when playing the stopped note as when playing the harmonic.

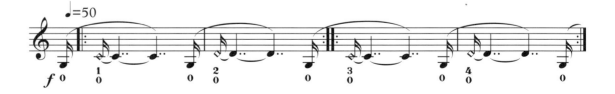

[1] In low positions you cannot play as near to the bridge on the G and D strings as you can on the A or E strings. See *Soundpoints,* page 41.

Also play on the other strings, using the equivalent harmonics.

Exercise 2

1 Play *ff*, but with the left fingers only just touching the surface of the string. The sound produced will be scratchy and distorted.

2 Keeping the bow heavy, play the same notes again while pushing the string a quarter-way down. Keep the left hand and fingers completely loose (floppy).

3 Always playing heavily with the bow, push the fingers halfway down. The tone will gradually improve as the fingers get firmer.

4 Push the fingers three-quarters down.

5 Finally, press the fingers down just enough to stop the note properly. It may be that the pressure is so light that although the pads touch the fingerboard, the string itself does not.

Play similar notes (avoiding natural harmonics) on each string, in low, middle and high positions. Also play double stops.

Practice method

A good practice method is to apply the exercise to pieces, although naturally the sound produced is harsh and whistling. Play whole passages – or even whole movements – with the fingers just touching the surface of the strings, then pushing the string a quarter-way down, and so on.

Releasing between notes

To avoid tension, there must always be as many *releases* as there are *muscular actions*. This exercise encourages the hand to release in between notes.

1 Play through the whole sequence as written. During the harmonic, relax the base joints and thumb – keep the feeling of relaxation as the new finger is dropped on to the string. Keep the finger that played the harmonic resting lightly on the string.

2 Repeat the sequence with a sixteenth-note (semiquaver) harmonic.

3 Repeat with a thirty-second-note (demisemiquaver) harmonic.

4 Repeat the sequence without harmonics, with the same feeling of release between the notes.

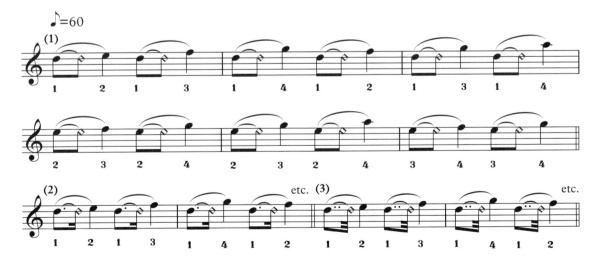

Also play on the other strings, using the equivalent harmonics.

Finger pressure in double stops

To play a double stop at the same volume as a single stop, the bow weight has to be much heavier.[1] But the finger pressure needed to stop each string is the same as for a single stop. Pressing too hard with the fingers in double stops is a common cause of tension. Although the bow is heavier, the fingers stopping the string must remain light. To lighten the hand in double stops, practise the passages as follows:

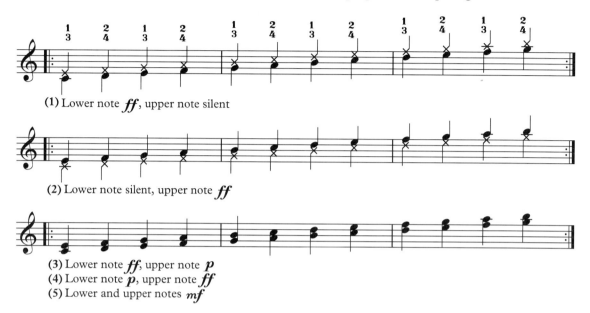

(1) Lower note *ff*, upper note silent

(2) Lower note silent, upper note *ff*

(3) Lower note *ff*, upper note *p*
(4) Lower note *p*, upper note *ff*
(5) Lower and upper notes *mf*

1 Play the passage with both fingers on the strings, but bow only the lower string.

Play loudly and heavily with the bow but keep the left hand very light, stopping the strings just enough to make the lower string speak. Use the fingers so lightly that they do not make the strings touch the fingerboard. Feel the lightness and looseness of the finger and hand, in contrast to the heaviness of the bow.

2 Repeat, bowing only the upper string.

3 Play both strings together, bowing the lower string heavily and the upper string lightly. Keep both fingers very light on the string, helped by the lightness of the bow on the upper string.

4 Repeat, bowing the upper string heavily and the lower string lightly.

5 Play both strings together equally. Use the same heaviness in the bow as before, which now does not seem so exaggerated because the weight is divided between two strings. Keep the same lightness in the left hand as before.

| Finger action |

About moving fingers from the base joint

Fingers, arms and legs all have a similar design in that they all have three main 'levers'. In each the upper lever is the strongest and the lower lever the weakest.

The following points roughly correspond to each other:

The shoulder–the hip–the base joint of the finger
The elbow–the knee–the middle joint of the finger
The wrist–the ankle–the nail joint of the finger

The strongest levers of the arms and legs are the upper arm and upper leg. In the broadest terms, these levers perform all the largest and strongest physical actions, moving from the shoulder and hip. Similarly, the main movement of the fingers should be from the base joint, which could be called the 'shoulder' of the finger.

Trying to work the fingers from the middle joint (the 'elbow' of the finger), or dropping them partly by moving the whole hand from the wrist, badly reduces ease of movement and is a major cause of tension.

Do not *lift* the fingers from the string: pull them back from the base joints without changing their shape. To see if the finger is moving correctly from the base joint, simply hold the hand in playing position without the violin. Move each finger forward from the base joint and back again, one at a time. The hand should remain perfectly still.

[1] When the bow plays on two strings at the same time, the weight of the bow on each string is halved – just as, if your weight is 50 kilos, 25 kilos goes into the floor through each foot, and 50 kilos goes into the floor if you balance on one foot.

Three warm-up exercises

Exercise 1

149

Hold the left hand in front of you in the shape of a loosely held fist – palm facing to the right, fingers touching together and rounded in their natural shape. The back of the hand, and the forearm, should form a straight line (Fig. 43a).

1 Suddenly pull the fingers back to the position shown in Fig. 43b. Keep the fingers curved.

2 Hold this position briefly and then push forward suddenly back to the starting position (Fig. 43a).

3 Wait again for a moment and then pull back again. Repeat several times.

Pull back as quickly and as far as possible – move the fingers only, not the hand and thumb – keep the back of the hand and the forearm in a straight line – keep the thumb still and relaxed when the fingers move – keep the space open between the base of the thumb and the first finger.

Fig. 43

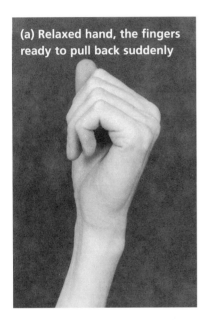

(a) Relaxed hand, the fingers ready to pull back suddenly

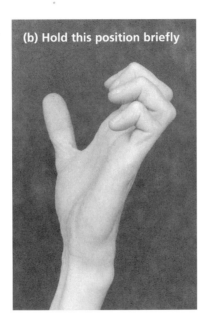

(b) Hold this position briefly

Exercise 2

150

- Hold three fingers down on the E string, and pluck the G and D strings with the remaining finger. Keep the forearm and the back of the hand in a straight line, without sticking the wrist out.

- Pluck loudly, pulling the finger back from the base joint *as fast as possible*.

- Pluck in an even rhythm: place the finger on the string – **wait** – pluck – **wait** – place – **wait** – pluck – **wait** – place, etc.

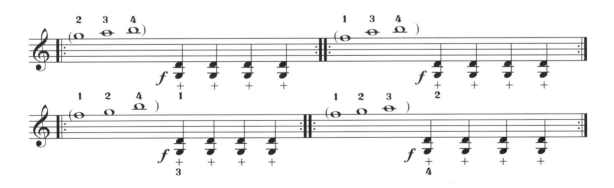

151 **Fig. 44** **Exercise 3**

Place the palm of the left hand flat against the shoulder of the violin (Fig. 44).

1 Pluck the open E string loudly with one finger at a time, pulling the finger back as fast as possible. Move the finger rhythmically: place the finger – pluck–place–pluck, etc.

2 Tap the finger up and down on the E string, lightly and quickly. Tap rhythmically in groups of fours, moving the fingers 'down–down–down–down', not 'up–up–up–up'.

The hand will need to be positioned differently for each finger, so that as each is used its base joint can sit just above the rim of the violin.

Move each finger from the base joint only, keeping the palm of the hand flat against the shoulder of the violin. The hand should not move at all, staying relaxed and still.

The hand positioned ready to tap the second finger on the E string

Silent tapping

Tapping exercises[1] are for the left hand the equivalent of tone production exercises for the right. Tone production exercises on one note are without all the other factors of playing – intonation, rhythm, co-ordination, and so on – leaving the player free to concentrate solely on what the bow is doing to the string. Silent tapping exercises leave the player free to concentrate solely on the movement of the fingers.

Finger action

- Tap 'down–down–down–down', so that you can hear the written pitches as the finger hits the string. ('Up–up–up–up' sounds the open string, whichever finger is used.)

- Rather than 'thudding' the fingers hard on to the fingerboard, feel the 'bounciness' of the string with each dropping of the finger.

- Pulling the finger back from the string, keep the same curve that the finger had on the string.

- Move the finger from the base joint, not from the hand, keeping the hand still. To check that the fingers are moving from the base joint, hold the left hand with the right hand. Put the right thumb just below the base joint of the finger that is moving, and the first finger below the knuckle on the other side (Fig. 45).

Elbow and hand position

Fig. 45

E string Place the elbow more to the left.

Base joints lower, nearer the level of the fingerboard. (See Figs. 40a and 40b, page 98.)

G string Place the elbow more to the right.

Base joints higher. (See Figs. 40c and 40d.)

In low positions on any string, lightly touch the neck with the side of the first finger.

Thumb

Keep the thumb loose, relaxed and uninvolved. Place it more forward than usual (approximately opposite the second finger), so that there is extra space between the base of the thumb and the first finger. Also practise without the thumb touching the neck, resting the scroll against the wall.

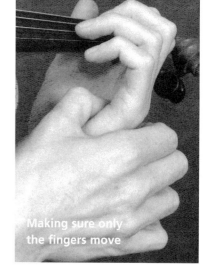

Making sure only the fingers move

[1] See also Carl Flesch: *Urstudien* (New York, 1911); Gaylord Yost: *Studies in Finger Action and Position Playing* (Pittsburgh, 1937)

Tempo

Begin at a medium speed, ♩ = 60–66, and work up to 80–92. At fast speeds keep the fingers close to the strings.

Exercise 1

(Tapping the fingers without the bow)

Keep the hand in one position and only change the shape of the fingers to reach the different notes. For example, tapping with the first finger on A♭ with a square finger should feel different to tapping on A♮ with an extended finger.[1]

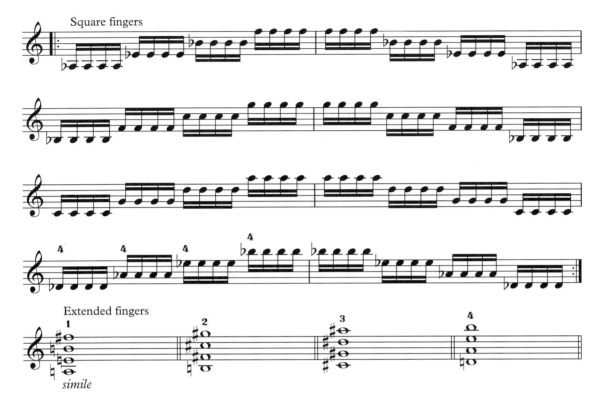

Exercise 2

□ = Square finger   ◊ = Extended finger

[1] See *Square and extended*, page 113

154

Exercise 3

Keep the hand in 1st position, moving only the fingers to the notes in 2nd position.

155

Exercise 4

Keep the hand in 1st position, moving only the fingers to the notes in 2nd position.

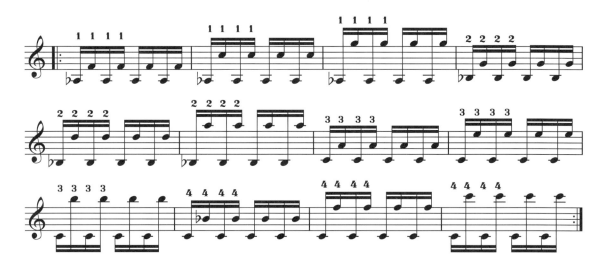

Keep the hand in 2nd position, moving only the fingers to the notes in 1st position.

Exercise 5

(Tapping the fingers without the bow)

To cover different intervals, play the exercise using the following key signatures:

Thirds

156

Fourths

157

158 Sixths

159 Octaves

Square and extended

□ = Square finger   ◊ = Extended finger

The terms 'square' and 'extended' describe the shape of the finger when it is placed on the string.[1] Fig. 46a shows the square shape (second finger C♮ on the A string). The angle between the nail joint and the middle joint is closer to a right angle than when the finger is 'extended'. Fig. 46b shows the extended shape (second finger C♯). The finger is now straighter from the nail joint to the middle joint (though still curved).

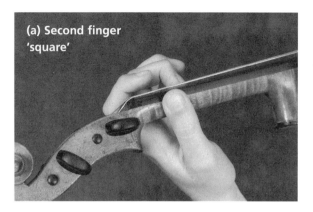

(a) Second finger 'square'

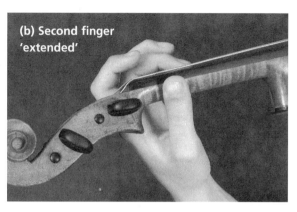

(b) Second finger 'extended'

Fig. 46

The square does not have to be a perfect right angle – it may often be 45° – but is simply more 'square' than the extended shape. This particularly applies to the fourth finger, which is never as square as the others. Whether a finger is square or extended depends on the position, and on what the surrounding notes are.

In Example 1 the second finger moves from square (□) to extended (◊), the hand staying in one position. During the sixteenth-notes (semiquavers) G–A (bar 2) the second finger moves back to the square shape ready for the C♮.

Example 1   Etude, op. 20, no. 3
                                                                              Kayser

In Example 2, the second and third fingers move from square to extended. A common fault is to keep the fingers square, and then to *shift the hand* up a semitone. This causes intonation problems because the hand is no longer in any particular position.

Example 2   Eine kleine Nachtmusik, K525, mov. IV
                                                                              Mozart

In Example 3, the first finger changes frequently from square to extended, the hand staying in one position. If the hand 'shifts' down to any of the square fingers, the notes that follow them are likely to be too flat.

Example 3   Nigun (no. 2 from 'Baal Shem')
                                                                              Bloch

Copyright © 1940 by Carl Fischer, Inc., New York.
Copyright Renewed. International copyright secured. Used by permission.

- In the following exercises, keep the hand still and move only the fingers. The base joints should remain relaxed and soft. Tempo: slow, medium and fast.

[1] 'The fingers fall...on the tips either in the "square" position or in an elongated position, depending upon the note being played. All fingers assume the elongated shape when they reach up a half step or more from their basic placement.' Ivan Galamian: *Principles of Violin Playing and Teaching* (New Jersey 1962), 17.

160

Exercise 1

This exercise exaggerates the change from square to extended.

- Keep the hand still, moving only the fingers along the string. (Do not raise the fingers between notes.)
- Release between the notes to minimise the sound of sliding.

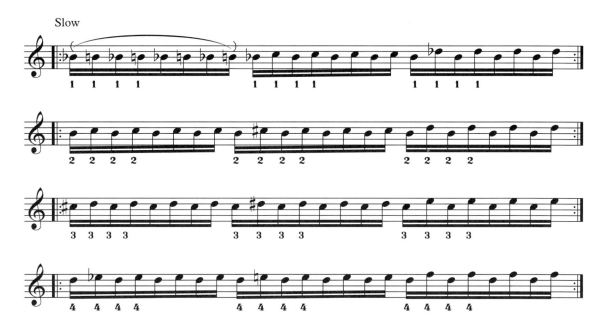

Play the same sequence on each string. Also play it one octave higher on each string.

161

Exercise 2

- Bars 1–6: keep the hand still, resting it on the finger that plays the second and fourth notes. Move the other finger from square to extended.
- Bars 7–12: feel the hand position resting on the finger that plays the first and third notes (hold this finger down), moving only the other finger, not the hand.

Play the same sequence on the other strings.

Exercise 3

Keep the hand still and move only the fingers.

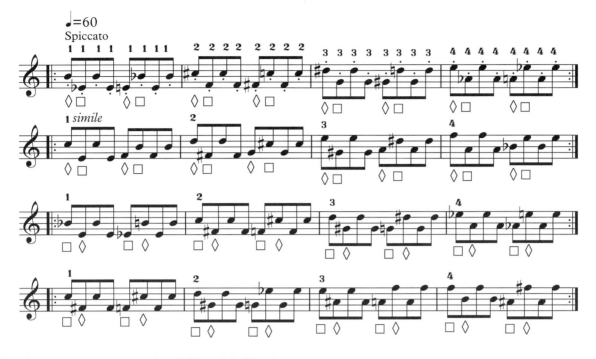

Play the same sequence on the G–D and A–E strings.

Exercise 4

Keep the hand still and move only the fingers.

Alternative

Other exercises

The exercises for *Finger preparation* are also useful for practising square and extended shapes.[1]

| Holding fingers down |

Overlapping

In an ascending scale (for example), crossing from the fourth finger to the first finger, hold the fourth finger down until *after* the first finger note begins. Other finger combinations work in the same way.

Similar to finger preparation,[2] this is another key element of left-hand technique. Think of placing the next finger on the new string, and then lifting the last finger off the old string, as two halves of one action, not two separate actions that happen at the same time (i.e., the first finger dropping while the fourth finger lifts).

Violin Concerto in G, K216, mov. I
Mozart

164

Exercise 1

This exercise forces early finger preparation and overlapping. At every string crossing, the finger *before* the crossing and the finger *after* the crossing are held down together like a double stop.

● Hold down the finger playing the second note of each bar (i.e., the note before the string crossing), until the beginning of the fifth beat of each bar.

● Silently place the next finger on the (next) string early, on the third beat of each bar. This 'prepared' finger is marked as an x-note.

[1,2] See *Finger Preparation*, page 130

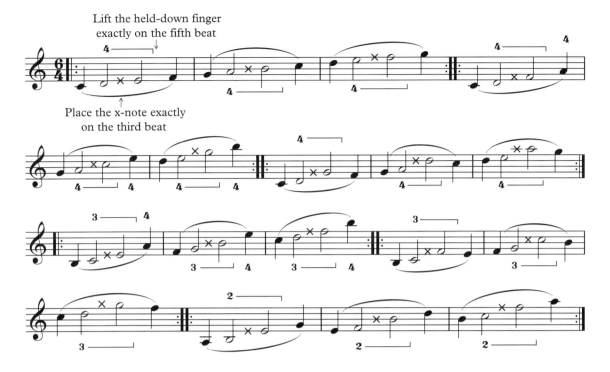

Play in a variety of keys to cover different tone–semitone possibilities:

Alternative

Instead of silently holding the fingers down, play them as double stops. The exercise then sounds as follows:

Exercise 2

Hold the fourth finger down as marked.

165

Holding down the first finger

In descending scales, and other scale-type passages, the hand (and therefore the intonation) may be more stable if you keep the first finger on the string for a few notes while the other fingers continue down the scale.

Sonata in G, op. 78, mov. I
Brahms

The exercises exaggerate the overlapping by holding the fingers down for longer than in normal playing.

166

Exercise 1

Keep the first finger lightly held down on the string throughout.

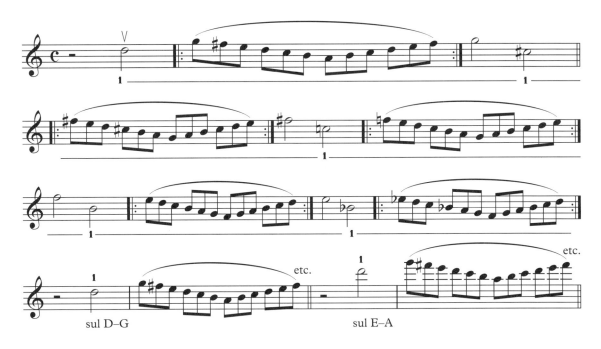

sul D–G   sul E–A

167

Exercise 2

- Keep the first finger lightly held down on the string throughout.

- At ★ extend back with the first finger while playing the fourth finger, and then let the hand follow into the new position. Do not push the wrist out while extending back.

- In 3rd, 2nd and 1st position in this exercise, there is a danger of squeezing the base of the first finger and thumb together while extending the first finger back: keep the space open between the thumb and first finger.

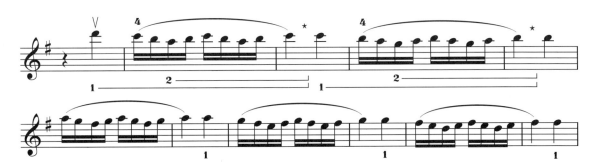

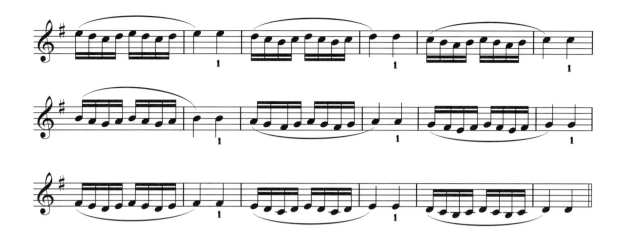

Fast fingers

Strong, hammer-like finger action is sometimes needed for extra articulation, but in general use it makes the fingers heavy and clumsy. What is important is the *speed* of the finger action. Sometimes fingers have to move slowly, but there are two reasons why fast fingers are often necessary.

First, the louder the volume, the wider the string vibrates; the wider the string vibrates, the faster the finger must drop on to the string.

Second, fast passages *feel slower* with fast fingers. The faster a finger drops on to a note, the later the dropping can start. So a fast passage, played with 'late' fingers all dropping very quickly 'at the last possible moment', feels slower than when played (at the same tempo) with slower-moving fingers, because there is a longer wait between each action.

About timing lifting and dropping

To play rhythmically evenly, you have to raise and drop the fingers *unevenly*.

Dropping a finger: the finger moves towards the string, and then the new note is played.

Lifting a finger: the new note is played as the finger moves away from the string.

Therefore the finger must begin to drop *before* the new note is required, and must be lifted *when* the new note is required.

In this example from Lalo, the second bar shows how the passage comes out unevenly if the lift-off is not left until the moment the new note is required.

Symphonie espagnole, op. 21, mov. I
Lalo

The difference in timing between lifting and dropping is one of the reasons why it is often best to move the fingers as late as possible, and then to move them very quickly. As well as improving clarity, giving the player a sense of extra time, and making it possible to play with a large tone, moving the fingers quickly at the last possible moment makes it easier to play with fine rhythm.

Practice method

A simple practice technique to equalise notes that 'drop out' is to play them longer and louder than the surrounding notes.[1]

[1] See *Drop-outs*, page 168

Lift-off

168

Exercise 1

- To play the up-bows, use a very short spiccato near to the point. Make the strokes sound similar to the left-hand pizzicato.

- For the purposes of the exercise, pluck using only the finger, pulling it back from the base joint, with no hand movement.

- Tempo: slow, medium and fast

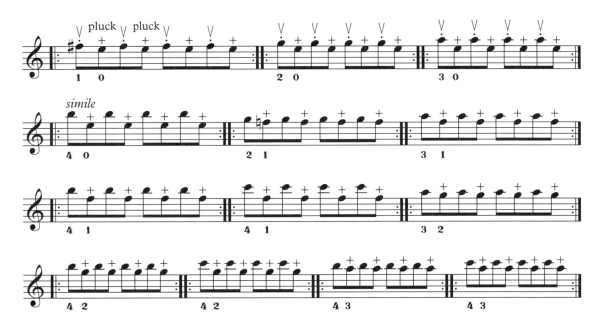

Repeat the same pattern on the G string. Position the elbow more to the left for plucking the E string, and more to the right for plucking the G string.

169

Exercise 2

Lifting off from high positions to the open string needs the fastest finger action to avoid 'fuzz' in the sound as the finger leaves the string. It is possible to avoid 'fuzz' by lifting the finger with a slight plucking movement (as in cello playing), but the point of the exercise is to lift the finger as fast as possible without plucking, and then to use the same lift-off speed in the lower position.

- Play strongly near the bridge: the louder the volume, the faster the finger has to lift.

- In the high position, lift the finger very fast so that the open string speaks immediately. Remember the feeling of the fast lift-off, and then use the same lift-off speed in first position.

- To make the exercise as effective as possible, lift the fingers vertically, without any sideways plucking. Keep the bow sustained, without playing a slight *diminuendo* before each lift-off.

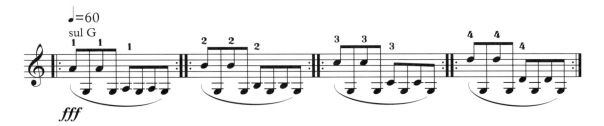

Play the same sequence on each string.

Gradually increasing speed

Exercise 1

The wider the string vibrates (i.e., the louder the volume), the faster the fingers have to touch or leave the string.

- Begin *pp*, dropping and raising the fingers slowly.
- As the volume increases *wait longer and longer* before dropping or raising, moving the finger faster and faster.
- Whatever the dynamic or speed of finger movement, the sound should always be pure, without any 'fuzz' as the finger touches or leaves the string. Playing *mf* or *ff*, listen to the 'ping' as the finger is dropped or raised.

See page 41 for a description of the soundpoints.

Play on each string.

Exercise 2

Play with the metronome at ♩ = 60 to make sure that only the speed of the finger changes, not the tempo.

1 Raise and drop the finger so slowly that it keeps moving without stopping – i.e., it begins to drop on the beat, moves down so slowly that it touches the string exactly on the next beat, and immediately begins to rise again. This will cause 'cracking' and 'fuzz' in the notes when the finger does not stop the string properly.

2 Increase the speed of the finger movement little by little so that, after dropping or lifting, you wait longer and longer for the next beat. The purity of the notes will gradually improve.

3 Finally play with such a fast finger movement that the finger is stationary most of the time – either up and waiting to go down, or down and waiting to go up.

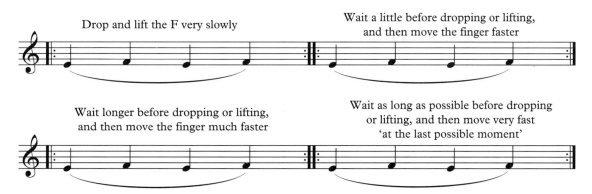

Play on each string using the following fingerings: 01, 02, 03, 04; 12, 13, 14; 23, 24; 34.

172

Slow tempo, fast fingers

Exercise 1

- Play f near the bridge with a sustained, even tone.

- Move the fingers as *late* and as *quickly* as possible, while playing at a very slow tempo.

- Each note should start with a 'ping' as the finger is dropped or raised. Lift the fingers higher than usual so that the finger has to move very fast.

- Use whole bows so that the bow speed is very fast, making the string vibrate as widely as possible.

- Place the lower fingers on the string before lifting a higher finger.[1]

Play the same sequence on each string.

Practice method

Play through any moderate-to-fast passage (or whole piece at a time) at a very slow tempo, while dropping and lifting the fingers very quickly. Wait until the last possible moment before moving each finger – keep the finger still for so long that waiting just another instant would cause the note to be late; then lift or drop extremely quickly. (Fingers that are prepared on the string should still be placed rather than dropped fast.)

173

Exercise 2

In this exercise the 'tempo' of the fingers is slow because they move only on each beat; but the speed of the finger movement, from one pair of notes to another, has to be fast to co-ordinate with the bow.

- Play as fast as possible so that the fingers have to move very quickly to get to their next positions in time. Start at ♪ = 92. Repeat the exercise at ♪ = 120, and then at ♪ = 144.

- There should be no extra sounds when changing fingers. Move so quickly that (1) the open strings are never touched by the bow, and (2) there is no 'fuzz' at the beginning of a group caused by bowing a not-completely-stopped string.

- For the purposes of the exercise, lift each pair of fingers and place them on the next string – do not hold fingers down on two strings at once.

- At first keep the fingers close to the strings. Later, lift them higher and higher so that you have to move them faster and faster.

[1] See *Finger preparation*, page 130

Fast spiccato or *sautillé*   *simile*

Also play on the G–D and D–A strings.

Easy variation

Begin at ♪ = 92. Repeat at 120, and then at 144.

simile

Play on each string.

Difficult variation

Place the lower note of each pair on the D string. Play only one line at a time, first the top line and then the bottom. Because the finger has so far to travel, it has to move even faster:

Also play on the G and A strings.

176

Exercise 3

Play very fast *détaché*, stopping on a sharply accented eighth-note (quaver). Play the eighth-note with a pure tone, however strong the accent is, with the finger completely stopping the note before the bow plays it.

Begin each bar up-bow as well as down-bow.

Fingerings

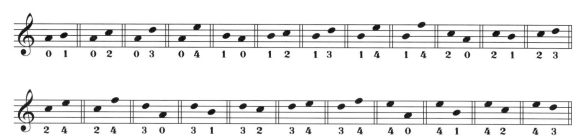

Play on each string.

177

Difficult variation

Place the upper finger of each pair on the G string without playing it (written as x-notes). Play the top line only, holding the finger on the G string until the instant it is needed on the A string. Because the finger has so far to travel, it has to move even faster:

Also play using the E and D strings.

178

Rhythms

● Play the rhythms exactly, with perfect bow and finger co-ordination. Play the thirty-second-notes (demisemiquavers) clearly.

● **Dropping fingers**

To force the fastest finger speed, keep the fingers slightly higher than usual before dropping. Drop at the last possible moment before the bow moves – do not lower the fingers near to the string ready to play (not as a rule, but in this exercise).

● **Lifting fingers**

Place the next finger on the string underneath before lifting;[1] lift the finger unusually high. Lift at the last possible moment before the bow moves.

[1] See *Finger preparation*, page 130

Also play these rhythm patterns, using the same notes as above:

Besides the five exercises below, play the fourth finger bars of Exercise 196. Also play scales, arpeggios and broken intervals using only the fourth finger (Exercises 211–3).

Fourth finger

Using the fourth finger:

- Keep the space open between the base of the thumb and the first finger (keep the thumb opposite the first finger, or between the first and second).
- Move the finger up and down from the base joint, without involving the hand.
- Keep a straight line from the elbow to the back of the hand.
- Drop and lift the finger as late and as quickly as possible.
- If the fourth finger collapses at its middle joint, play more on the tip of the fourth finger than the pad.

Never strain. Leave out any stretches in these exercises that are genuinely too difficult for your hand. In many cases you can easily increase the distance the finger can reach by keeping the hand, finger and thumb entirely loose, opening the hand at the first and second finger, and widening at the base joints – a common fault is to tense the hand and base joints, and to try to *stretch* upwards with the fourth finger. Relax the hand and finger into the stretch.

To open the base joints wider between the third and fourth fingers, play the third finger slightly more on the left side of the fingertip, and the fourth finger slightly more on the right side of the tip. In other words, tilt the third finger slightly more towards the scroll, and the fourth finger slightly more towards the bridge.

Play the exercises on each string.

179

Exercise 1

- Hold the third finger down throughout. Keep the first finger resting lightly on the string (shown by the notes in brackets).

- Move the fourth finger entirely on its own, from the base joint. Do not use the hand to move the finger.

- To open the base joints wider, play the third finger slightly more on the left side of the fingertip, and the fourth finger slightly more on the right side of the tip.

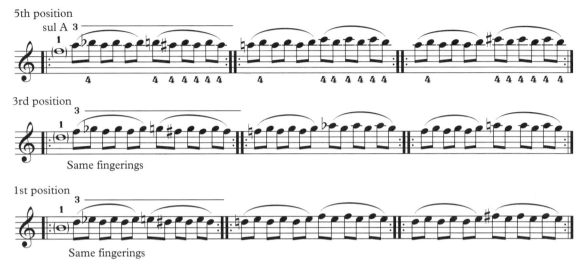

180

Exercise 2

- To open the base joints wider, play the third finger slightly more on the left side of the fingertip, and the fourth finger slightly more on the right side of the tip.

- Sustain the whole-note (semibreve) while plucking with the fourth finger.

- Pluck loudly, to exercise the finger as much as possible.

- Keep the hand, thumb and wrist still and relaxed while using the fourth finger. Keep the first finger resting lightly on the string (shown by the notes in brackets).

181

Exercise 3

- Play loudly to exercise the fourth finger as much as possible.

- To open the base joints wider, play the third finger slightly more on the left side of the fingertip, and the fourth finger slightly more on the right side of the tip.

- Hold the third finger down throughout. Keep the first finger resting lightly on the string (shown by the notes in brackets).

- Also play on the G–D and the D–A strings.

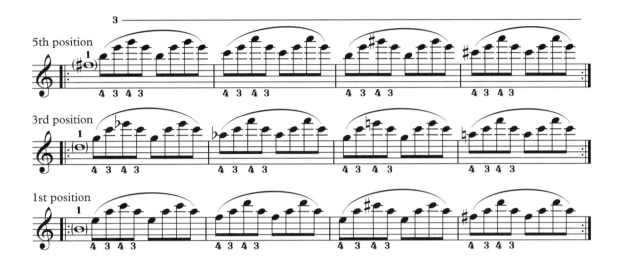

182

Exercise 4

- Hold down the first and second fingers on the string as long as possible. Hold the third finger down while playing the fourth finger.

- Raise and drop the fourth finger as *late* and as *quickly* as possible, moving from the base joint.

- Before lifting the fourth finger, the next finger must already be placed on the string underneath. This applies to the 3rd, 5th, 7th, 9th and 11th notes of each bar.

- Listen to the 'ping' as the finger stops or leaves the string.

Rhythm variations

Play the same sequence on the other strings starting in 1st position.

183

Exercise 5

- Hold the first finger down throughout.
- Whenever possible, hold down the second finger.

Play the same sequence on the other strings in 7th, 4th and 1st positions.

Co-ordination

In many cases it is easier for the bow to be ready to play a note than it is for the left hand fingers to be ready on the string.

The fingers may need to change shape from note to note, or be placed after moving the whole hand in a shift; depending on what has come before, they may drop from different heights or have to move across from another string; some fingers may need to be placed on the string before lifting another, and so on. Meanwhile the bow may simply be moving up and down on the same string.

The left hand fingers must always lead. If the finger is late, a moment of 'fuzz' is caused by bowing a half-stopped string.

Either the finger has found the string too late, and the bow has already begun to move without the finger stopping the note properly – or it lifts off too late, and the next bow catches it again momentarily before playing the lower note. These two exercises work from the opposite extreme by making the fingers too early.

A simple way to demonstrate perfect co-ordination is to play pizzicato: the difference in timing between putting the finger down and plucking it is obvious. In the following example first play pizzicato, and then bow with the same timing as when plucking.

Violin Concerto in D, op. 61, mov. I
Beethoven
(1) pizzicato
(2) arco
409

Fingers 'leading'

Exercise 1

184

- Sustain the first note of each bar evenly and solidly, stopping the bow suddenly on the second beat. Leave the bow on the string without lightening the pressure.

- On the third beat, place the new finger on the string silently (written as an x-note).

- Play the whole sequence through with the metronome at $\quad$ = 100, then gradually speed up to 200, or faster. At each metronome speed repeat each bar several times.

Example (bars 5 and 6 of the fingering pattern – see ⋆)

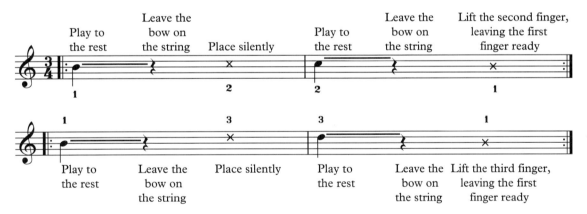

Fingering pattern

Also play the same pattern on the other strings.

185

Exercise 2

- Play with the metronome beating quarter-notes (crotchets).
- Hold the first note longer and longer, so that the second note comes closer and closer to the bow change.
- Continue until the second note is only a fraction ahead of the bow change, and then play only two notes with perfect co-ordination.

Fingerings

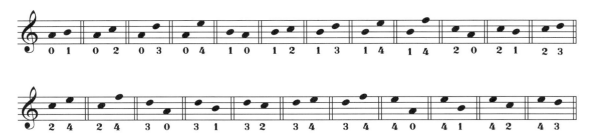

Also play the same fingerings on the other strings.

Practice method

Winter (The Four Seasons) op. 8 no. 4, mov. I
Vivaldi

Begin at a slow tempo, playing the dots as long as possible and the short notes as short as possible. Gradually increase the tempo until the dotted pattern is as fast as it can practically be played, always feeling the fingers a fraction ahead of the bow. This is one of the single most effective practice methods, and gives instant results.

Finger preparation

Finger preparation is another example of 'technical timing' as opposed to 'musical timing' (see footnote on page 27). To play any descending notes smoothly and seamlessly, the lower fingers have to be ready on the string before lifting the upper fingers.

42 Etudes ou caprices, no. 2
Kreutzer

In the example above, although the fingers playing the first and third notes obviously have to be on the string before the bow moves, that is a question of co-ordination – they are not 'prepared' fingers as such. The fourth note (first finger F) is a prepared finger. Whatever the tempo, this finger is placed on the string while playing the note before (second finger G). At first the prepared first finger does not press hard, only half stopping the note. Then, as the second finger lifts, the first finger stops the F fully.

The seventh note (third finger D) is a prepared finger, and fully stops the string an instant before the bow arrives on the A string. The ninth note (second finger C) is similar to the fourth note (F).

186

Exercise 1

Exaggerate the finger preparation by placing the prepared fingers very early, like a syncopation, as shown by the x-notes in the example. *Do not press the prepared fingers down* – gently rest them on the string and then *stop the string at the same time as raising the previous finger.* In other words, stopping the new note, and finishing the old note, are *two halves of one action*, not two separate actions.

Example

187

Exercise 2

Here the third note of each group is on the lower string. Place it early, like a syncopation, as shown in the example:

Example

Other positions

Start in 5th position on the D and G strings, and in 4th position on the E and A strings:

188

Exercise 3

Here the fourth note is prepared. Place it early, like a syncopation.

Other positions

Start in 5th position on the G and D strings, and in 4th position on the A and E strings:

Exercise 4

189

Here the second and fourth notes of each group are prepared fingers. Place them early, like a syncopation, as shown in the example.

Example

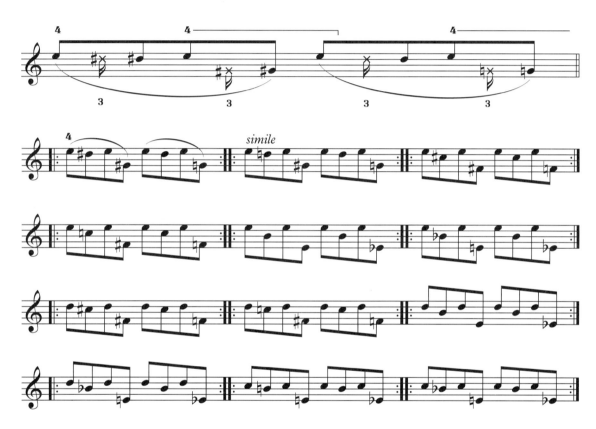

Other positions

Start in 5th position on the D and G strings, and in 4th position on the E and A strings:

190

Exercise 5

Prepare the second and fourth notes of each group, placing them early like a syncopation.

Other positions

Start in 5th position on the G and D strings, and in 4th position on the A and E strings:

Trills

Releasing the lower finger

For most actions on the violin there is a counter-action, usually in contrary motion to the principal movement. In the case of trills, the lower finger moves (almost invisibly) in the opposite direction to the upper finger.

The lower, held-down finger in a trill must not press too hard, otherwise the upper finger is unable to move freely.

191

Exercise 1

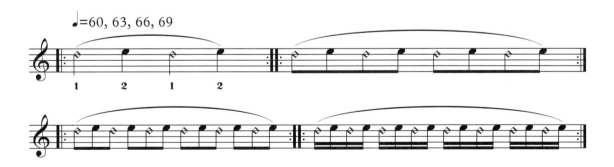

As the speed of the notes increases, the harmonic should still speak clearly.

Fingerings

- During the harmonic, completely relax the wrist, hand, fingers and thumb. Keep that feeling of relaxation as you play the upper finger.
- Leave the harmonic finger lightly touching the string when playing the upper finger.
- Playing with the metronome, begin slowly at ♩ = 60 and gradually increase the tempo to 63, 66 and 69.

Also play the same pattern on the other strings.

Exercise 2

192

As you drop the upper finger, raise the lower finger quite high, moving the two fingers in contrary motion.

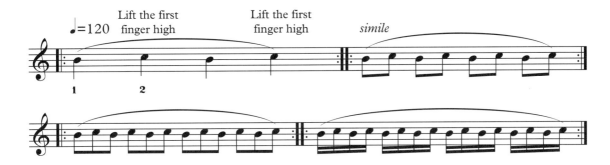

Fingerings

Play the same patterns on the other strings.

193

Exercise 3

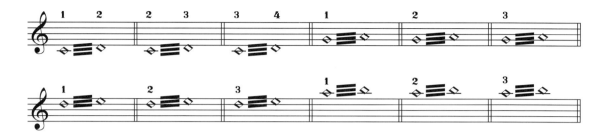

When the trill is fast enough, the higher of each pair of harmonics in this exercise comes out a fifth higher than normal (because the lower finger remains touching the string), so that the trills sound as follows:

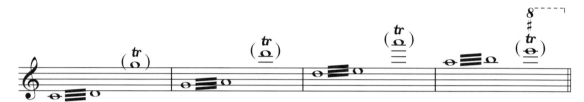

If the trill does not sound clearly, try playing nearer to the bridge or with a faster bow speed, and make sure the lower finger (which must remain on the string) is neither too heavy nor too light.

Trilling harmonics like this gives the fingers a feeling of extraordinary ease and lightness. Aim at the fastest possible trill with the least possible effort. There should be almost no sensation at all in the hand and fingers. Then find the same effortlessness in ordinary trills.

194

Building trills note by note

Sustain long, f bows near the bridge before playing each trill, making the string vibrate as widely as possible. Play without vibrato.

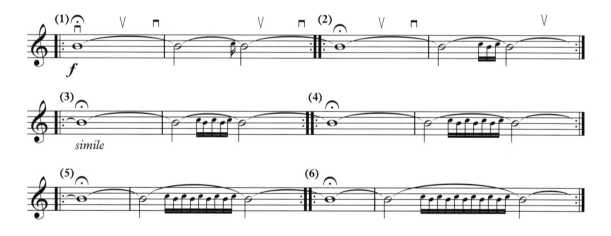

1   Raise the trilling finger a little above its normal height – drop very quickly on to the string – lift off quickly back to its slightly-higher-than-normal position, and then relax. Move the fingers from the base joints.

   Listen to the 'ping' as the finger hits or leaves the string. Keep the sound sustained as you use the fingers.

2   Raise the finger a little above its normal height – drop quickly on to the string – raise only *slightly* – drop again quickly – raise quickly back to the starting position.

3   Raise the finger a little above its normal height – drop quickly on to the string – raise *slightly* – drop again quickly – raise *slightly* – drop again quickly – raise quickly back to the starting position.

4–6 The examples show up to six trill notes. Continue up to about eight or nine.

Play every note of the trill clearly and cleanly, making the violin ring. There should be no 'fuzz' caused by raising the finger too soon, or by dropping or lifting too slowly.

Three questions of timing apply to this exercise: (1) how fast the finger drops, (2) how long it stays down on the string, and (3) how fast it is raised.

Particularly in double stops, do not overpress with the fingers that stay on the string.

Fingerings

Play the same patterns on the other strings.

Direction

195

The trilling finger moves up–up–up–up, not down–down–down–down or down–up–down–up. If Heifetz's recording of the Bruch Concerto[1] (or the recording of many other artists) is played at half speed, the trill passage in the first movement does not come out sounding even, but actually sounds approximately like this:

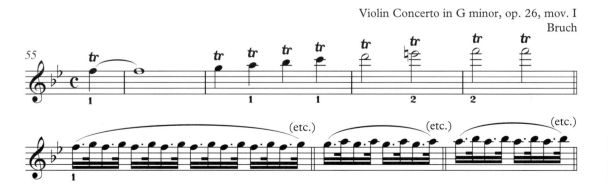

Violin Concerto in G minor, op. 26, mov. I
Bruch

[1] New Symphony Orchestra of London, cond. Malcolm Sargent, RCA, LSB 4061

The following simple exercise can be used either to build technique for trills or else as a practice method for specific passages in trills. Lift the trilling finger quickly, as if the string were very hot.

Fingerings

Use the same patterns as in Exercise 194, playing on each string or pair of strings.

196 Rhythm exercise

This is a quick substitute for Ševcík-type exercises and is excellent as a general quick warm-up exercise, covering all the possible combinations of two fingers.

- Play with the metronome, starting slowly at ♩ = 60 and gradually speeding up to about 80.

- Drop and lift the fingers as *late* and as *fast* as possible, making a clean beginning and end to each note.

- Play loudly, to exercise the fingers as much as possible.

- Move the fingers from the base joints, without the whole hand also moving from the wrist. If this is not entirely working, hold down unused fingers on another string to get the feeling of the fingers moving without the hand.

Fingerings

Use the same patterns as in Exercise 194, playing on each string or pair of strings.

Blocks

Dropping or lifting each finger individually, as a separate action, is possible only up to a certain speed. After that, it is easier to play very fast by dropping or lifting groups of fingers all at once, in a fan-like shape, with *one action,* so that the notes are played almost simultaneously. There are then fewer finger actions to perform, and *fast passages feel slower.* In the example below (see *Practice method*) the number of finger actions (not counting shifts) is reduced from seventeen to six.

Ascending   While playing the quarter-note (crotchet) at the beginning of the bar, prepare the other fingers above the string in their tone–semitone pattern. Bring the fingers down together as one action. Although very fast, each note should still be clear.

Descending   Prepare the underneath notes on the string, in tune, and then 'tilt' the whole group off the string with one action.

Then continue by playing the same patterns as before, but now without stopping on the first note. Drop or lift the fingers an instant after the bow begins to move, 'tilting' them on or off the string.

Play the whole exercise on each string. Use a variety of key signatures to cover different tone–semitone possibilities.

Practice method

Practise fast runs as follows, dropping the fingers together as one action:

Violin Concerto in G minor, op. 26, mov. I
Bruch

152

Practise descending runs in the same way.

Extensions and contractions

Extensions

If any of the following stretches, when played in 1st position, are impossible for your size of hand, simply move the fingers as far as you can.

- Keep the wrist in approximately a straight line with the forearm, without pushing it forward as the extending finger reaches upwards. (See Fig. 39, page 97.)

- Place the thumb well forward, opening the space between the base of the thumb and the first finger.

- Increase the stretch of the fingers by widening at the base joint, using the part of the fingertip that produces the most space between the fingers.[1] Basically, try to keep the second, third and fourth fingers as upright on the string as possible (not as a rule, but in these exercises).

- The pitch of the note being played should not change while extending another finger above or below.

198

Exercise 1

Ascending

Keep the lower of the two fingers lightly on the string, without lifting off as you place the upper finger. For example, in the first bar do not lift the first finger.

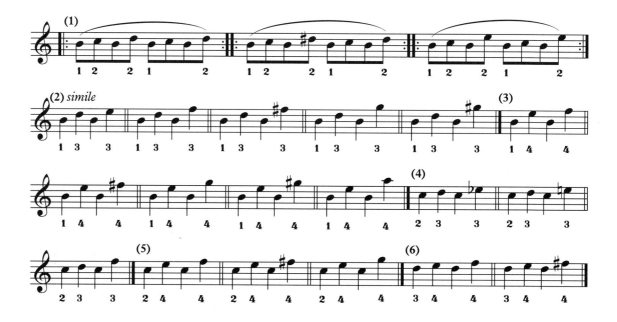

[1] See *Widening at the base joints*, page 93

Descending

Place the second and fourth notes of each bar on the string, before lifting the first and third notes.[1]

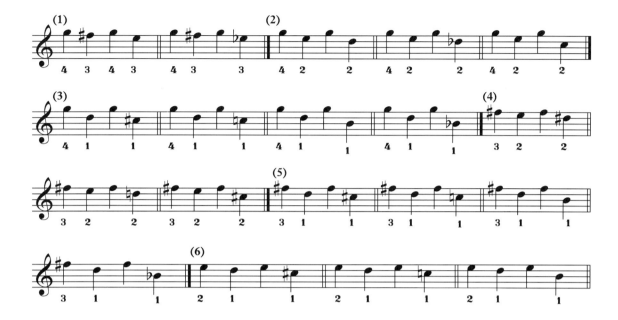

Other positions

Play the same notes on the other strings in various octaves:

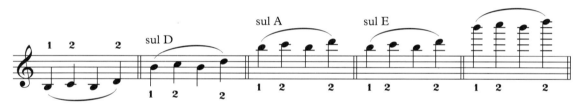

Exercise 2

- **Ascending**   Hold the lower of the two fingers down on the string throughout.
- **Descending**   Do not lift the upper finger until the lower finger is firmly in place on the string.

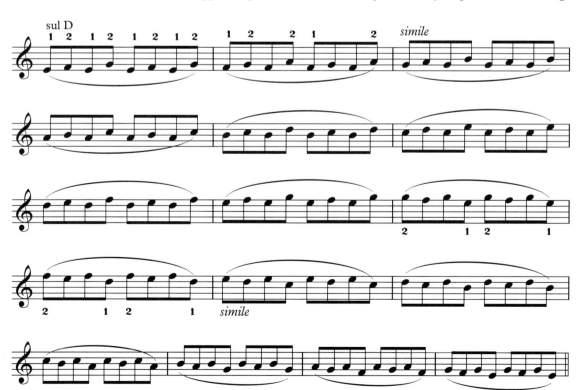

[1] See *Finger preparation*, page 130

Continue in the same way, slurring and repeating each bar at least twice:

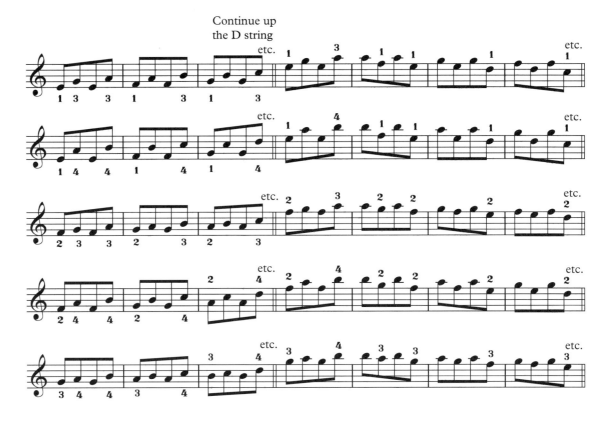

Play the exercise using the following key signatures:

Play the same patterns on the other strings, starting in 1st position.

200

Exercise 3

- **Ascending**   Hold the lower of the two fingers down on the string throughout.
- **Descending**   Do not lift the upper finger until the lower finger is firmly in place on the string.

Play the exercise using the following key signatures:

Play the same patterns on the other strings, starting in 1st position.

Exercise 4

- **Ascending**   Hold the first finger down on the string.
- **Descending**   Keep the hand position balanced on the fourth finger and reach back with the first finger. Do not lift the fourth finger until the first finger is firmly in place on the string.
- Play separate bows and slurred.

201

Play the exercise using the following key signatures:

Play the same sequence on the other strings, starting in 1st position.

Practice method

Learn how to measure an extension by also practising extending to the surrounding notes:

Sonata in G, op. 78, mov. I
Brahms

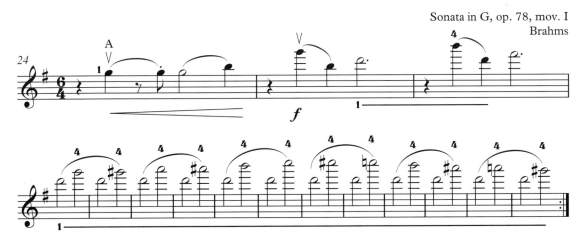

Contractions

202

Exercise 1

Hold down the first finger throughout

Play the exercise in the same positions on the other strings.

203

Exercise 2

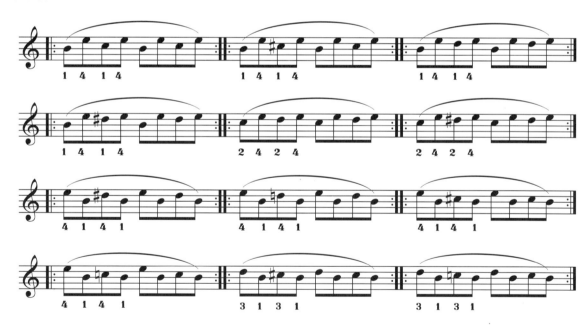

Other positions

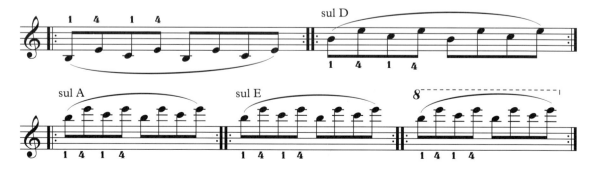

Shifting

'Ghosting'

Some of the exercises in this section use 'ghost' notes, which are played as follows:

1 Lighten the finger as though playing a harmonic.

2 Use the least bow pressure.

3 Use the least length of bow.

Arm movement

Low positions (up to 4th): the hand moves up and down the neck without the elbow having to move left or right.

Middle positions (from 5th to 7th): the hand goes 'up and over' the shoulder of the violin, supported on the thumb. The hand should not move 'around' the shoulder, otherwise the elbow is forced to move too far in to the centre of the body. The elbow should move to the right only as far as necessary – as little as possible.

High positions (8th onwards): shifts are made more with the hand moving from the wrist, with almost no arm.

In shifting from high or middle positions to low positions, the elbow must move to the left again. Figs. 47a and 47b show a one-octave shift from first finger A in 8th position down to the first finger in 1st position. Note how the elbow is more to the left in Fig. 47b, and how it has got 'stuck' in a position too far to the right in Fig. 47c.

Fig. 47

(a)

First finger A, 8th position

(b)

First finger A, 1st position

(c)

Having descended from 8th position, the elbow has remained too far to the right

204

Exercise 1

Bar 1 Move the hand up and down the neck without moving the elbow to left or right.

Bar 2 Move the elbow to the right when ascending, and to the left again when descending. Move the hand 'up and over' the shoulder of the violin, supported on the thumb (Fig. 47a).

Bar 3 Keep the arm still, with the elbow positioned to the right (just as far right as necessary). Shift by moving the hand from the wrist.

Repeat on the other strings. On the E string, position the elbow well to the left in the lower positions. In the high positions, move the elbow to the right only as far as necessary.

205

Exercise 2

Having separated the arm movement into three parts in Exercise 204, put all three together by playing two-octave shifts on one string.

- Feel the different movements smoothly joined together – only the hand/forearm moving in the lower positions; the elbow moving to the right in the middle positions; mainly moving with the hand alone in the upper positions.

- Descending, make sure that the upper arm returns to its normal position under the violin, i.e., not too far to the right (Figs. 47b and 47c).

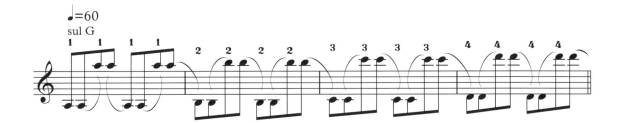

Play the same shifts on each string.

206

Leading the shift

Thumb preparation

There are various rules governing when the finger/hand/arm moves before the thumb, or when the thumb moves first. The exact action depends on the size of the hand and the length of the thumb, the actual notes and the speed of the shift, but in the most general terms:

1. 1st or 2nd position to higher: thumb and hand together.

2. 3rd position to higher: the thumb sometimes slightly precedes the hand.

3. 3rd, 4th or 5th position to 1st: the thumb precedes the hand.

4. 6th position and higher down to 1st: the thumb, hand and arm together in one single movement.

5. Higher position down to 3rd: keep the thumb in place while shifting, then move the thumb into the new position.

A simple way to discover the natural use of the thumb without having to think about 'rules' is to play without a shoulder rest. The thumb is then forced to make exactly the right movements at the right time. When the shoulder rest is put back on, the thumb 'remembers' the same movements.

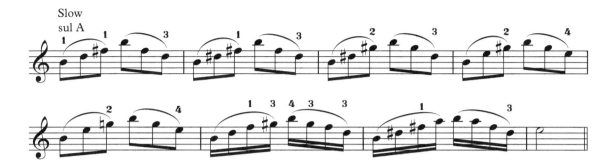

- Without a shoulder rest, play arpeggios on one string, as in the Ševčík sequence above. The thumb must now always support the violin, and therefore automatically makes correctly timed movements of preparation and support.

- Play very slowly, noticing where the thumb instinctively wants to move to, and when it wants to move.

- Do not clamp the violin between the chin and shoulder (do not raise the shoulder). Simply rest the instrument on the collar bone, and relax the weight of the head into the chin rest. Using some padding underneath the violin does not affect the exercise.

- Start the arpeggio sequence in different positions to cover all possibilities.

Practice method

Play through whole pieces without a shoulder rest (always making sure that the shoulder does not come up to try to clamp the violin in place). Practise the difficult shifting passages until the thumb/finger/hand/arm all operate smoothly *without the scroll moving*. When the shoulder rest is put back on, the thumb remembers the same actions. You will probably find that many passages have to be played very slowly.

Fingers leading

The impulse for the shift often comes from the finger rather than the hand or arm, with the hand (and then the arm) *following*. 'Aim' with the fingertip into the new note. In these exercises the timing is exaggerated, the finger moving on its own followed by the thumb, hand and arm.

Exercise 1

207

□ = Square finger   ◊ = extended finger[1]

In the first bar move only the finger, keeping the hand in first position. Do not move the thumb. In the second bar shift normally from position to position.

- In the first bar begin with the finger square, extend the finger to the upper note, change it back into a square to return to the lower note. Take care to move only the finger, not the hand.

- In the second bar shift normally with the hand/arm, but still make the very smallest amount of the finger movement as in the first bar. In every shift, aim with the fingertip into the new note.

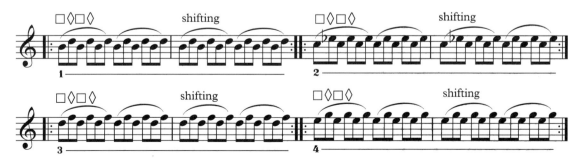

Play on each string.

[1] See *Square and extended,* page 113

208

Exercise 2

- To make each shift, only move the finger. At the arrow move the thumb, hand and arm into the new position.

  → = move the thumb up (towards the bridge)   ← = move the thumb back (towards the scroll).

- Time the movements in a regular rhythm: finger–thumb–finger–thumb, etc.

Play on each string.

About slow arrival speed

In long shifts (and very often in shorter shifts as well),[1] the shift does not move at one single speed. One of the secrets of great accuracy is to shift fast to *somewhere just below the arrival note*, and then to continue more slowly into the arrival note itself. Singers typically reach notes in the same way, the key point being that you must never go too far and then come down into the arrival note. One of the chief advantages of slow arrival speed is that it does not matter where you shift to – a little higher, a little lower – so long as you 'arrive' a little below the actual arrival note and then move more slowly into it.

Very often the slow arrival speed is not noticeable at all. Sometimes it is audible, as in singing, and is used as part of the expression of the passage (although this is completely different to an actual slide or *portamento*).

In these exercises the slow arrival speed is written into each shift as an extra note a semitone below the arrival note. The dotted rhythm forces the speed of the shift to be fast–slow.

Practice method

[1] For example, every shift in the octave variation (Variation 3) of Paganini Caprice no.24 (24 Caprices op.1) requires a slow arrival speed. Even the semitone shift from A to G♯ feels more comfortable and accurate after practising it with a fast–slow shift.

Sonata no. 3 in D minor, op. 108, mov. I
Brahms

One-finger exercises

- While playing with one finger keep all the unused fingers relaxed and uninvolved, above or near to the string.

- When playing with just the first finger, sometimes practise with the fourth finger silently down on an adjacent string (as lightly as a harmonic); or keep the first finger down when playing with just the fourth finger.

Slow arrival speed

Exercise 1

209

1 First play each section through as written (see example below). Play *f* with an evenly sustained tone, and with a light left hand. Shift to the dotted eighth-notes (quavers) *quickly,* shift to the half-notes (minims) *slowly.*

2 Repeat the section, ghosting the dotted eighth-notes.[1]

3 Play without the dotted eighth-notes, but still with fast shifts that slow down into the arrival note.

Other fingers and positions

Play the sequence on the other strings in various octaves, continuing up the string as high as possible.

[1] See *Ghosting*, page 145

210

Exercise 2

1. First play through the whole sequence as written, playing all the notes with equal tone (see example below). Shift to the eighth-notes (quavers) *quickly,* shift to the dotted quarter-notes (crotchets) *slowly.*

2. Then play through, ghosting the eighth-notes.

3. Play through without the eighth-notes, but still with a fast shift that slows down into the arrival note.

Other fingers and positions

Play the sequence on the other strings in various octaves:

Scales and arpeggios

- When using the first finger, keep the fourth finger near to the string to maintain a good hand position.
- When using the third and fourth fingers, keep the first finger close to the string.
- Use separate bows as well as slurs.

Exercise 1

211

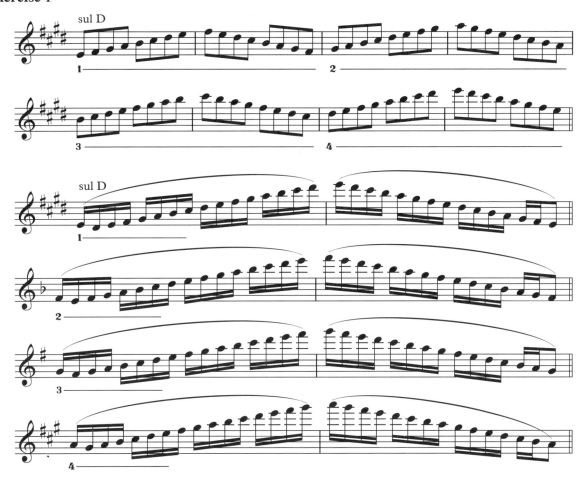

Play the same patterns, starting in 1st position, on each string. Use a variety of major and minor scales.

Exercise 2

212

(Leave out the notes in brackets to play just one octave of each arpeggio.)

Bowing variations

As well as slurring, also play fast spiccato or *sautillé*, three and four strokes to a note. Then the shifts must be very fast to co-ordinate with the bow, so that it sounds the same as if played with a normal fingering.

Play the same arpeggio pattern with the other fingers. Start on different key notes on each string.

Broken thirds, fourths, etc.

Play in a variety of keys to cover different notes and intervals:

Bowing variations

Other fingers

Play the exercise on each string, with each finger.

Semitones

Also see *Dividing semitones*, Exercise 293.

In these two exercises play the first two beats of each bar across the strings in one position. In the last two beats play the same notes up the string. Play so that somebody listening but not seeing your left hand would not realise that you were changing the fingering.

- Move the whole hand to shift – do not just move the finger.
- Lift and drop the fingers 'late' and fast, especially when playing at slow and medium speeds.
- Play slurred as written, and also separate bows.
- Tempo: slow, medium and fast.

Exercise 1

214

Other positions

Play the same notes on the G–D strings, starting in 2nd position, and on the D–A strings starting in 5th position.

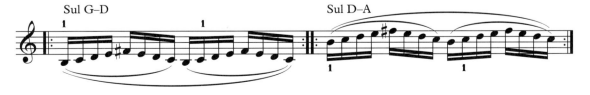

Exercise 2

At the bar marked *simile* play the upper fingering first, and repeat using the lower fingering.

Play the same notes on the G and D strings, starting in 2nd position:

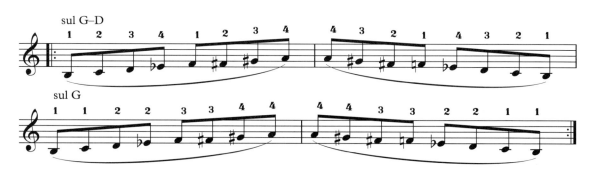

Chromatic glissando

Violin Concerto no. 2 in D Minor, op. 22, mov. I
Wieniawski

The chromatic glissando can be likened to the movement of the right arm in staccato, the left arm/hand making a vibrato-like movement while it pushes the hand down (or up) the string. Keep the wrist pushed outwards, with the finger solidly in the string throughout. In this example from Wieniawski, the run is started with a movement from the hand, with the arm taking over after a few notes. Each note in a perfectly executed chromatic glissando sounds as clear as in a fingered chromatic run.

Practice method

The first step is to find the correct speed of the glissando in relation to the tempo of the passage. If the glissando is too slow the semitones become quarter-tones or less, and you end up only part of the way down the string by the time you should have reached the bottom. If the glissando is too fast the semitones become too wide, and you reach the bottom too soon. The speed must be even, otherwise some semitones will be played wider than others.

To find the correct speed play an ordinary glissando, sliding evenly without individual notes. You need to slide at such a speed that you pass – without stopping – the first note of each group of four exactly on each beat. Think of a descending elevator, passing each floor at regular intervals without stopping. In this example count: 4–1–2–3–4–1 (the first '4' being the C♯, which is the second note of the run).

Having found the speed of the slide, the next step is to slide in stages – still without the individual semitones – working from the bottom up:

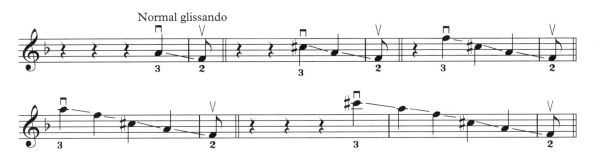

Also work in stages from the top down, making sure that the note on which you stop is always exactly in tune:

Then begin to make the individual semitones, again working in stages from the bottom up:

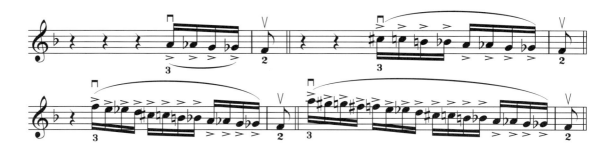

Also start at the top and work down in stages, always arriving exactly in tune on the first note of a beat:

Metronome exercise

- Do not just slide the fingers in these exercises – shift the whole hand from one position to another. Release the fingers during the shifts, relaxing the thumb, wrist, upper arm and neck.
- At the slow speeds, shift at the last possible moment and very fast, almost moving on the beat.

Example

Fingerings and Intervals

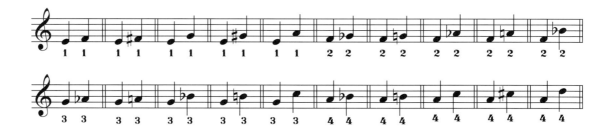

Other positions

Play the same patterns in the following positions:

Classical shifts

Classical shifts are also known as 'beginning' shifts, the hand moving on the finger that begins the shift.

- **Ascending**   Move the hand up on the finger that is playing the lower note. Drop the new finger directly on the upper note.
- **Descending**   Move the hand down on the finger that is playing the upper note. Place the lower finger on its note before lifting the upper finger.
- **Co-ordination**   In separate-bow shifts, shift with the 'old' finger on the 'old' bow, play the 'new' finger on the 'new' bow.

1. First play each line through as written (see example below). Play ***f*** with an evenly sustained tone, and with a light left hand. The lower bowing gives the correct co-ordination for separate-bow shifts.

2. Then ghost the middle note of each triplet, playing it as a grace note.

3. Finally play without the middle note at all, as simply one note followed by another. In other words, play 'note–note' rather than 'note–shift–note'.

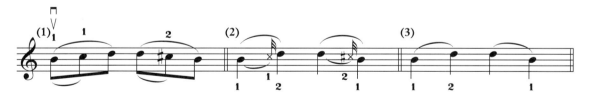

Other positions

Play the same notes on the other strings in various octaves:

219

Romantic shifts

Romantic shifts are also known as 'end' shifts, the hand moving on the finger that ends the shift.

- Romantic shifts are only played ascending, never descending. Having played the lower finger, place the higher finger on the surface of the string, without pressing. Shift up on the higher finger.[1]

- *The speed of the shift is fast–slow:* shift quickly to just below the arrival note, and then slow down into the note. This has been built into the exercise with extra notes between the actual notes of the shift.[2]

- **Co-ordination:** In separate-bow shifts, play the 'old' finger on the 'old' bow, and shift with the 'new' finger on the 'new' bow. (Having finished the lower note, place the upper finger – on the surface of the string, without pressing – *at the same time* as beginning the new bow. Then move the bow and the finger together.)

[1] Because the finger shifts on the surface of the string without pressing, it moves into the arrival note *diagonally*, from just below the arrival note. In other words, (1) shift most of the way with the finger light on the string, (2) just a little below the arrival note begin gradually to stop the string more, until (3) arriving on the note with enough finger weight to sound it. Do not shift lightly all the way to the arrival note, and then press the string down vertically; do not fully stop the string a long way below the arrival note, and then slide up heavily into it.

[2] See *About slow arrival speed*, page 148

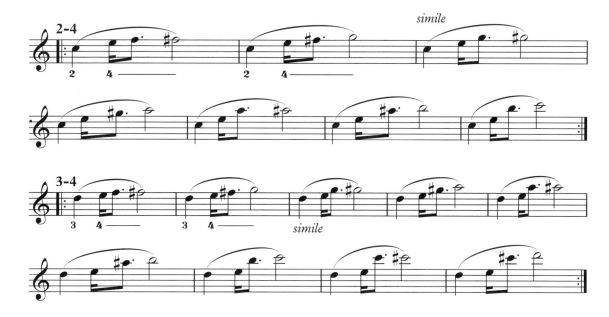

1 First play each section through as written (see example below). Play f with an evenly sustained tone, and with a light left hand. The lower bowing gives the correct co-ordination for separate-bow shifts.

Shift quickly to the dotted eighth-note (quaver) fast, and slowly into the half-note (minim).

2 Repeat the section, ghosting the sixteenth-note (semiquaver).

3 Ghost both middle notes, still playing in the dotted rhythm.

4 Play the shift without the middle notes, as simply one note followed by another. Still shift fast, and slow down into the arrival note.

Other positions

Play the same notes on the other strings in various octaves:

220 Combination shifts

In a combination shift, both fingers do the shifting. The shift begins with the finger that is already playing, and ends with the finger that plays the new note.

- Having played the first note, lighten the finger and move it up (or down) the string. During the shift place the new finger lightly on the surface of the string, and continue on it to the arrival note.

- The speed of the shift into the arrival note should be slow, like a Romantic shift. This has been built into the exercise with extra notes between the actual notes of the shift.

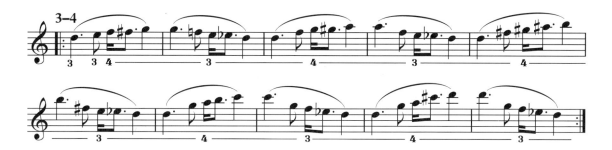

1 First play each section through as written (see example below). Play *f* with an evenly sustained tone, and with a light left hand.

2 Ghost the three middle notes between the actual notes of the shift, still playing the dotted rhythms.

3 Play without the extra notes, as simply one note to another, with hardly any glissando.

Other positions

Play the same notes on the other strings in various octaves:

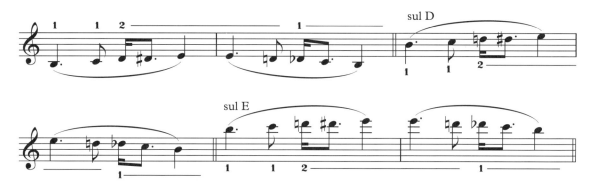

Practice method

Wherever possible practise each shift all three ways, with Classical, Romantic and Combination intermediates.

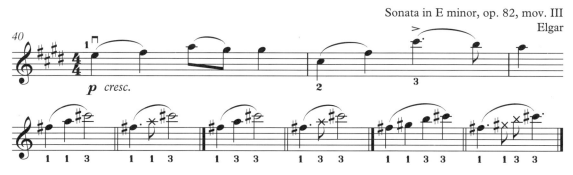

Sonata in E minor, op. 82, mov. III
Elgar

Used by permission of Novello & Co Ltd

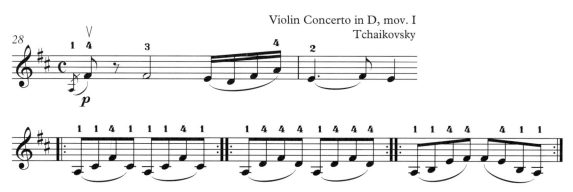

Violin Concerto in D, mov. I
Tchaikovsky

221

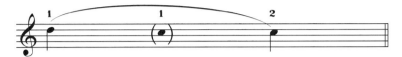

Exchange shifts are those where the fingers 'cross over' during the shift, e.g., shifting from 2–1 in an ascending shift or 1–2 in a descending shift.

Using substitutions

Also see *Substitutions,* page 170

- Move the hand down on the finger that is playing the upper note. Once the shifting finger is on the note being shifted to, substitute the new finger.

- **Co-ordination:** In separate-bow shifts, shift with the 'old' finger on the 'old' bow, and play the 'new' finger on the 'new' bow.

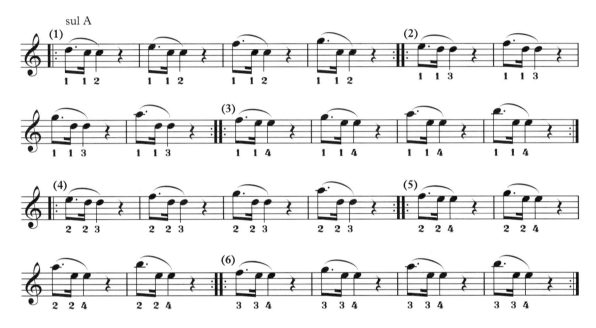

Use a variety of key signatures to cover different intervals:

1 First play each section through as written (see example below). Shift to the sixteenth-note (semiquaver) slowly, with a heavy glissando. The lower bowing gives the correct co-ordination for separate-bow shifts.

2 Then ghost the sixteenth-note, playing it as a grace note.

3 Play without the middle note at all, as simply one note to another.

Other positions

Play the same notes on the other strings in various octaves:

Shifting below the note[1]

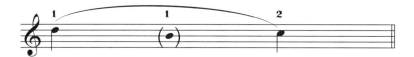

- Move the hand down on the finger that is playing the upper note. Once the shifting finger has gone below the note being shifted to, drop the new finger directly on the new note.

- **Co-ordination:** In separate-bow shifts, shift with the 'old' finger on the 'old' bow, and play the 'new' finger on the 'new' bow.

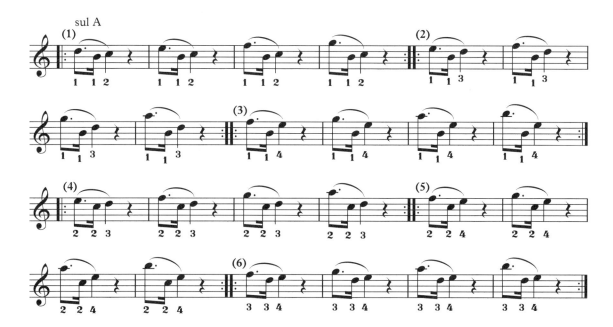

Use a variety of key signatures to cover different intervals:

1 First play each section through as written (see example below). Shift to the sixteenth-note (semiquaver) slowly, with a heavy glissando. The lower bowing gives the correct co-ordination for separate-bow shifts.

2 Then ghost the sixteenth-note, playing it as a grace note.

3 Play without the middle note at all, as simply one note to another.

Other positions

Play the same notes on the other strings in various octaves:

[1] These exchange shifts are similar to Exercise 221 (which used substitutions). While substitutions are more usual, shifting below the note can also be used. This exercise improves both kinds of shift at the same time.

223

Shifting with both fingers

- These exchange shifts work in the same way as combination shifts: the shift begins with the finger that is already playing, and ends with the finger that plays the new note.
- Begin to move the hand up or down on the finger that is playing the first note of the shift. During the shift, lighten the finger and exchange the new finger, and continue like a Romantic shift.
- The arrival speed into the destination note should be slow. This has been built in to the exercise as an extra note.[1]

1 First play each section through as written (see example below). Play *f* with an evenly sustained tone, and with a light left hand.

2 Ghost the three middle notes between the actual notes of the shift, still playing the dotted rhythms.

3 Without playing the middle notes, shift with hardly any glissando, as simply one note to another. Begin the shift with the finger that plays the first note, lighten the finger during the shift and exchange the new finger.

Other positions

Play the same notes on the other strings in various octaves:

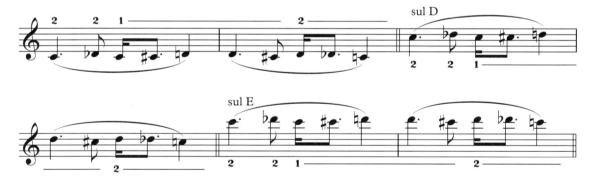

224

Broken intervals

Play on each string starting in 1st position, playing in the minor as well as the major. Also play the same patterns in broken fourths, fifths and sixths:

Bowing variations

Double stops

Playing on each pair of strings, use the same method to practise thirds, sixths and fingered octaves – a key practice technique. Examples:

Metronome exercise

Begin at ♩ = 60 and gradually increase up to about 80.

- Playing the quarter-notes (crotchets) and eighth-notes (quavers) shift 'late' and very fast, almost moving on the beat.
- Release the finger during the shift. The thumb, wrist, upper arm and neck must remain relaxed.
- Descending, move the thumb back before the shift. (See *Thumb preparation*, page 146.)

Exercise 1

225

Example

Fingerings and intervals:

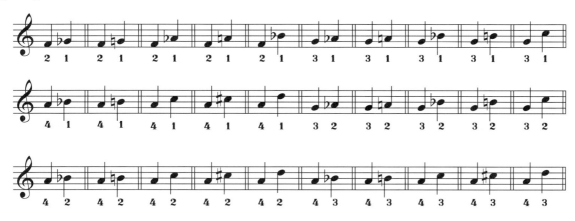

Other positions

Play the same patterns in the following positions:

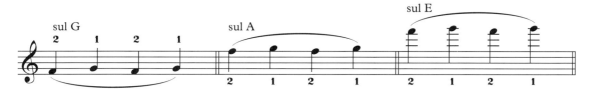

Practice method

Make each shift into a sort of 'trill', playing it as fast as possible. Encourage the fingers to be very light on the string by bowing lightly over the fingerboard.

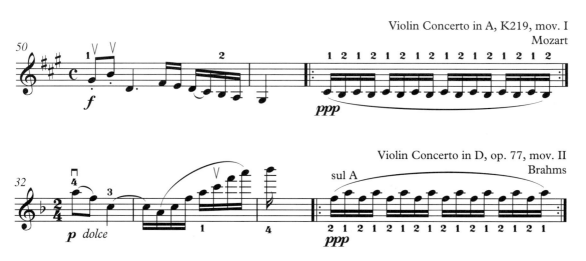

Violin Concerto in A, K219, mov. I
Mozart

Violin Concerto in D, op. 77, mov. II
Brahms

226

Scales

Play two-finger scales on each string, playing slurred and separate bows:

Play the same pattern using 2–3 and 3–4, starting on different key notes and playing both major and minor (harmonic and melodic) scales.

227

> ### Drop-outs
>
> See also *Practice method*, page 119.

For fast passages to have brilliance, every note must be clear, without any notes 'dropping out'. The most common notes to drop out are those before or after a change of position, a change of string, or a change of bow.

This exercise strengthens the notes that might drop out before or after position changes. Practising it improves scales in general, and is also a good way to practise specific runs in a piece.

2–1, 3–1 and 4–1 are obviously the usual fingerings for fast runs, but practising 3–2, 4–2 and 4–3 is good for improving overall technical facility.

Example

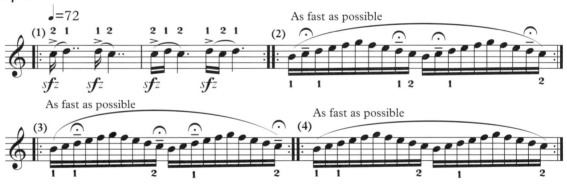

1 Play the sixteenth-notes (semiquavers) clearly, and as quickly as possible, beginning with a powerful *sfz*.

2 Play all the notes of the run as quickly as possible, except the notes *before* the shifts. Pause on these slightly, playing them *longer* and *louder* than the other notes. Leave the fingers down on the way up without lifting them when a new finger is placed.

3 Pause on the notes *after* the shifts, playing them longer and louder than the other notes.

4 Play as quickly as possible, up and down many times without stopping. Make sure that all the notes have exactly the same length and volume. The shifts should not be audible, and should not cause any bump or unevenness. Leave the fingers down on the string. If the suggested metronome speed is too fast, start a little more slowly and increase the speed of the metronome gradually.

The left thumb must remain very light against the neck of the violin. If the scroll of the instrument shakes during the shift (disturbing the bow), the thumb or fingers may be pressing too hard or not releasing sufficiently. Keep the bow solidly and evenly in the string throughout, *mf* or *f*.

Also play in other keys to include different tone–semitone patterns:

Shifts of a tone or semitone

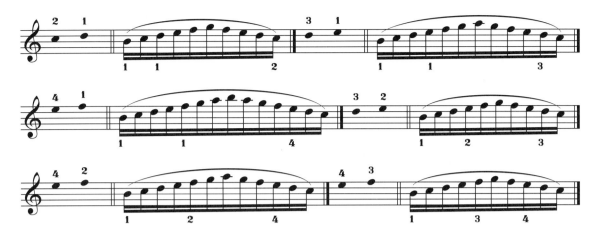

Shifts of a third

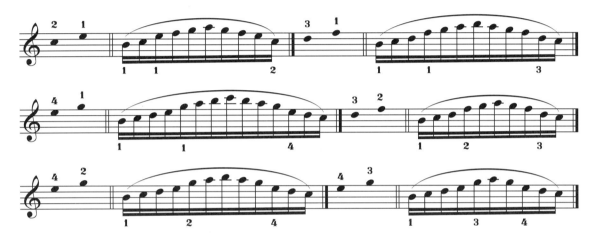

Shifts of a fourth

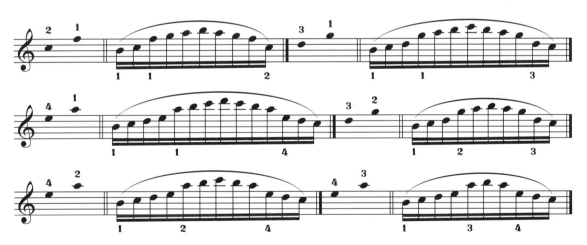

Other positions

To play the exercise in different positions, play the same notes on the other strings:

G string   Down an octave, in 2nd position.

D string   As written, in 5th position.

E string   Up an octave, in 4th position.

228

Substitutions

See also *Using substitutions*, page 162.

Exercise 1

- Play *f*, keeping the bow sustained without lightening it before each substitution.

- Move the fingers quickly, making the shifts as inaudible as possible.

- Keep the lower of the two fingers on the string, without lifting off during the shifts (lighten the held-down finger during the shift).

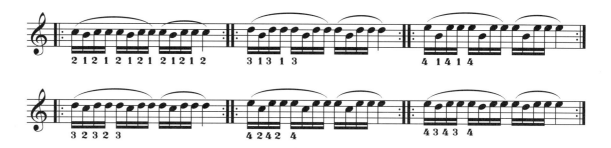

Other positions

Play the same notes on the other strings in various octaves:

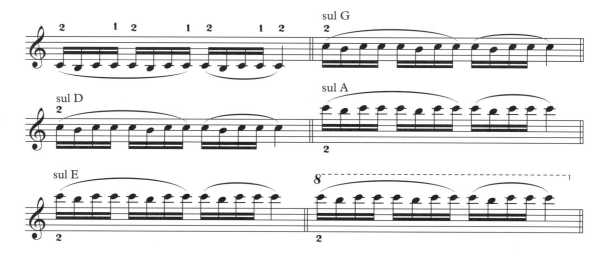

Also play in the following keys:

229

Exercise 2

- Play *f*, keeping the bow sustained without lightening it before each substitution.

- Move the fingers quickly, making the shifts as inaudible as possible.

- Continue the example as high up the string as possible.

- As well as slurring one bar to a bow, play fast spiccato or *sautillé*, three and four strokes to a note. The shifts must be very fast to co-ordinate with the bow, so that it sounds the same as if played with one finger throughout.

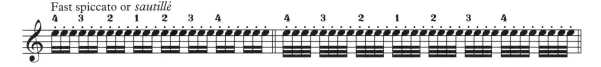

Play the same pattern on the other strings.

Exercise 3

230

- Continue each note pattern up the string, as shown in the example. Play as high up the string as possible.
- Keep the lower of the two fingers on the string all the time.

Example

Note patterns

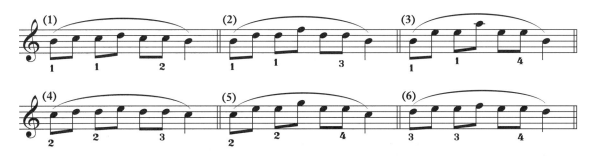

As well as slurring one bar to a bow, also play fast spiccato or *sautillé*, three and four strokes to a note (see Exercise 229).

Also play in the following keys:

Play the same patterns on the other strings.

231

Exercise 4

- Play separate bows, and also slur four or eight notes to a bow.
- Keep the lower of the two fingers on the string when playing the upper finger.

Also play in the following keys:

Play the same patterns on the other strings.

232

Exercise 5

- Play separate bows, and also slur four or eight notes to a bow.
- Keep the lower of the two fingers on the string when playing the upper finger.
- **Ascending**   To begin each group (for example, the fifth note of the first bar), extend the finger back and follow with the hand, rather than using a complete shift.
- **Descending**   Extend the finger up (for example, the fifth note of the second bar), and follow with the hand.

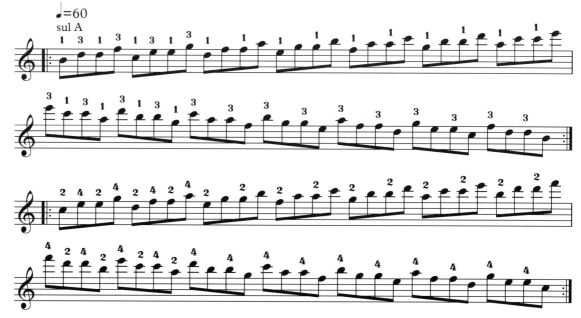

Also play in the following keys:

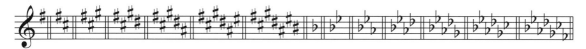

Play the same patterns on the other strings.

Octaves and tenths

Octaves

Exercise 1

233

- Play slowly, at about ♪ = 40. As with all shifts, it is important to 'hear' the note in advance.

- First play slurred, and then with separate bows.

- Crescendo into the upper note, moving closer to the bridge. Sustain the sound through the change of bow.

- Written out here as far as 4th position, continue higher up the string.

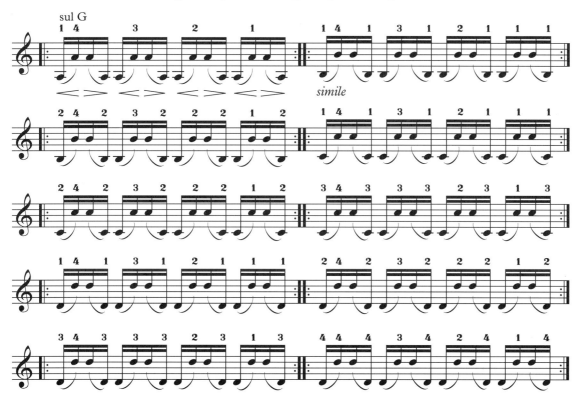

- Then play the same notes and fingerings with a sharp attack, as shown below. Attack each note decisively, without testing the notes by banging the fingers down hard on the string.

- Also play with four (or eight) fast strokes to a note. The faster the strokes, the faster the shift must be for the finger to arrive in time for the bow stroke. Play with machine-like regularity, timing the shifts so that they are inaudible, and the passage sounds the same as if you were playing in one position across two strings.

Play on each string.

Exercise 2

- In the first three bars of each group shift slowly, with a glissando. Memorise the feel of the hand in both the lower and the higher position. In the fourth bar play the octave as simply two notes, connecting the notes well but without a glissando. In other words, play 'note–note' rather than 'note–shift–note'.

- Crescendo into the upper note, moving closer to the bridge. Sustain the sound through the change of bow.

Play on each string.

Exercise 3

Play the same as Exercise 234.

- In the first bar extend the third finger to the B♭ without shifting.
- In the second bar extend the third finger to the E♭ without shifting.

235

Play on each string.

Tenths

236

Exercise 1

- First play slurred, and then with separate bows.
- Play slowly, at about ♪ = 40.
- Crescendo into the upper note, moving closer to the bridge. Sustain the sound through the change of bow.

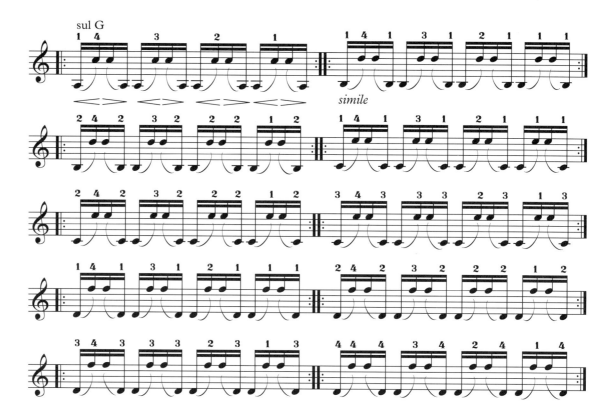

Then play the same notes and fingerings with a sharp attack, and with four (or eight) fast strokes to a note, as in Exercise 233.

Play on each string.

Exercise 2

Play the same as Exercise 234.

Play on each string.

238

All shifts in one complete sequence

Continue the first bar of each pair up one octave, and then come down as shown in the second bar.

Other strings

Play through the sequence on the other strings as follows:

Bowing

Play the sequence using overlapping bowing:

Also slur with one or two bows to a bar, and play separate bows.

Double stops

Feel the hand balanced slightly more on the upper finger than on the lower finger, and reach back with the lower finger. Do not base the hand on the lower finger, since then you have to stretch the upper finger forward.[1]

239

Exercise 1

Example

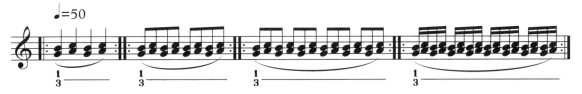

Fingerings and intervals:

Play in a variety of keys to cover different tone–semitone possibilities:

Other positions

Play the same patterns in the following positions:

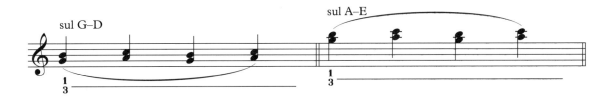

[1] See *Positioning the hand for thirds,* page 102

240

Exercise 2

1 First play through as written (see example below). Play f with an evenly sustained tone, and a light left hand. The lower bowing gives the correct co-ordination for separate-bow shifts.

2 'Ghost' the sixteenth-notes (semiquavers).

3 Play without the sixteenth-notes, joining the double stops together as though there were no shifts.

Play in a variety of keys to cover different tone–semitone possibilities:

241

Exercise 3

Also see Exercise 225.

Example

Fingerings and intervals:

Play the patterns in a variety of keys to cover different tone–semitone possibilities:

Other positions

Play the same patterns in the following positions:

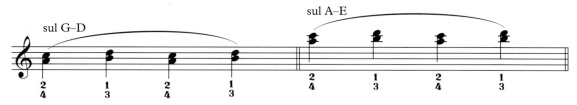

Exercise 4

242

(Continue up
the string)

Bowing

Use overlapping bowing:

Also slur with one or two bows to a bar, and play separate bows.

Rhythm variations

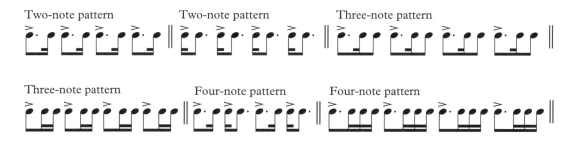

Play two-note rhythms starting on the first note of the passage, and starting on the second note. Play three-note rhythms starting on the first, second and third notes of the pasage. Play four-note rhythms starting on the first note, the second note, the third note, and the fourth note.

Exercise 5

243

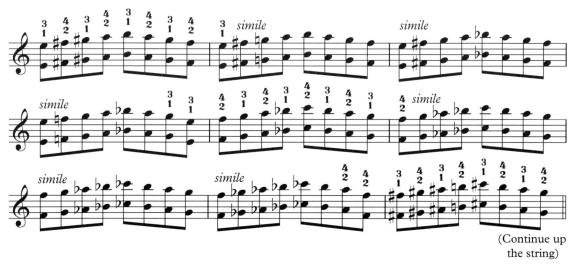

(Continue up
the string)

Use the same bowings and rhythms as Exercise 242.

244

Exercise 6

Keep the hand position based on the fourth finger, and reach back with the first finger. Open the hand at the base joints, particularly making a wide space between the first and second fingers.

(Continue up
the string)

Use the same bowings and rhythms as Exercise 242.

245

Exercise 7

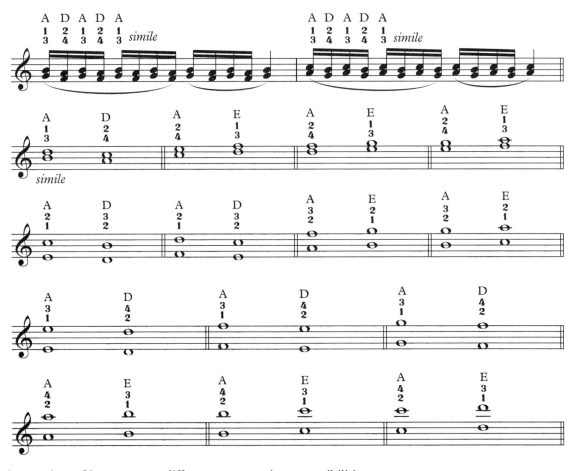

Play in a variety of keys to cover different tone–semitone possibilities.

Use the same bowings and rhythms as Exercise 242.

Exercise 8

Play f, keeping the bow sustained and deep in the string. Keep the left fingers light.

As well as playing through the sequence as written, from beginning to end, also practise one bar at a time as follows, playing with the metronome:

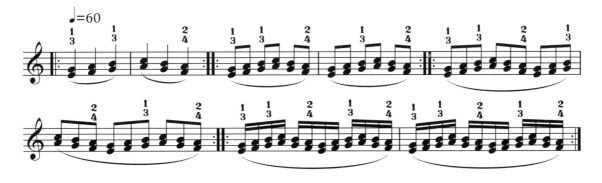

Use the same bowings and rhythms as Exercise 242.

247

Exercise 9

1 First play through as written (see example below). Play f with an evenly sustained tone, and a light left hand. Pivot to the tied notes smoothly. The lower bowing gives the correct co-ordination for separate-bow string crossings.

2 'Ghost' the eighth-notes (quavers).

3 Play without the eighth-notes, joining the double stops together as though there were no string crossings.

Play in a variety of keys to cover different tone–semitone possibilities:

Intonation

Sympathetic vibrations

Open strings vibrate sympathetically when a stopped G, D, A or E is played, making the violin sound much more resonant and open. For this reason, good intonation is an important aspect of tone production.

248

An open string *above* a stopped note of the same pitch vibrates as a whole. An open string *below* a stopped note divides into several parts, each vibrating separately. Third finger G on the D string makes the open G vibrate (visibly) in halves. Third finger D on the A string makes the open G divide into thirds. Second finger G on the E string makes the open G divide into quarters.

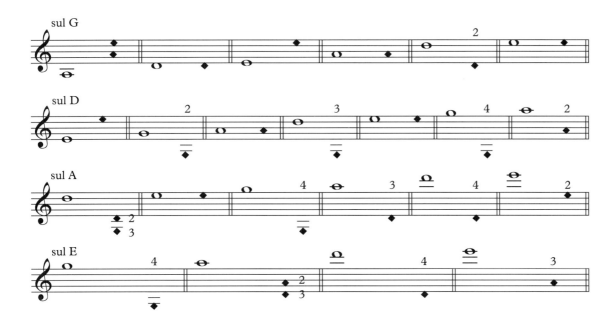

The diamond notes show the open strings that vibrate sympathetically with the stopped notes. The numbers show how many sections the string divides into.

- Play A (for example), a tone above open G. Play without vibrato. Roll the finger very slightly higher and lower, to find where the open A vibrates the widest.

- Listen to the sound gaining and losing edge: when the finger is in the very centre of the note, the sound has an open, 'soft-centred' quality, and the open A vibrates the most. When the finger is a fraction too high or low, the sound becomes tighter and slightly hard-edged, and the open A vibrates less.

- Depending on the instrument, its strings or its set-up, it is sometimes not possible to see the lower open string vibrate. But the hard edge, which comes into the stopped note if it is not in tune, will still be clear.

| The feel of the hand and fingers |

Like the right hand feeling the give of the wood, hair and string, the left hand *feels* its way around the neck of the violin. The left hand knows where it is by feeling the relationship of the fingers to each other, by measuring against the nut and against the shoulder of the violin, by measuring the different thicknesses of the neck, measuring from the part of the neck that joins on to the violin body, and so on.

249

Memorising the hand position

1 Play a note in tune, leaving the finger on the string for some time while *memorising the feel of the hand and fingers* on the instrument.

2 Name the note and position. In the last bar of the example above, say to yourself: '4th position, fourth finger, D' – '5th position, third finger, D' – '6th position, second finger, D' – '7th position, first finger, D'.

3 During the // take the left hand away from the instrument, dropping it to your side or turning the hand anticlockwise to face palm-outwards (Fig. 48).

4 Return the hand to the violin and play the next note exactly in tune, without testing or adjusting. 'Hear' the note mentally in advance. Do not look at the fingers and string – *feel* where to place the notes.

5 Play and remove and play the same finger on the same note several times.

Play on each string, continuing up into higher positions. Play each note with all the fingers, in any order.

Fig. 48

From this position go straight to the in-tune note

250

Pitching spaces between fingers

To measure the right tuning of a note from the previous note, you not only judge by the sound, but by the relationship of the fingers to each other. When the playing fingers are not next to each other, you need to imagine the missing fingers. For example, play first to third finger B to D: as well as measuring the third finger from the first, you also have to imagine the feeling of second finger C or C$\sharp$, and measure the third finger from *the imagined second finger*.

(A simple way to demonstrate how important this is: hold down first finger B on the A string – move the second finger down by the side of the neck of the violin so that the fingertip touches the palm of your hand – keeping the second finger there, now try to place the third finger in tune on the note D on the A string. Notice how different it feels, trying to judge the distance without the help of the second finger.)

This is one reason why fingers that are not being used should stay close to the strings – they remain involved in the playing by helping to measure distances accurately.

Ascending

Descending

Each bar contains two ordinary quarter-notes (crotchets), and one or two x-notes. Play each bar in three different ways, using the x-notes as follows:

1   Play the x-note as an ordinary quarter-note, playing it equally with the others (see example below). Play each bar or group several times, memorising the feel of each note and the feel of the fingers in relation to each other.

2   Play the first quarter-note and lift the bow off the string.
    Without playing it, place the x-note (or notes) silently on the string.
    Play the last quarter-note of the bar. *Feel* the relation of the fingers to each other.

3   Do not put the x-note (or notes) on the string. While playing the first quarter-note mentally pitch the x-note, and recall the feeling of it on the string. Put the second quarter-note down next to this *imagined* x-note.

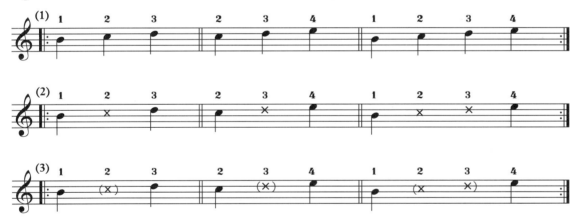

Play in a variety of keys to cover different tone–semitone possibilities:

Other positions

Play the same notes in other octaves:

251

Guide-notes

Guide-notes are a secure way to find the correct hand position or note, either after a rest or as part of shifting technique.[1] In the following two examples, the stemless notes are quickly placed on the string without being bowed:

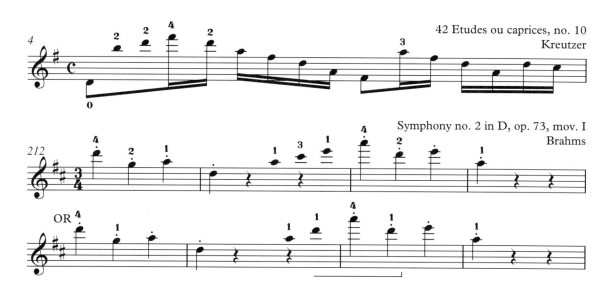

This exercise includes a wide variety of different routes to each note. Although some of them may never be used in actual playing, it is still useful to practise them because they increase the ability of the fingers to feel their way around the fingerboard. Add your own possibilities.

1 Play all the guide-notes of a group equally (see example below).

2 Place the first guide-note on the string without playing it (written as an x-note), and then play all the others.

3 Place the first and second guide-notes without playing them, and play all the others.

4 Silently place the first three guide-notes, and only play the fourth.

5 Play the 'destination note' only, getting to it by silently placing each guide-note.

6 Silently place the guide-notes on the string together as 'blocks' (as though playing a double stop on one string). Sound the destination note only.

7 Silently place the blocks so quickly, in the space of half a second or so, that it feels as though you reach the destination note with one movement.

To save time play bars 1, 6 and 7 only.

Play on each string. Add sharps and flats to the arrival note to cover more possibilities.

Note: To speed up the work practise *Substitutions* (page 170), since many guide-notes use them.

[1] The obvious ideal is simply to be able to put fingers down, in tune, anywhere on the fingerboard. In many cases this is possible, and many players do not need guide-notes to help find a particular position. There are also many passages where you have to go to a high note suddenly, and there is no time for any kind of preparation. Practising guide-notes makes it more possible *then* to dispense with them and simply go straight to the note.

2nd position

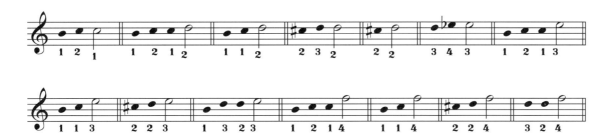

3rd position

4th position

5th position

6th position

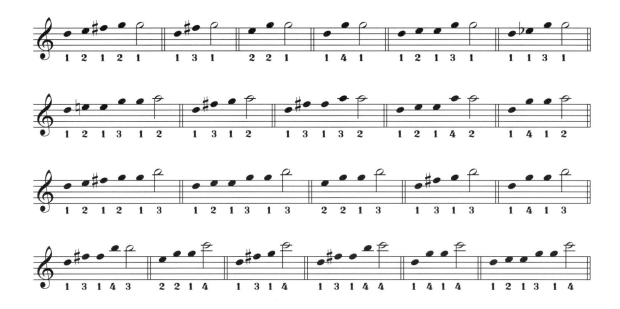

7th position

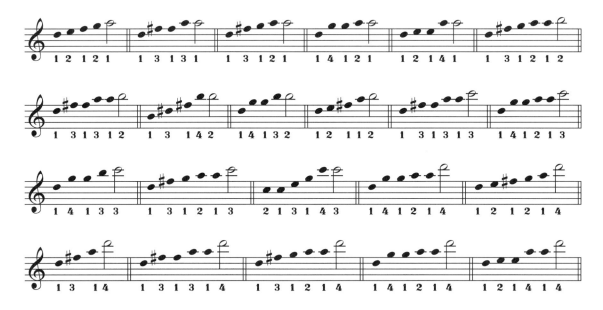

8th position

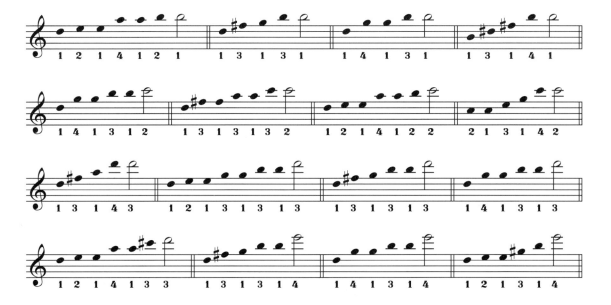

Uniform intonation

'Playing in tune' means that there is a definite structure to the intonation. Uniform intonation exercises are a quick and effective way to make intonation consistent, so that the same notes, played with any finger in any octave, are the same pitch. They are excellent either for developing technique, or as time-saving warm-up exercises.

In the opening of the Bruch Concerto, the G's, D's and A's should be in tune with the open strings. The F♯ can be played high, close to the G. Every B♭ should be identical, and tuned low (as a 'leading note' down to A) to help create the dark, G minor character of the passage:

Violin Concerto in G minor, op. 26, mov. I
Bruch

In passages like the following, every E, C♯ and A must be identical, so that from E down to A is a true perfect fifth, A down to E is a true perfect fourth, and each major third from C♯ to A is the same width. Tune the C♯ high (as a 'leading note' to D) to add brightness to the A major:

Violin Concerto in D, op. 61, mov. I
Beethoven

In these exercises, constantly check that notes are in tune by comparing them against the following:[1]

G	Tune to the open G	C♯	Tune from D
A♭	Tune from G	D	Tune to the open D
G♯	Tune from A	E♭	Tune from D
A	Tune to the open A	F♭	Tune from E♭
B♭	Tune from A	D♯	Tune from E
C♭	Tune from B♭	E	Tune to the open E
A♯	Tune from B	F	Tune from E
B	Tune from C	G♭	Tune from F
C	Perfect fourth/fifth from G	E♯	Tune from F♯
D♭	Tune from C	F♯	Tune from G

If there is a clear mental picture of the exact position of each note, and the relationships of each note to the surrounding notes, it is then possible to play the same letter names, whichever octave they occur in, exactly in tune with each other.

Practice method

42 Etudes ou caprices, no. 10
Kreutzer

Compare the F♯'s with each other, playing them *f*. Play the x-notes *ppp*.

[1] The exact tuning of a sharp or flat depends on the key, style and character of the music. For example, B♭ as the tonic of B♭ major is higher than the B♭ as the third of G minor. Tuning also depends on whether it is a single or double stop, and what notes other instruments are playing.

252

Exercise 1

- Play all the B's, in every possible place on each string, and then all the C's, C♯'s, D's and so on. Use any fingering.
- Constantly check the notes as described above. For example, if you are tuning all the A's, test the stopped notes by playing open A's in between. If you are tuning F♯'s, keep checking the pitch by playing third finger G on the D string followed by second finger F♯.

Example

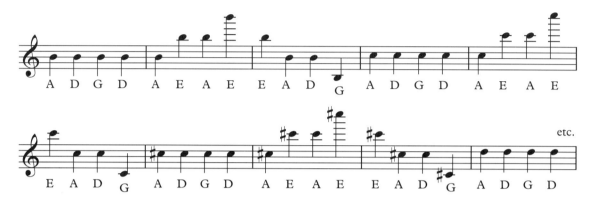

253

Exercise 2

Continue each of these bars up the string. The example below shows bar 2 written out in full.

- The pitch of the second and the fourth notes should be identical.
- Use separate bows, making it sound *as if there were no shifts*. Also play slurred.

Example (using bar 2)

Play in a variety of keys to cover different tone–semitone possibilities:

Play the same patterns on the other strings, starting in 1st position and working up the string.

Exercise 3

254

- Continue the exercise on B, C, etc., as far up the string as possible.
- Constantly check notes against others as described on page 191.

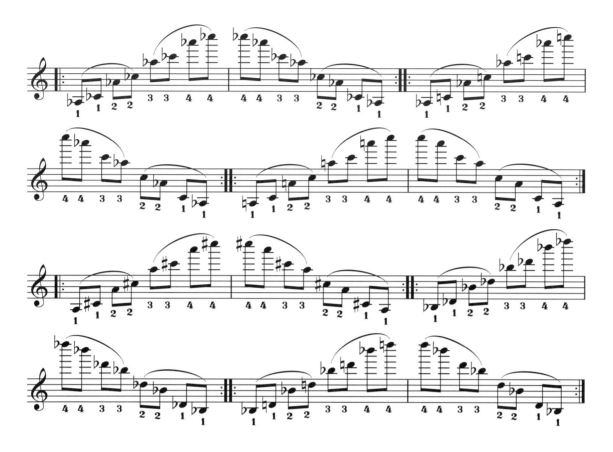

Finger patterns

255

Practise this exercise in the key and related keys of your current repertoire.[1] Doing this as a matter of routine, before playing the piece itself, solves many intonation problems before they arise.

- Tune each bar exactly the same so that every note is identical, whatever the position.
- It is not necessarily the point of this exercise to be able to play all the notes continuously, in tune, without stopping. Rather, play through from beginning to end, repeating particular bars several times to find exactly the right tuning. Play slowly, using either separate bows or slurred, and *memorise the feel* of each group of notes.
- First play without vibrato, and then with vibrato.
- Play through in different keys to cover all the notes and tone–semitone patterns:

[1] If you are playing anything that uses high positions, for example a major concerto or a virtuoso piece, play this exercise in all positions, including the highest. If you are playing a piece that mainly uses lower positions, to save time play this exercise only in the positions needed in the piece. If you are playing Bach, for example, there may be little point in practising this exercise at the top of the G string.

Major and minor thirds

256

- Make the pitches of each interval identical. Constantly check notes against others as described on page 191.

- It is not necessarily the point of this exercise to be able to play all the notes continuously, in tune, without stopping. Rather, play groups of notes several times, learning the feeling of where the hand and fingers are, while seeking to make the notes identical.

- First play without vibrato, and then with vibrato.

- Tempo: slow, medium and fast.

Bowing

First play separate bows, *martelé*, with a space between each note; then play slurred:

Play in a variety of keys:

Lower positions

Higher positions

Tuning scales

Basing the tuning of scales around perfect intervals is the method Pablo Casals used, and Dorothy DeLay teaches scales in the same way today.

The exact tuning of major, minor, augmented and diminished intervals depends, to a certain extent, on individual taste and the character of the music. For example, some players prefer wider (brighter) major thirds, or narrower (darker) minor thirds, than others. But perfect intervals – fourths, fifths and octaves – are either in tune or not, and cannot be adjusted according to taste.

Therefore the first notes to tune in a scale are those of the perfect intervals – the 1st, 4th and 5th degrees of the scale. The next notes to add are the 3rd and the 7th. These are tuned high so that the 3rd 'wants' to resolve into the 4th just as the 7th 'wants' to resolve into the octave.

Then the 2nd is placed between the 1st and 3rd, and the 6th between the 5th and 7th. If the player is using a high 3rd and 7th, the 2nd and 6th must also be high; if using a lower 3rd and 7th, the 2nd and 6th must be lower.

Practice method

Before playing complete scales in their usual order, tune each note individually.

1 Begin with perfect intervals. Tune the 4th, the 5th and the octave to the tonic. (In this key, all these notes should be tuned to the open strings.)

Alternative: play only the 4th, 5th and octave, but silently finger the left-out notes, written here as x-notes:

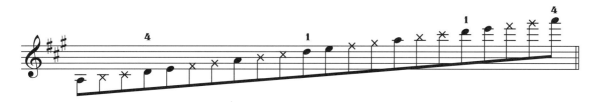

2 Then add the 3rd and the 7th. Feel the 3rd leading up to the 4th, and the 7th leading up to the octave.

3 Add the two remaining notes, the 2nd and the 6th. Place the 2nd midway between the 1st and the 3rd, and the 6th midway between the 5th and the 7th. So if you prefer quite high leading notes, the 2nd and the 6th also have to be higher.

Alternative note order

1 1, 4, 5, 8.

2 1, 4, 3 – 5, 8, 7. This order makes it easy to measure the 3rd from the 4th and the 7th from the 8th.

3 1, 4, 3, 2, 1 – 5, 8, 7, 6, 5. This order makes it easy to place the 2nd in the middle between the 1st and 3rd, and the 6th in the middle between the 5th and 7th.

4 Then play the complete scale in the proper order.

Tuning accidentals from naturals

- In these 'expressive intonation' exercises,[1] tune every semitone close to a natural: squeeze the flats close to the natural below, and squeeze the sharps close to the natural above. Feel the sharps 'leading' up and the flats 'leading' down.
- First play without vibrato, and then with vibrato.

258

Exercise 1

Take each of the following note patterns one by one, and play it in every possible octave on the fingerboard. The group marked with an asterisk is written out in full in the example below.

As shown in the example below, play each group of four notes with four fingerings (wherever possible): start each group on the first finger, then on the second, third and fourth finger.

* Example

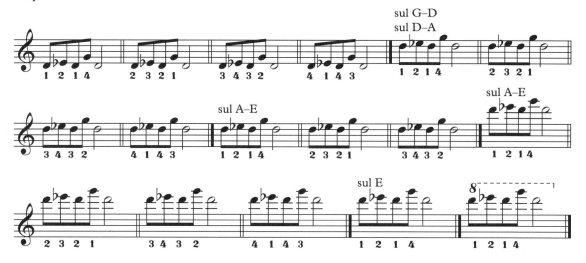

259

Exercise 2

The group marked with an asterisk is written out in full in the example below.

[1] The term 'expressive intonation', often associated with the great cellist Pablo Casals, means sharpening sharps and flattening flats to heighten the musical expression of a passage. This is partly a matter of personal taste, some players preferring sharper sharps and flatter flats to others.

As shown in the example below, play each group of four notes with four fingerings (wherever possible): start each group on the first finger, then on the second, third and fourth finger.

* Example

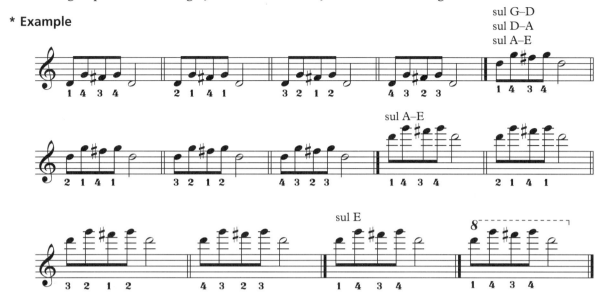

Exercise 3

260

- Take each of the following note patterns one by one, and play them in many different positions as shown in the example below. Use a variety of fingerings.

- Constantly check that all G's, D's, A's and E's are in tune with the open strings. Tune C♮ as a perfect fourth above open G, or as a perfect fifth below third finger G on the D string.

Example

Wide and narrow semitones

Basic rule: the semitone is wide whenever the letter names are the same, e.g., C–C♯, D–D♯ the semitone is narrow whenever the letter names are different, e.g., E–F, C♯–D.

In this example, narrow semitones are marked with a V, wide semitones with a bracket:

Violin Concerto in D, mov. III
Tchaikovsky

Each bar in this exercise includes sharps and flats that, on the keyboard, would be identical.[1] For the purposes of the exercise, play the sharps *as close to the natural above*, and the flats *as close to the natural below* as acceptably possible. Feel the sharps 'leading up' to the natural above, and the flats 'leading down' to the natural below. A–A♯ (fingered 1–1), feels much further apart than A–B♭ (1–2).

- Play each group of two bars with three fingerings: start on the first, second and third fingers as shown in the first line. Also start on the open string where possible.

- Play each group of two bars in different octaves everywhere on the fingerboard. No. 1 is written out in full in the example below.

- First play without vibrato, and then with vibrato.

[1] 'Chromatic half-steps such as A♯ –B♭, D♯ –E♭, G♯ –A♭, E♯ –F, are also known as "enharmonic intervals". On the piano their keyboard position and sound is identical but on stringed instruments and brass instruments like the trombone, their actual pitch is not the same but subject to finer distinction in accordance with the higher and lower tonal character of sharp and flat keys. This "enharmonic" relationship exists throughout the entire system of established musical notation.'
Leopold Auer:
Graded Course of Violin Playing, Volume 2 (New York, 1926), 1.

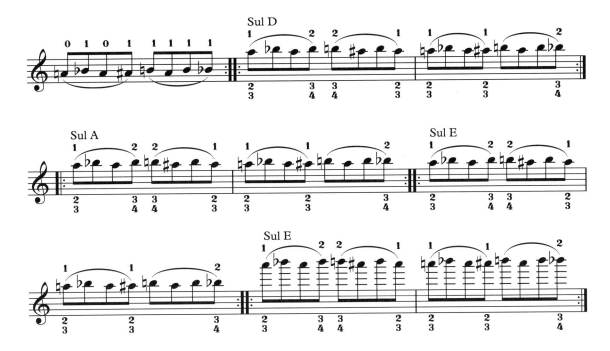

About tuning double stops

When two notes are played together they produce a third tone. This is a low note that has the same number of vibrations as the difference between the two actual notes. You can hear the third tone clearly, especially in high double stops. You cannot hear the third tone of an in-tune octave because it is the same as the lower note of the octave. (For example: A=440 cycles per second, one octave up is 880, and the difference is 440.)

Perfect intervals do not sound in tune unless the third tone is also in tune. The third tone of a major or minor interval does not have to be in tune. To a certain extent it is a matter of personal taste how wide or narrow major or minor intervals are played. It can be enlightening to practise tuning thirds and sixths so that their third tones are in tune; but in normal playing major and minor intervals can sound out of tune when the third tone is in tune, so you have to ignore the third tone.

For example, in the opening of the third movement of the Brahms Concerto, the D should be in tune with the open D; for the third tone to be in tune, the F♯ must be played slightly too flat.[1] This produces an 'in-tune' major third, but because the listener's ear catches the higher note as the melody, the F♯ comes out sounding too flat. If a sharper F♯ is used, the passage sounds in tune, but the third tone is out of tune. In the third bar, if the top B is played in tune with the D it comes out sounding too flat and must be played higher, out of tune with the D.

Violin Concerto in D, op. 77, mov. III
Brahms

In the opening solo of the Haydn Concerto, the C (second note, bar 1) sounds too sharp if it is played in tune with the open E; the B (second note, bar 3) sounds too flat if it is in tune with the open D; the F (third note, bar 3) sounds too sharp if it is in tune with the D.

Violin Concerto no. 1 in C, H VII:I
Haydn

[1] The exact pitches of the notes in a third or sixth are either 'fixed' or 'moveable'. Most G's, D's, A's and E's should be in tune with the open strings, and are therefore fixed notes. All other notes are moveable, but may also be fixed depending on their place in the melody or harmony. To play the third tone in tune in a third or sixth:

If the fixed note is the lower of the two notes, the upper note has to be flattened. If the fixed note is the higher of the two notes, the lower note has to be sharpened.

262

Tone–semitone groups

Single notes

Play various tone–semitone groups (e.g., semitone–tone–tone, tone–semitone–tone, tone–tone–semitone, etc.) using the fingering sequence: 12, 13, 14; 23, 24; 34; 43, 42, 41; 32, 31; 21.

Repeat the fingering sequence up the string, a semitone higher each time, as far as an octave or more.

- Play each group up the string as far as possible, a semitone higher each time.
- Constantly check G's, D's, A's and E's with the open strings. Also check groups of notes by playing them in first position, and then finding the same pitches in the correct position.
- Leave the first finger lightly down on the string, and leave every other finger down wherever possible.
- As you lift each finger, keep the finger in the same shape as it was when it was on the string. Lift the finger from the base joint.
- Play on each string.

Example: the first two bars of the exercise (marked ★), written out in full.

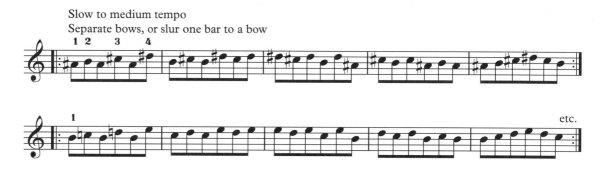

Quick practice

Play just one or two sequences of each group in low, middle and high positions; or play straight through using the following sequence:

Complete tone–semitone patterns

Finger all of these bars 1–2–3–4, and play on the A string using the sequence shown in the example above.

Play on each string.

Double stops[1]

Each exercise is written out six times, each time a semitone higher. Continue higher up the string if possible.

263

Exercise 1 – Semitone–tone–tone

264

Exercise 2 – Tone–semitone–tone

[1] See *About tuning double stops*, page 201

Exercise 3 – Tone–tone–semitone

Exercise 4 – Semitone–tone–semitone

267

Exercise 5 – Tone–tone–tone

268

Thirds

This one-line sequence contains every tone–semitone possibility for pairs of thirds.

The sequence is written out five times, a semitone higher each time. Continue higher up the string if possible.

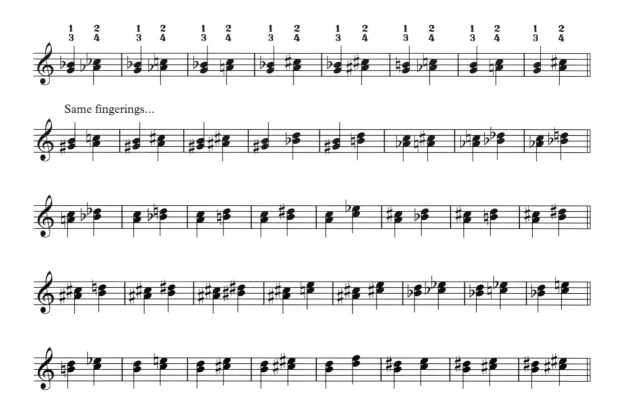

Practice methods

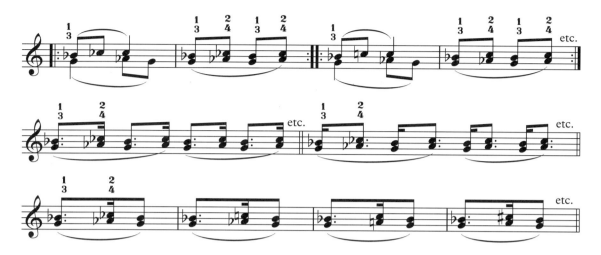

Also play the same sequence on the G–D and A–E strings.

> **Sequences transposed up the string**

- Hold down the first finger throughout. Keep the hand in one position, without changing it to suit each individual finger. Keep all the fingers over the strings ready to drop, rather than pulling them back away from the strings.

- Drop and lift fingers quickly, as late as possible.[1] Listen to the 'ping' as the fingers touch or leave the string.

- Prepare lower fingers lightly on the string before lifting higher fingers. Then raise the playing finger very quickly at the last possible moment.[2]

Chromatic sequence

Hold down the first finger throughout.

269

[1] See *Fast fingers*, page 119

[2] See *Finger preparation*, page 130

Other strings

270

Harmonic sequence

Hold down the first finger throughout.

Other strings

Perfect fourths

Perfect intervals are good for setting intonation because they are either in tune or out of tune, without any choice, whereas other intervals can, to a certain degree, be wider or narrower according to taste or context.

- Play the same patterns on each pair of strings, continuing the examples higher up the string as far as possible.

- Always drop both fingers together. Do not place one and then the other.

- Play slowly, but drop the fingers on to the string quickly and decisively.

- It is not necessarily the point of the exercise to be able to play all the notes continuously, in tune, without stopping. Repeat groups, or particular pairs of double stops, as many times as necessary to get them perfectly in tune. Playing fourths, make sure that the 'third tone' is exactly in tune, two octaves below the top note of the interval.

- Leave the fingers down on the string wherever possible.

- Always compare any G, D, A or E with the open strings.

Bowings

Play slurred and separate bows, as well as overlapping:

271

Exercise 1

272

Exercise 2

Exercise 3

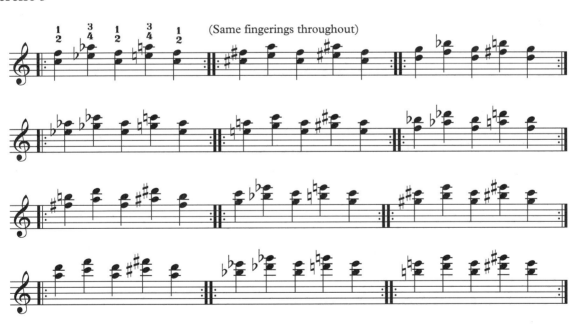

(Same fingerings throughout)

274

Exercise 4

(Same fingerings throughout)

Practice method for scales in thirds

Vibrato

part g

Whether you have an arm vibrato or a hand vibrato, it is helpful to practise both types since each contains elements of the other.

Occasionally play vibrato exercises with the scroll resting against a wall.

Flexibility

First joint

Play without the bow.

The first joint of the finger, the joint nearest the nail, acts like a brake on the vibrato. The more the joint is allowed to give, the wider and slower the vibrato becomes. It is important not to play with the 'brake' set in one position all the time – it is always changing according to the vibrato required. The 'brake' should rarely be completely on or completely off.

Bend and straighten each finger at the first joint. Either bend the finger itself, on its own, or use the hand and finger to bend the joint. Note that the angle of the vibrato into the string is diagonal to the string.

- Place a finger on the string in its normal, curved shape (Fig. 49a). Straighten the finger from the middle joint to the tip (Fig. 49b); bend again, straighten again, etc. Make the movement quickly and loosely.

- Begin with the finger resting lightly on the surface of the string. While bending and straightening, gradually press harder until pressing the finger to its maximum; then gradually release again to the surface of the string.

- Repeat in a continuous motion. Feel how relaxed the finger and hand is when resting lightly on the string, and keep that relaxation while pressing the string.

Bend – straighten – bend, etc.

Fingertip lightly on the string – heavier – heavier, etc. – lighter – lighter, etc.

Repeat with each finger, in various positions, on each string.

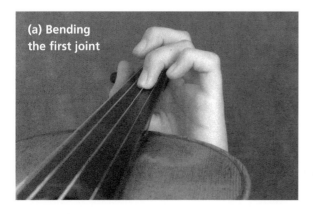

(a) Bending the first joint

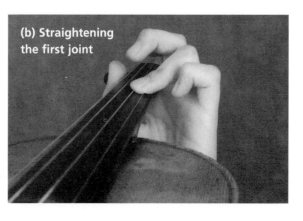

(b) Straightening the first joint

Fig. 49

275

276 Base joint

Play without the bow.

Like the first joint, the base joint also acts as a brake on the vibrato if it is prevented from moving. The actual amount it moves may be so little as to be invisible, but if it is not able to move at all the whole hand may become tight.

Press and release the string, as in the exercise above, but this time move the base joint in and out as well as the first joint.

- Begin with the fingertip resting lightly on the surface of the string (Fig. 50a).
- Move the finger at the base joint by pulling and pushing the knuckles out and in.
- The finger straightens slightly as you pull the knuckle away from the neck of the violin (Fig. 50b). The finger curves again as you push the knuckle back in (Fig. 50a).
- While moving the knuckles out and in, gradually press the finger harder and harder into the string, until pressing to the maximum. Then gradually release again to the surface of the string, still moving the knuckles in and out.

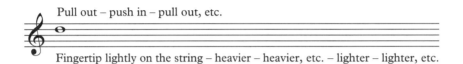

Pull out – push in – pull out, etc.

Fingertip lightly on the string – heavier – heavier, etc. – lighter – lighter, etc.

Repeat with each finger, in various positions, on each string.

Fig. 50

Pushing the base joint in

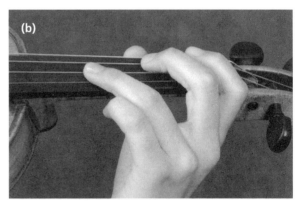

Pulling the base joint out

277 Circles

Play with or without the bow.

Movements in violin playing are never in straight lines. Every movement is circular, or moving in an arc. In vibrato, the hand does not move backwards and forwards in a straight line. This is partly because the finger releases the string slightly on the backward movement of the vibrato, making the fingertip move in a circular manner. This exercise exaggerates the circular movement.

- Rest the scroll against the wall. Use one finger on the string at a time.
- Move the hand in clockwise circles (Fig. 51). Think of the movement as forward-and-down on the dotted eighth-note (quaver), back-and-up on the sixteenth-note (semiquaver).
- **Forward movement (dotted eighth-note):** The fingertip goes deeper into the string; the finger curves more.
- **Backward movement (x-note):** The fingertip releases the string; the finger straightens slightly.

Make this circular movement with each finger, in various positions, on each string.

Fig. 51

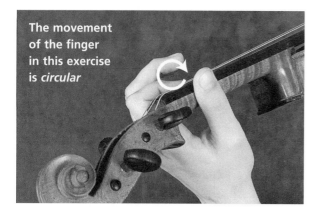

The movement of the finger in this exercise is *circular*

Hand and arm movements

Sliding exercises

Play with or without the bow.

Keep the fingers relaxed, without squeezing together, and touch the neck with the thumb as lightly as possible.

Exercise 1

278

Play each bar as fast as possible. The idea is to begin with a large sliding movement up and down the string, and gradually to make it smaller and smaller until it becomes the width of a vibrato. The actual notes need not be exact: you can make the sliding movement smaller by quarter-tones.

- **Bars 1–3**   Begin with a large sliding movement (using the arm or hand), and reduce the distance gradually. Move the thumb as well as the hand until the movement is very small; then keep the thumb in one place while only the finger slides on the string.

- **Bar 4**   When the sliding is only a quarter-tone or so, gradually fix the finger on the string so that the fingertip rocks to and fro without sliding. The backward movement is written as an x-note.

- **Bar 5**   Using the same hand or arm movement as in bars 1–4, play a very narrow vibrato, the finger rocking without sliding.

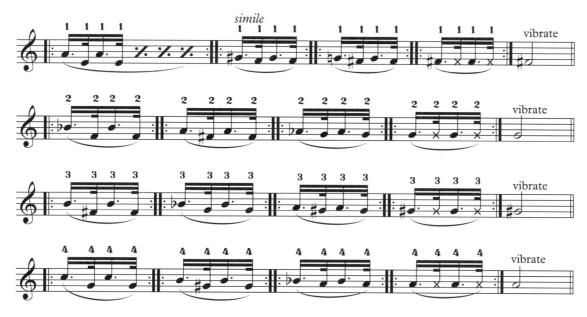

Hand vibrato

- Move the finger up and down along the string, moving the hand from the wrist, and leading the movement from the finger.

Arm vibrato

- Move the arm and hand together. Although the main movement is from the elbow, still lead the movement from the fingertip, and still allow the hand to give at the wrist.

Play on each string.

279

Exercise 2

Alternate between a semitone shift, in which the fingertip slides on the string, and a vibrato movement.

- **First bar:** Shift lightly. Keep the thumb in one place as the finger slides.
- **Second bar:** Vibrate (without sliding the finger on the string) using the same arm or hand movement as in the first bar. The x-notes represent the backward movement of the vibrato, which should not be heard. Keep the joint nearest the nail *loose*.

Hand vibrato

Move the hand up and down the string from the wrist, without actively moving the arm. Lead the movement with the finger.

Arm vibrato

Move the arm and hand together. Although the main movement is from the elbow, keep the wrist very relaxed. Lead the movement with the finger.

Play on each string.

280

Tapping

Play this exercise without the bow.

Place the base of the thumb along the top rim of the violin (Fig. 52). Place the pad of the thumb in its usual place for high positions, at the top of the violin neck. Do not move the fingers themselves – move the hand up and down from the wrist.

1. Tap the fingers (all four at once) on the violin table to the left of the fingerboard. Tap rapidly in fours, leaving the finger down on the fifth tap, i.e.:

    tap, tap, tap, tap, tap-and-stop

    tap, tap, tap, tap, tap-and-stop, etc.

2. Do the same on the strings near the top of the fingerboard.

3. Tap with one finger at a time, on each string, near the top of the fingerboard.

Arm vibrato

Keep the pad of the thumb at the top of the violin neck, but keep the base of the thumb away from the top rim. Tap the fingers by moving the forearm, not the hand.

Fig. 52

Place the thumb along the top rim of the violin

Wall exercise

281

Stand with your left forearm flat against a wall.

- Rapidly move the hand backwards and forwards, from the wrist, without the forearm coming away from the wall. Steady the forearm with your right hand (Fig. 53a).

- Make the same movement, but moving the whole forearm from the elbow, the hand and forearm moving in one piece (Fig. 53b).

Fig. 53

(a) Moving the hand

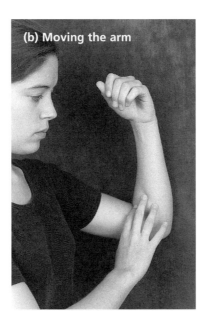

(b) Moving the arm

Forearm rotation

The chief movement of the forearm is backwards and forwards, but there is also an *almost-invisible* sideways turning movement.

Exercise 1

282

Without the violin, hold the left hand in playing position, level with the shoulder.

1 Turn the forearm anticlockwise so that the palm faces away from you. Then turn clockwise back again to violin position.

2 Make this movement continuously, back and forth, as quickly as possible – the hand should become a blur. Keep everything loose – the wrist, hand and fingers, and the upper arm and shoulder.

3 While making this turning movement, very slowly move the elbow to the left and up (until the palm faces the floor and the arm is horizontal).

4 Continuing to make the turning movement, move the elbow back down and to the right, until the arm is in playing position for the G string (elbow turned to the right).

5 Do not stop the turning movement, while continuously moving the arm from playing position to palm-facing-down position, and back again.

Exercise 2

283

Without the bow, tap the fingers up and down on the string quite quickly, one at a time. For the purposes of the exercise, do not move the finger much – tap by rotating the hand sideways.

- As you put each finger down, turn the forearm clockwise. As you raise each finger, turn the forearm anticlockwise away from the fingerboard.

- Keep the thumb relaxed, and feel it turning on the violin neck.

Repeat on each string.

284

Exercise 3 – Thumb

Partly as a result of forearm rotation, the thumb moves in the opposite direction to the finger. This is never an active, conscious movement, but when the finger vibrates forwards the thumb moves backwards, and vice versa. This movement is a slight *rolling* on the neck of the violin: a fraction more of the left side of the thumb (the side furthest from the player) touches the neck when the finger vibrates forwards (towards the bridge), and a fraction more of the pad touches the neck when the finger vibrates backwards.

The movement is so slight as to be almost invisible, but if it is blocked the vibrato may become tense. It is just as much a part of arm vibrato as of hand vibrato.[1]

The x-notes represent the backward movement of the vibrato, which should not be heard.

[1] This thumb movement is not always a part of arm vibrato. The thumb does not move in the opposite direction to the finger if the arm and hand move together as one unbroken unit (when there is always a straight line from the elbow to the knuckles). Although at times this vibrato works well, it may be too wide and slow as well as too tense. The thumb does move in contrary motion to the finger when the arm movement 'swings' the hand backwards and forwards as a passive movement (see Exercise 286). This gives a feeling of the vibrato 'motor' being shared between the finger, hand and arm, rather than being only somewhere just above the elbow. Whatever vibrato you use, it is good to practise every type of exercise.

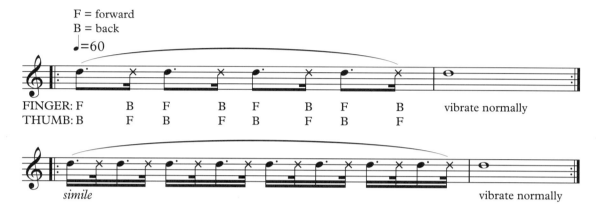

- Using a normal hand or arm vibrato movement, roll the finger forwards four times, in a firmly dotted rhythm. At the same time, roll the thumb in the opposite direction.
- On the next forward movement (the fifth), make a normal arm or hand vibrato, i.e.:

    forward, forward, forward, forward, forward-and-vibrate

    forward, forward, forward, forward, forward-and-vibrate, etc.

- During the notes with normal vibrato, feel how the vibrato seems to be powered from the fingers as much as from the hand or arm.

Repeat with each finger on each string.

285

Relaxation exercises

Releasing to a harmonic

During the forward movement of the vibrato, the finger leans slightly more heavily into the string. The finger releases the string slightly during the backward movement. The pressure differences are an automatic result of leaning the finger forward – never press the finger deliberately.[2]

A vibrato with equal finger pressure backwards and forwards is a major cause of left hand tension.

[2] See *Rolling fingers into the string*, Exercise 130.

[3] Normally, the forward pitch of vibrato is the in-tune pitch of the note. Here, the backward pitch is an in-tune note, because of needing to use the harmonic to lighten the finger. A 'flat F' is used because rolling from an in-tune F to an E harmonic would be too big a movement.

1 Start on a very flat F, just above E♮ on the A string.[3] Position the finger on the string closer to the *tip* of the finger than to the *pad*, i.e., quite upright (Fig. 54a).

2 Using a normal hand or arm vibrato movement, roll the finger back towards the pad. At the same time *completely release the string* to play the harmonic E. More of the pad now touches the string, with the finger flatter (Fig. 54b). Do not slide the finger along the string as though shifting.

3 Roll forward towards the fingertip. At the same time the finger bends slightly at the nail joint and goes deeper into the string. The flat F is played automatically, without the finger having to 'press'.

The harmonic should sound clearly. Play *f*, with an even sound.

Repeat with each finger, and on the other strings using the equivalent harmonics.

(a)

The finger in its forward, 'into-the-note' position

(b)

The finger rolled back, releasing the string

Fig. 54

'Swinging' the hand in arm vibrato

286

The movement of the arm, in arm vibrato, causes a passive movement in the hand. There is no active hand movement, but an *almost-invisible* backwards-and-forwards movement in the opposite direction to the arm.

If the forearm and hand move as one unbroken unit, this tends to produce slow and wide vibratos, and you have to work much harder than necessary. In arm vibrato it is possible to continue vibrating even if someone tries to prevent you by holding the forearm firmly, just below the wrist.

In this exercise, none of the hand movements is an active movement.

Without the violin, hold the left arm in playing position, palm facing you (so that if you were playing, the fourth finger would not be able to reach the E string).

Using a movement from the arm, loosely 'swing' the hand.

1   Swing the hand backwards and forwards. If you really allow the hand to go floppy, a small movement in the arm produces a large movement in the hand.

2   Swing the hand from side to side, as though waving to yourself.

3   Swing the hand in circles, clockwise and anticlockwise. Relax the fingers, hand and wrist, and let a small circular movement in the forearm produce a large circular movement in the hand.

Vibrating harmonics

287

Alternate between a harmonic and a stopped note. Vibrate all the time without stopping, during both the harmonic and the stopped note.

●   Completely relax the hand, fingers and thumb during the harmonic, and *keep that relaxation while playing the stopped note.*

●   To change from the harmonic to the stopped note, move the finger down into the string *very slowly,* without stopping the vibrato, and release the string back to the harmonic very slowly.

Repeat on the other strings using the equivalent harmonics.

288

Keeping the scroll still

The aim of this exercise is to be able to make a forceful vibrato without the scroll of the violin moving. This is not possible if the hand is tight.

1 Play a very slow, very narrow vibrato.

2 Look at the scroll. If it moves even the smallest amount, relax the thumb, hand and fingers, or change the direction of the vibrato, until the scroll stays perfectly still.

3 Gradually increase the speed and width of the vibrato. If the scroll begins to move even slightly, gradually decrease the speed and width again until the scroll is still.

4 Discover what makes the scroll shake: tight thumb? – side of first finger clamping against the neck of the violin? – inflexible finger? – tight wrist? – wrong direction of the vibrato movement?

5 Relax the hand or alter the movement, and then gradually increase the speed and width again.

6 Continue until the vibrato is very fast and wide without making the violin shake.

Practise each finger in low, middle and high positions on each string. Also play double stops.

289

Upper arm

A common cause of tension is the upper arm being pulled close in to the body as part of the vibrato movement, instead of the upper arm staying relaxed and 'hanging' naturally. This exercise separates the vibrato action from the action of pulling the upper arm sideways.

Use the right hand as a violin 'neck' – put the left thumb in the palm of the right hand, the fingers using the back of the hand as a 'fingerboard' (Fig. 55a).

- Holding the left hand in playing position, make a normal vibrato movement (a wrist or an arm vibrato).

- While vibrating, move the right hand back so that it is above the left shoulder (Fig. 55b), making as large a space as possible between the upper arm and the body.

- Also vibrate in guitar or cello position, or with the left hand behind your head, etc. Feel how the vibrato movement can continue without the upper arm tensing, or pulling in to the right.

The violin itself can be used instead of the hand (Fig. 55c).

Fig. 55

Using the hand as a violin 'neck'

Note the open space between the upper arm and chest

The violin can be used if preferred

Vibrating at any speed

Like tone production exercises on one note, this key exercise is a straightforward practice or warm-up method which often becomes part of the routine of everyday practice.

Vibrato is made with only one active movement, which is *forward* to the in-tune note. The backward movement is like a rebound. This is similar to clapping, where there is only one active movement to bring the hands together, not an active movement 'out' to bring them apart: the hands go 'in–in–in–in', not 'in–out–in–out'. Similarly the vibrato movement is 'forward–forward–forward–forward', not 'forward–back–forward–back'.

The forward movement of the vibrato pushes slightly more deeply into the string. The backward movement slightly releases the string.

The **dotted eighth-note** = the forward, in-tune pitch of the vibrato.

The **x-note** = the backward movement which releases the string and hardly sounds.

Practise on long, sustained notes, with the metronome, always playing four beats on the down-bow and four beats on the up-bow. Begin slowly at 60. Then repeat at 66, 72, 80, etc., up to about 108.

1   One vibrato per beat (bars 1–2).

2   Two vibratos per beat (bars 3–4).

3   Four vibratos on the first beat, and then stop the finger, in tune, on the second beat (bars 5–6).

Play forward, forward, forward, forward, forward-and-stop on the in-tune note.

Play a few notes on each string with each finger, in low, middle and high positions. Also play double stops.

Vibrato accents

Usually you have to guard against one hand being influenced by what the other hand is doing. Here, that problem can be turned into an advantage: to speed up vibrato let the left hand be affected by the right, so that the attack in the bow helps to give a 'kick' to the beginning of the vibrato.

Bow   Fast–slow, heavy–light.

Vibrato   Fast–slow, wide–narrow.

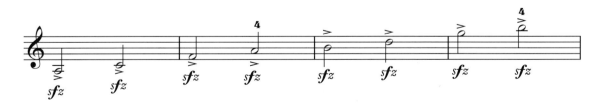

Play a few notes on each string with each finger, in low, middle and high positions.

292

Changing speed without changing width

The easiest way to increase vibrato speed is to make it narrower. But in this exercise, in order to isolate the elements, the width remains the same while the speed changes.

The **dotted eighth-note** = the forward, in-tune pitch of the vibrato.

The **x-note** = the backward movement which releases the string and hardly sounds.

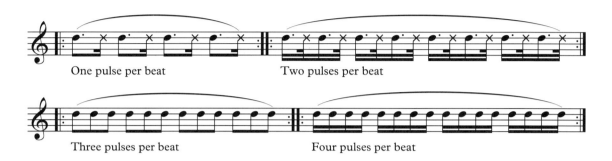

One pulse per beat   Two pulses per beat

Three pulses per beat   Four pulses per beat

Play continuous whole bows, down- and up-bow, on one note.

- Play four metronome beats on each bow. Start at 60, then repeat at 66, 72, 80, etc., up to about 108.
- At each metronome speed, play one vibrato to a beat, and then 2, 3 and 4 vibratos.
- At each metronome speed, first play the 1, 2, 3 and 4 vibratos with a very narrow vibrato, then with a medium, and finally a wide vibrato.
- Make sure that you increase only the number of vibratos per beat, and that the width of vibrato – whether narrow, medium or wide – stays the same.

Also play the exercise in reverse order to decrease speed, or jump from one number of pulses to another, e.g., 4, 3, 4, 2, 3, 1, etc.

Play a few notes on each string with each finger, in low, middle and high positions.

293

Width

Dividing semitones

This exercise sensitises the ear and the finger to the slightest variation in pitch, making it easier to play with the narrowest, purest vibrato which sounds like BBBBBBBB, CCCCCCCC, etc. – in other words, sounding like one pitch which throbs rather than a wide sliding of the pitch between the note itself and the same note flattened. It is also an excellent intonation exercise: after playing a 64th or 128th of a tone, a semitone seems a huge distance.

Play each stage completely without vibrato.

1 In third position on the A string, play E–D–E. Play firmly, with separate bows. Tune both notes to the open strings.

2 Measuring exactly halfway between the D–E, play a 'tempered' D♯: play E–D♯–E.

3 Measuring exactly halfway between the D♯–E, play a quarter-tone: play E–D♯ plus a quarter-tone–E.

4 Now only using one finger (rock slightly up or down to find the pitches), play E – then the note an eighth-tone lower – then the E again.

5 Continue halving through the 16th, 32nd, 64th and 128th of a tone. Always play E, then the fraction of a tone below, and then the E again. Continually check the E to make sure that it is always in tune with the open string.

Play a few notes on each string with each finger, in low, middle and high positions.

Variation

1 Play D–E.

2 Play equal semitones: D–D♯–E.

3 Play four equal quarter-tones: D–D plus a quarter-tone–D♯–D♯ plus a quarter-tone–E.

4 Play eight eighths, and so on as far as possible.

Fingertip and pad

Vibrato is narrower when the finger is placed very upright on the string, so that the tip of the finger stops the string. Placing the finger flatter, so that more of the pad touches the string, produces a wider vibrato.

In this exercise, change the vibrato from very narrow to very wide, and then back to very narrow again. Use only the different parts of the fingertip and pad to make the different vibratos – do not use extra hand or arm movements.

Vibrate on one long D: each sixteenth-note (semiquaver) represents the forward, in-tune pitch of the vibrato.

1 Begin with a narrow vibrato, playing with the finger vertical on the fingertip.

2 Very gradually flatten the finger so that you use more and more of the pad. Do not let the pitch of the note waver – the only change should be that the vibrato gradually becomes wider.

3 Continue to widen the vibrato to the maximum; then gradually narrow it to the minimum by moving back on to the fingertip.

Play a few notes on each string with each finger, in low, middle and high positions.

Changing width without changing speed

Play continuous whole bows, down and up, on one note. Play four beats on each bow.

● Play four vibratos to a beat (like vibrato 'sixteenth-notes'). Vibrate with the metronome at 60, then repeat at 66, 72, 80, etc., up to about 100.

● At each metronome speed begin with the narrowest possible vibrato. Very gradually widen it, little by little, to the widest possible vibrato. Then gradually narrow it down to the smallest again.

● Always play four vibratos on each beat, so that the vibrato speed does not change whatever the change of width.

Play a few notes on each string with each finger, in low, middle and high positions.

Practice method: 'Pulsing'

Sonata no. 3 in D minor, op. 108, mov. II
Brahms

Each note below represents one vibrato 'pulse'. Keep the bow smooth, making the pulsing or 'throbbing' with the vibrato only. Vibrate each finger 'forward–forward–forward–forward' to the in-tune note.

Begin with two pulses on each sixteenth-note (semiquaver), and go on with four pulses on each sixteenth-note:

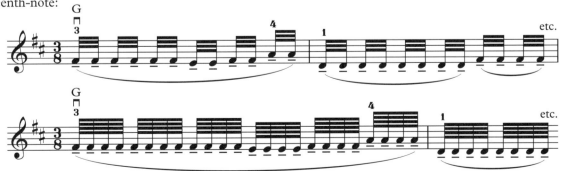

296

Continuous vibrato

Moving fingers in slow motion

In this exercise keep the hand vibrating without stopping, using a normal hand or arm vibrato. Lower and raise each finger very, very slowly. Because the hand is vibrating, the finger also 'vibrates' as it slowly nears or leaves the string.

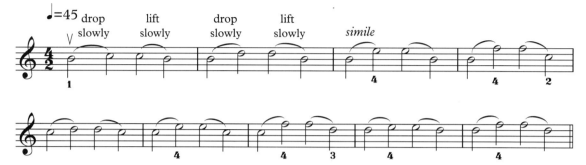

Dropping fingers

- As the finger gets closer to the string, each forward movement of the vibrato begins to make the finger touch the string. At first this produces a broken, distorted sound, and then gradually the new note is fully stopped. Make this stage – between the finger just beginning to touch the string and it fully stopping the string – as long as possible by lowering the finger very slowly. Keep vibrating without stopping as the finger nears, begins to stop, and fully stops, the string.

Lifting fingers

- Lift the finger off very, very slowly, vibrating all the time. As the finger begins to release the string there is an in-between stage where each backward movement of the vibrato causes the sound to break, and then finally the finger is completely clear of the string. Make this stage, between the finger stopping the string and being completely clear of the string, as long as possible by lifting the finger very slowly.

- When descending from, say, second finger to first finger, make sure that the lower finger is already on the string. Both fingers vibrate together as the upper finger slowly lifts.

Play the same patterns on the other strings.

297

Pulsing

The **dotted eighth-note** = the forward, in-tune pitch of the vibrato.

The **x-note** = the backward movement which releases the string and hardly sounds.

- Play with the metronome, starting at 60. Speed up gradually to about 80.
- First play one vibrato 'pulse' on each beat, then two on each beat, and then four on each beat.
- When moving from a lower note to a higher note (e.g., from the fourth note of the first bar to the fifth note), the finger must drop *in tune* on the higher note and then roll back. In other words, the first vibrato 'pulse' is really simply the beginning of the in-tune note, made by dropping the finger.
- Timing in this exercise is important when moving from a higher note to a lower note (e.g., the last x-note of the first bar going into the first note of the second bar). During the x-note the finger/hand has already moved back, and then *as the finger is lifted* the lower finger has to go forward into the new note.

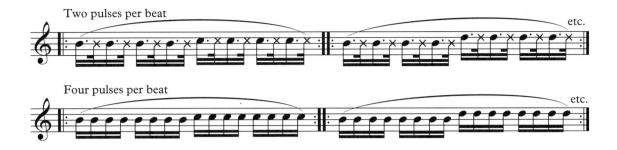

Play the same patterns on the other strings.

Silent raising and dropping

While playing the upper string, silently raise and drop the fingers on the lower string (written as x-notes).

- Vibrate the finger on the upper string continuously, without stopping the vibrato momentarily as you drop or raise the finger on the lower string.
- Also vibrate the silent fingers on the lower string, without stopping the vibrato as the finger touches or leaves the string.

Make the continuous vibrato on the upper note sound the same as if you were not using the fingers on the lower string.

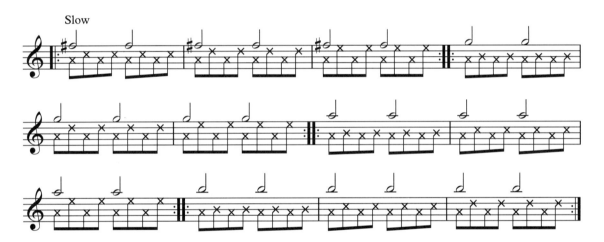

Also play on the G–D and D–A strings.

Practice method: hold down fingers

Although fast sixteenth-notes (semiquavers) may seem impossible to vibrate, any held-down fingers are, in effect, longer-value notes. By vibrating these fingers, the other fingers naturally vibrate too. (The vibrato must be very slight for the notes not to become 'wobbly', but there is still an important difference between this slight vibrato and no vibrato at all.)

299

Equal vibrato on different fingers

Comparing fingers

- Vibrate each finger, one at a time, on the same note.

- Make the vibrato of each finger sound exactly the same as the others (the same width and speed), so that a listener would not be able to tell which finger is being used. It does not matter in what order you use the fingers.

Cover the following possibilities:

1 Slow, wide vibrato with each finger.

2 Slow, narrow vibrato with each finger.

3 Fast, wide vibrato with each finger.

4 Fast, narrow vibrato with each finger.

Play all four possibilities in low, middle and high positions, on each string. Examples:

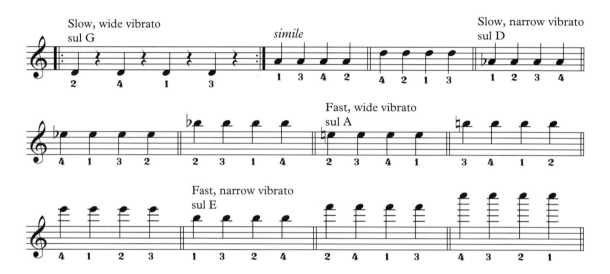

Also play double stops, for example alternating 1–3 and 2–4 in thirds.

300

Even pitch

- Vibrate at exactly the same speed as the spiccato stroke. Use a metronome, starting slowly and gradually speeding up.

- Make the *forward movement of the vibrato* coincide exactly with each spiccato, so that every note has the same pitch. The x-notes represent the backward movement of the vibrato, which should not be heard. The sound should be *the same as if there were no vibrato*, i.e., BBBBBBBB, CCCCCCCC, etc.

- If the pitch changes from note to note, it means that the width of the vibrato movement is not always the same; or else the spiccato is missing the highest pitch of the vibrato.

Play the exercise on each string in low, middle and high positions.

General index

Index *of musical examples*